CHAPTER 2

BIRTH CONTROL BANNED IN BOSTON

Ultimately, it was about sex and control. In Boston, it was also about Catholicism. A law known as Chapter 272, which described "crimes against chastity, morality, decency and good order," was enacted in the 19th century when the anti-sex Comstock movement swept the country. By that law, it was illegal to:

> ...sell, exhibit or offer to sell, lend or give away any drug, medicine, instrument or article whatever for the prevention of conception or for causing unlawful abortion, or advertise the same or write, print or cause to be written or printed, a card, circular, book, pamphlet, advertisement or notice of any kind stating when, where, how or by what means such article can be purchased or obtained.

The punishment for this crime was five years in jail and a fine of $1,000. The leaders of the birth control movement wanted to overturn 272 and resented the power of the Catholic Church over all Bostonians' access to contraceptives. The birth control movement pitted Protestants against Catholics, turned Catholics against their church and men against women in a struggle for power and control.

Women, naturally, led the charge for birth control. They were the generals in this revolution for liberation. They circulated petitions, lobbied legislators, started clinics, recruited men into their ranks and took on the hierarchy of both the government and the Catholic Church. They knew that women's health was jeopardized by repeated and frequent pregnancies. By the 1920s, these women revolutionaries established Mothers' Health offices in and around Boston, which were, in reality, family planning clinics. Not able to stop clinics with pickets and other forms of harassment, those in power who were opposed to birth control had the clinics raided by the police. Supplies and patients' records were confiscated, and the women running the clinics were arrested.

In 1931, Margaret Sanger, who established America's first birth control clinic in New York, came to Boston for a series of speeches and to launch another petition drive to repeal Massachusetts' Chapter 272. She and the women of Massachusetts enlisted the help of Boston's most eminent physicians, many of who were staff members of the most prestigious Harvard teaching hospitals.

Thousands signed the petition. As a result, a referendum to repeal Chapter 272 was once again placed on the ballot. Catholic priests, acting under instructions from the new head of the archdiocese, Archbishop Richard Cardinal Cushing, denounced birth control from their pulpits. It was a long and bloody battle fought on many fronts. It was a battle that the birth control advocates lost again and again.

Finally, in 1966, after millions of signatures, hundreds of petitions and countless miles of marching, Massachusetts amended Chapter 272 so that physicians could finally prescribe contraceptives to married couples. In a final attempt to stop the spread of birth control, Massachusetts passed a law that prohibited the dispensing of birth control to unmarried women. Women in Boston were still not free, but they were one step closer.

CHAPTER 3

BOSTON CITY HOSPITAL

It was a hot, cloudless July morning in 1971 when I arrived at Boston City Hospital to start my residency. BCH was a place of life, death and everything in between. It had been born in a barren landfill in the South End of Boston in 1864 during a cholera epidemic which swept the city. What started as a single building in a muddy field had become a cacophony of more than a dozen buildings, built at different times but of the same dull, cold, red brick. The buildings sprouted over an entire city block to make an uneven edifice of care. Each building was connected to the other by a labyrinth of catacomb-like tunnels which carried trash, waste, patients, doctors, nurses, ideas, misery, life, death and sometimes even diseases from one part of this sprawling complex to another.

BCH's original mission was to heal the poor of Boston and to respond to the fevers which invaded the city—cholera, yellow, typhoid, rheumatic and childbed fevers. In more recent times, it treated the scourges of malnutrition, diabetes, hypertension, syphilis, tuberculosis, AIDS, violence and poverty. When those who had no place else to go arrived at the doors of other hospitals or doctors' offices, the order was always, "Send them to City."

The sick and poor of Boston entered through the rear of the hospital—the emergency room. By ambulance, car, cab and foot, they arrived to be triaged and treated by a team of interns, residents, nurses and medical and nursing students. City Hospital's ER was the busiest and the best in Boston.

Rising like a majestic giant, nine stories above the emergency room, was the Dowling Building. On its top floor were 12 operating rooms, where doctors were always busy stitching up bodies pierced by bullets, broken by car accidents, slashed by knives or carried to the brink of

9

death by ruptured bowels, infected appendices, tubal pregnancies and exploding gall bladders.

BCH surgeons knew everything, made instantaneous decisions; they were in total control of the operating room. They saw a problem, made a diagnosis, operated on the problem and moved on to the next one. They didn't see patients; they saw problems. Men and women brought before them became the gall bladder in bed three, the appendix next to the window, the motor vehicle accident in bed six or the aneurysm in the Intensive Care Unit. Surgery at BCH was a man's world. There were no women on the surgery staff and none in training. It was a world of blood, guts and balls.

Next to the Dowling was Pediatrics, known to everybody as "Peedie." The Peedie building was open, light and airy, with play spaces for its little patients, the children who were unwanted and unloved. They came from whorehouses, sick houses, orphan houses, drug houses, group houses, halfway houses and treatment houses, but mainly poor houses. Children were brought to BCH when there was no place else for them to go.

The second-largest brick building in this vast, eclectic complex of structures was the six-story Medical Building, with its wraparound rotting porches, where patients used to be wheeled to absorb the healing rays of the sun. The porches had long since become useless, rusted and separated from the outside walls of the building. The open wards of the medical building stripped patients of their privacy and the little dignity they clung to. Arranged in imperfect rows around the wall of each ward, the beds were separated from each other by old, frayed, cotton curtains. The narrow windows in these wards rose to the ceiling, letting in the sun during the day and the bitter chill during the winter nights.

Interns and residents from the medical, surgical and pediatric services used the House Officers Building to catch some sleep when they were on-call. It was a six-story brick dormitory standing halfway between the front and back of this Lego-like array of buildings. The top four floors were sleep rooms, each equipped with a bed, chair and telephone. There was a common bathroom and shower on each floor. On the first floor was a large, open room with a TV, a Coke machine, a phone, a couple of tables, a few couches and chairs. Liver Rounds—so called because the large amount of beer consumed certainly assaulted the livers of those who attended—were held in the lounge after work every Friday. Interns, residents and nurses gathered to drink beer and relax after a grueling week of taking care of Boston's sickest patients. It was also a place to hook up. All the sleep rooms in the House Officers Building were fully occupied on Friday nights, but no one got much sleep.

My home away from home for the next three years was located on the far corner of the block: the Maternity Building, where the obstetrics and gynecology service was located. OB/GYN at BCH was where I wanted to be, providing care to poor black women. It was to be my contribution to the revolutions that were taking place in America.

The entire six-story Maternity Building—two floors dedicated to gynecology, four to obstetrics—was undergoing renovations at a slow, one-floor-at-a-time pace. The top floor of the building—called Maternity 4, or just MAT 4—was where the labor and delivery rooms were located. Here, the renovations were at their worst. There were bare pipes protruding through the floors, wires hanging from the ceilings and women in labor, having babies in the mixture of dust and chaos. The summer heat was oppressive and the nurses placed fans around MAT 4 to provide some relief for the women who sweated through the pains of labor. It helped, but not much.

Also on the top floor was the infamous Tub Room—a large, stark room located near the entrance to the labor and delivery area. It was like a decontamination chamber through which all the patients had to pass before being admitted in labor. This cold room contained two shallow marble tubs raised on pedestals and an open drain in the floor. Women in labor were hosed down with a spray of water before being allowed back to The Porch to await the arrival of their babies.

The Porch was the labor room. It was a large, open room with no windows, no partitions between the six labor beds and only a couple of movable cotton screens, which could be placed around a woman during an exam. There was one large floor fan which struggled to blow away the heavy summer air. Since families were not allowed on The Porch, women in labor were alone in the throes of their pain.

There were four delivery rooms. Each was simple, bare and functional. The metal delivery table was flat with a sheet covering a thin mattress. Attached to the end of the table were two cane-shaped rods with canvas straps hanging from their ends. The entire contraption looked like a medieval rack. During delivery, the patient's buttocks were at the edge of the table and her feet were put in the straps to allow a clear view of her vagina and the emerging baby as it made its way into the world.

The residents' lounge was a large, all-purpose room on MAT 4. It was a hang-out, a classroom, a sleep room, a dining room and, occasionally, a place to sneak in a little sex. There was a large, dirty window overlooking the fume-engulfed southeast expressway and a blackboard with patients' names listed on it. There were dilapidated wooden and plastic chairs, a small round table that rocked on uneven legs and a Naugahyde couch that sank in the middle like an old swayback horse. When residents were not working or sleeping, they could be found in the lounge, talking, reading or watching TV.

Tucked in the corner of MAT 4 were two sleep rooms for the residents on call. They were conveniently located right behind the nurses' desk, so if a woman in labor developed an emergency or was about to deliver, the resident could be quickly summoned. Being able to instantaneously go from a deep sleep to assisting a woman about to give birth was part of the training of a resident in OB/GYN.

CHAPTER 4

NEW LIFE

Seeing and feeling a new life emerge from the body of another is both exciting and awesome. The experience of witnessing a new human, slowly, with alternating advances and retreats, bulge through and enlarge the tiny opening of the vagina, is unmatched by any other I had ever had. First the head emerges, misshapen, with its skin and hair covered with vernix—that white, cheesy substance made up of skin cells and fine hair protecting it from the fluid in which it floated for nine months. After the head emerges, the rest of this new person—the neck, shoulders, arms, chest and abdomen with the attached, pulsating umbilical cord—quickly follows and it is, in turn, followed by hips, buttocks, thighs, knees, legs and feet.

"Is it alright?" she wants to know. "Is it a boy or a girl?" she asks.

A boy. A girl. Every time I held a new baby in my hands, I watched as it breathed in this new sea of air. It extended its arms and legs, grimaced, opened its eyes, took its first breath and began to cry. It was no longer in the warm, fluid-filled, protective embrace of its mother's womb. Now it was here, in this new, cold, outside world. It had gone from being totally dependent, a parasite in the truest sense, to a detached being, continuing on its journey to independence. No longer did it get its mother's oxygen; it breathed and got its own. No longer did it need its mother's blood to provide nutrition; it could suck and get its own.

It had been born.

CHAPTER 5

THE CHIEF AND THE MASTER

———

After they had their babies, new mothers at BCH were transferred to one of the open wards on any of the three floors below MAT 4. There were 15 beds around the perimeter of each of the cavernous rooms, one bathroom and one pay phone at the end of the hall.

Also admitted to these wards were women who had complicated pregnancies—diabetes, heart disease, hypertension, bleeding and sickle cell anemia. Both they and their babies were at risk of death.

The first two floors of the building, GYN 1 and GYN 2, were open wards for gynecology patients—women who were having miscarriages, had infections in their wombs and tubes, cancer, large fibroid tumors or were waiting to have abortions. The operating and recovery rooms were on GYN 2. All of our surgery was done in this separate, isolated building, located on the corner of this city block in Boston's South End.

There were two archaic elevators in the building, both of which were frequently out of service. One was a freight elevator used to remove trash, dirty linen and human waste from each of the wards in the building; the other was the passenger elevator. When the latter was broken, patients, doctors and nurses rode in the freight elevator with the rubbish.

The outpatient OB/GYN clinic at City Hospital was a block away from the Maternity Building. It consisted of a large waiting room filled with wooden chairs and benches and an old wooden table in the middle of the room. Surrounding the waiting area, which was always filled with women, were a series of closet-sized examining rooms just large enough for one examining table, one patient, one nurse and one resident doctor.

After being examined, the patient got dressed and met with the resident at the large table in the waiting room, along with other patients talking to their residents. There, the patient was told the intimate

14

details of the doctor's findings and diagnosis—whether it be that the discharge she had was a sexually transmitted disease, that she was pregnant (whether she wanted to be or not), or that the six-month fetus she was carrying had a serious congenital abnormality. Whatever the news, after hearing this very personal diagnosis, the patient left the clinic quickly and silently, horrified and embarrassed by what she had been told so publicly, and absorbed by the private decisions she had to make.

This vast complex of BCH was under the control of the commissioner of health and hospitals, who was appointed by the mayor of Boston. The commissioner, in turn, appointed the administrator and all other members of the hospital's bureaucracy, most of who were important to the election and re-election of the mayor. Since the days of boss-man Michael Curley, BCH was a place of patronage, where relatives, friends and friends of friends of the mayor got jobs. They were the ones who were supposed to make sure that each building and each medical unit worked and functioned.

Each of the patient care units, however, was controlled by a doctor called the chief. The chief was the essence of power, having achieved his exalted position through research, discovery, writing, lecturing, leadership and political cunning. The chief was a mythic figure with aura, prestige and control of everything in his domain.

Because it was a hospital for the poor, BCH was a valuable and important teaching site for all three of Boston's medical schools—Harvard, Tufts and Boston University, each of which had training programs there. The surgical and medical departments at the hospital were divided into five separate patient care units, two staffed by Harvard doctors, two staffed by Tufts and one by Boston University. Through a convoluted admissions system, a patient could be admitted to the Harvard, BU or Tufts teaching service. Each was run with the iron fist of the chief, who was also a professor at his medical school. His medical staff consisted of a large number of doctors-in-training—interns and residents—and volunteer doctors, often referred to as "visits" because of their transient and brief visits to the hospital. Mixed in with all of these was a small and dedicated group of "attending" doctors who believed that it was their calling to provide humane care to the poor and the indigent. There were never enough of these idealists.

The chief controlled everyone's schedule, pay and laboratory space if they did research. He controlled the future of the young doctors in training, all of who had fought and struggled to get to BCH, and a few who, like some of their patients, would not survive. The chief controlled everyone's life.

The leaders of American medicine were teachers at BCH. Those who were trying to become leaders received their training and carried out research there. It was one of the great training Meccas of American medicine because its poor and uneducated patients were ideal for teaching and learning. There was no other place in Boston that had such a large number of patients and potential research subjects with such complicated and interesting illnesses. There was no other place where young doctors could practice and be trained under the expert and experienced, albeit distant, eyes of some of the world's most famous doctors. Being subjects for research and objects for learning was the trade-off that poor patients at BCH made for not being able to pay for their health care.

Dr. David Charles, a BU faculty member, was the chairman and chief of the three-school unified OB/GYN department. Originally from Wales and educated in Great Britain, he spent time in the British military and in the British colonies in Africa. He was a big, broad man, well over six feet tall, wore black rimmed glasses and kept his chin tucked against his chest, which expanded his already large, round face. He spoke through clenched teeth, his accent crisp and flat as the words squeezed through his lips. He always started his sentences with, "The thing is…"

David Charles really wanted to be a Harvard professor. Most of his research was carried out with Harvard faculty and scientists. Often, it appeared, he despised Boston University.

The vice chairman from Harvard was the unpredictable Cuban, Dr. Bernardo Santamarina, whom everyone called "Santa." He was tall, old and handsome, always carried a Cuban cigar between his fingers and had a speech impediment in addition to his thick Spanish accent, which made understanding him nearly impossible. He was a skilled surgeon, and always willing to operate on the edge. He prided himself on being able to carry out the most heroic of vaginal deliveries. Watching Santa deliver the most precarious of babies vaginally— whether they were large, small, breech or with their backs lying across the mouth of the womb—was an awe-inspiring experience. He would don his special rubber gauntlet glove that extended up his right arm past his elbow and, with blind manipulation of his hand inside of the pregnant womb, convert a second twin lying crossways over the mouth of the womb into a breech and deliver it by grabbing both feet and pulling it through the gaping cervix and vagina of the mother. To those of us in training, he was the master obstetrician. He had a busy private practice, located on prestigious Beacon Street, on Doctors Row in Boston. It was rumored that he performed abortions for his patients in his office. In 1971, that was illegal.

CHAPTER 6

Transformation: Year One

I had three years of OB experience in the Air Force. I had given spinal anesthesia to women getting ready to deliver, delivered scores of babies and taken care of many women with complicated pregnancies. I had delivered twins and breeches, used forceps and even done cesarean sections. I performed minor surgery and assisted in many major GYN operations during my stint as a medical officer in the Air Force. Now in Boston, at BCH, I was ready to go through my formal training to become a specialist and give care to those I cared about most—poor, black women.

My training in OB/GYN would last three long years. The residency program at BCH in obstetrics and gynecology was a resident-teach-resident program. The senior residents taught senior assistant residents, who in turn taught us, the junior assistant residents. We taught the medical students. The instruction from attending physicians, those seasoned and experienced physicians who should have been our teachers, was sporadic, episodic and irregular. Many times, they were not in the operating room during surgery, or the delivery room during a birth. Attending physician presence in the outpatient department—the clinic— was practically non-existent. There were conferences and rounds with Dr. Charles and some of the attending physicians, but they never saw most of the patients. Care was provided by the residents in training.

There were 15 residents, five in each year of training. My first year was mainly in obstetrics—taking care of pregnant women and delivering their babies. Every morning, the residents assigned to the obstetrical service met in the residents' lounge on MAT 4 to discuss the patients who were in the hospital. There were pregnant women with uncontrolled diabetes whose unborn babies were going to be too big or could die in the womb before they were born. There were women whose blood pressure was so high that they were at risk of having a stroke. There were women hooked on heroin who were being detoxed and given methadone to control their cravings for "heron." There were women who delivered and then left the hospital without taking their babies. There were women abused by their husbands or boyfriends and came to the emergency room beaten and bruised, and were admitted to provide them with shelter and safety.

As a first-year resident, I performed plenty of difficult and complicated deliveries. I performed c-sections, breech and forceps deliveries, took care of women who hemorrhaged after their deliveries and performed post-delivery tubal ligations for women who did not want to have any more children...as long as it had been approved by the Abortion and Sterilization Committee.

CHAPTER 7

The Committee

——————

One of the things I learned early in my residency was how to take a quick nap to refresh myself. I never knew when I was going to be able to sleep again. After a long night on call, I took advantage of the quiet on MAT 4 to take a mid-morning nap in the lounge. There was no one in labor, rounds had been made, and there was nothing else to do—for now.

As usual, my nap was interrupted, this time by the sound of the squeaking lounge door and the nurse's voice saying my name.

"Ken, there is a 40-year-old multip in labor in the exam room. I think she's a repeat c-section."

Awake and alert, I hopped up from the couch in the lounge and made my way directly to the examining room. Lying on the table was a woman who looked much older than her 40 years. She moaned with each labor pain. I examined her and asked her a few questions. She was at term—40 weeks pregnant. Between contractions, she gave me a brief history of herself: she had not come to the clinic for prenatal care, had diabetes and the last 2 of her 13 children had been delivered by cesarean section.

She needed to have a repeat cesarean immediately, or the scar on her womb might burst with the force of her labor. She could die.

There was another contraction. She panted and moaned with pain. When it was finished, she grabbed my arm. Her face was weary and glistening with sweat.

"Please. Give me a tubalagation. I can't go through this again."

I wanted to nod in agreement, but this was Boston. Though her request made sense, she hadn't come to the clinic, and neither she nor her husband had signed the consent form needed for us to legally tie her tubes. Her case had not been presented to *The Committee*.

Hospital rules stated that if a woman wanted to have her tubes tied, she needed to 1) be married and 2) have the permission of both her husband and the Abortion and Sterilization Committee. Her husband hadn't come to the hospital with her. He was at home, taking care of their other children.

I asked the nurses to get the patient ready for a cesarean, and left the examining room to make some phone calls.

The first person I dialed was Dr. James Penza, one of the few attending physicians available. "Jim," I said, "there is a gravida 14 who just came in. She needs a repeat c-section."

"Let me know when she's ready," said Jim Penza on the other end. "I'll come up and scrub with you."

I hung up the phone and glanced down at the patient's chart. I skimmed through it for a second, then looked back toward the examining room. Having her tubes tied would have been best for her, especially since that was what she wanted. Being pregnant, diabetic, needing a c-section and 40 put her life at risk. Another pregnancy would only increase the risks involved.

I called her husband. When he answered, I could hear a baby crying in the background.

"This is Dr. Edelin. I'm a resident at City Hospital and I'm calling regarding your wife."

"She all right?"

"She's in labor right now and in a lot of pain. It's going to be a difficult birth, but so far, there haven't been any serious complications. The reason I'm calling is because your wife asked for a tubal ligation when she was—"

"Hell no."

I paused, but only for a moment. "But she told us she didn't want to have any more children. If she gets pregnant again, it could be very rough on her. Plus, she's diabetic."

"I said, 'No.'"

"It will be easy to do since we have to do a c-section anyway. Her tubes will be right there."

"You deaf? I said, 'No!'" he shouted. I held the phone a few inches from my ear as he screamed something about not wanting to deal with her family if he gave his permission for the operation.

A cluster of anger began to form in my chest and attempted to claw its way to the surface. "Sir, I need you to understand how important this is. Another pregnancy could potentially kill her."

"I've made up my mind, doctor," he said and hung up.

I slammed the phone down. When I returned to the examining room, the patient looked at me with that tired face, her eyes desperate.

"I spoke to your husband. I'm sorry. He does not give his permission for the tubal ligation."

Her face, already contorted in pain, crunched up as she began to cry. "No! No! No! I can't go through this no more!" she choked out, sobbing uncontrollably as we wheeled her to the operating room for her c-section.

I met up with Dr. Penza to scrub for surgery. He took one look at me and cocked his head to the side.

"You look like you're ready to punch something."

I told Dr. Penza about the patient's request for a tubal ligation and her husband's stubborn refusal. He frowned.

"Such a shame. Best time for it, too. Even if she gets her husband's permission in, say, two months, it'd be much more dangerous for her."

I knew it, and the injustice of it all made my blood boil. It was what she wanted and it was what was best for her, but because this was Boston and 1971, she was not entitled to make that decision for herself.

We performed the c-section and delivered a healthy, 10-pound baby girl. After sewing up the incision in her womb, Dr. Penza and I looked at each other.

I gently grasped one of her fallopian tubes with a surgical instrument. "I think we should remove her appendix," I said.

After a moment, Dr. Penza nodded. "Okay. Be sure to get both of them."

Jim Penza left the operating room.

I tied her tubes.

It was not the first, nor would it be the last time that the rules and good patient care clashed in the operating room at BCH.

CHAPTER 8

The Chief

———

October 1971

Dr. David Charles, the Chief, sat with two visitors in his pale green office on the first floor of the OB/GYN building. Tucked in a corner across from the freight elevator, most of the space in the office was taken up by a large, ornate, wooden desk. Hands folded, he leaned his massive body back and propped one foot up on the edge of the desk.

"The thing is," he said, "we do two or three second trimester abortions a week. I mean, after all, this is City Hospital."

Across from him, seated in brightly colored plastic chairs, were two Harvard researchers who had just presented to him an idea for a project they wanted to carry out.

Dr. Leon Sabath was an associate professor of medicine at Harvard Medical School and worked in the world-renowned Thorndike Memorial Laboratory at BCH. A research position in the Thorndike was unparalleled anywhere else in academic medicine, and usually led to lucrative research grants, many published papers and a rapid rise up the academic ladder.

Sabath had the look of a Harvard professor—thin and of medium height, bald on top, with the thick, "Coke bottle" glasses in clear plastic frames. He was dressed in a button-down shirt and wore a crimson tie adorned with Harvard crests. Although he was not British like David Charles, his crisp, Harvard accent rivaled Charles' enunciations syllable for syllable.

Sitting next to Sabath was Dr. Agneta Philipson, a tall, big-boned, attractive, blond woman who had come to Boston from Sweden to spend a year in research at the Thorndike. She had four children, but no one would

23

ever have guessed it from her looks and manner. She wore her long, white lab coat opened, and sat with her lean, shapely, slightly tanned legs crossed, her calf muscles bulging and gaining definition. Her short, European-style skirt revealed most of her thin, firm thighs.

She and Sabath wanted to know how much of two different antibiotics, when given to pregnant women, would enter the body of the fetus inside of her. Philipson had written the outline of a research protocol which involved giving these antibiotics to pregnant women who were coming to BCH for abortions. After the abortions, the fetal tissue would be analyzed for levels of the antibiotics. As she, Sabath and Charles discussed the project, they all agreed that it would be even better if they could analyze the levels of the antibiotics in specific fetal organs. That would mean, of course, that the fetuses would have to be aborted intact so that a pathologist could dissect out the organs and analyze each separately for antibiotic content.

"We probably need no more than 20 specimens," Philipson said. "That should give us enough information to answer the question."

David Charles jumped at the idea. This research would link his name with the Thorndike and that, he thought, was where he really belonged. It was bad enough that he was at BCH, but he was a Boston University professor, not a Harvard one.

"Let me make sure we have residents who don't mind doing hysterotomies," he said. He reached for the phone.

———

"Ken, Dr. Charles is on the phone for you," the nurse said as she stuck her head into the examining room where I was seeing a patient. When the chief called, a resident always took the call—mid-exam or not. I excused myself and went to the small office in the clinic and picked up the phone.

"The thing is, Edelin, do you do abortions?" Charles said as soon and he heard my voice on the other end. No greeting, no preamble. Right to business.

"Yes," I said, puzzled by the question.

He then asked me if I objected to doing hysterotomies for second trimester abortions.

I had assisted one of the senior residents with a few hysterotomies, so I knew how to do the operation. It was a rare, major surgery, but sometimes the only option for patients. They weighed heavily on everybody's emotions—the patient, me, the nurses, the scrub techs, the anesthetists.

"Well, Edelin?"

Pulling myself back from my confused thoughts, I again responded that I would be willing to do hysterotomies.

"Good. You're going to get lots of surgery to do."

Click.

I stared at the earpiece of the phone for a few seconds before slowly hanging up. There was something overwhelming about being called by the chief, and something seductive about being able to do more surgeries. I was flattered. And I was ready.

CHAPTER 9

ABORTION

Of course I performed abortions. Why wouldn't I? I remembered the 17-year-old girl who'd died from an illegal abortion when I was a third-year medical student. That awful scene was seared into my brain, clear and fresh as the day it happened. There were other memories, too, just as vivid, with feelings of fear and desperation that were all too personal.

July 1957

"Kenny, I've missed my period."

I was working the summer before college in a mail room in a New York City office building. Time froze. I couldn't think. Those five words changed everything. No college. No doctor. No dreams.

"Are you there?" she asked. I moved my jaw, but no words came out. Elbows on the desk, I supported my head in my hands. How could I have been so stupid?

We had made out passionately many times, but had intercourse only once. That one time raced through my mind at lightening speed and the memory of it morphed from pleasure to horror.

It had been a warm June day, just before our graduation from Stockbridge School in Massachusetts. Gerry and I had walked to Cathedral Field, a wide, flat meadow at the base of Stockbridge Mountain.

The field was named after the rows of pine trees that had been planted to resemble the pews of a grand European cathedral. In front of the pews was a cluster of oak and maple trees shaped like an altar.

Hidden within the altar was a hay stack invisible to anyone who might be passing by. As we'd held hands and walked through the trees on that glorious day, we'd known what was about to happen. We'd known what we wanted to do. Gerry was wearing loose fitting shorts which had given me a full view of her beautiful, brown thighs. I had tried to get a rubber, but none of my friends had any to give and I couldn't buy any in the towns near the school. Buying or selling rubbers was illegal in Massachusetts.

In the seclusion of the altar and in the comfort of a blanket thrown over the soft hay, we'd made love. It had been clumsy, awkward and wonderful. I'd tried to be careful, but I hadn't been fast enough to interrupt the explosion let loose inside of her warm body. I knew immediately that it was a mistake. It was too late. I was too late.

"Kenny?"

"Yeah, I'm here." My voice sounded weaker than I intended it to be.

"I've missed my period," she repeated.

How could I have been so stupid? Hopelessness, fear and the loss of my future overwhelmed me.

"Maybe it'll come tomorrow," I managed to whisper. She started to protest, but I had to get back to work. "I'll call you tomorrow," I said, and hung up the phone.

I did call her the next day and every day after that, asking, consoling, begging and asking her again.

"Have you had your period yet?"

Every day for two weeks, I called and asked and every day for two weeks, the answer was the same. The only thing that changed was that Gerry sounded more fragile as each day passed. Her life, too, was about to change. After two weeks of phone calls, we had to figure out what we were going to do next. In the end, we decided that I would come to her house on Saturday and we would tell her mother.

The early evening train ride from New York City to the suburbs was long and lonely. The train jerked, allowing me no peace. Life was about to get as hard as the iron wheels of the train running along the steel tracks. I dreaded what we had to do.

How could I have been so stupid?

It was over. We would get married, I would continue to work in the mail room and we would have a baby. I would never become a doctor.

The inside of Gerry's house was as dark and dreary as our mood. Her mother was in another room, watching television. Gerry and I sat in the living room, on the edge of the couch, holding hands but saying nothing. The silence and the gloom engulfed us—drowned us. What words could I string together to tell her mother? Nothing came to either of us. Nothing. We just sat, looking at each other in silence. My stomach was in knots and I was hungry for air. Gerry finally left me alone in the living room, alone in my thoughts and the reality of what we were about to face. The loss of our futures, our families' hopes for us and our dreams. The darkness of the house became the darkness of my life.

When Gerry returned, she looked different. The furrow in her forehead was gone. The dimples which had enthralled me were back, and tears ran in them and onto her cheeks.

"It's here," she said. "My period just started."

The gloom rushed from my body as the light and our lives returned. Gerry and I hugged for a long time. Tears of relief poured from her eyes. Tomorrow would come. As we sat back down on the couch, relief replaced fear.

Her mother finally came into the living room and asked me how I was doing.

"Very well," I said, smiling for the first time in over two weeks. "Very well."

Gerry and I had been lucky. We had been to the precipice and been saved from the abyss.

We saw little of each other for the rest of the summer. In the fall, I started Columbia and she, too, went off to college. Our love affair ended quietly with a few tears. That was my first encounter with the knot in my stomach. It would not be my last.

December 1962

For two years after college, I went back to the Stockbridge School to teach science and math. I needed the isolation of the Berkshire Mountains to recover from the distractions and temptations of New York City, and I needed a break from being a student before going off to medical school. There, I submerged myself in teaching and learning. My only outlet and release came from Ellie.

Ellie was a young teacher from the white state of Vermont. She was fascinated by working so closely with a Negro. Her only knowledge of us had been through newspapers and grainy pictures on black-and-white televisions. She was mesmerized by the Civil Rights movement and the heroism of southern Negroes in the struggle for freedom. And like many white women, she was fascinated by Negro men.

As a new teacher at Stockbridge, she felt liberated, independent and wanted to experience what life had to offer. She attached herself to me and I did not resist. At first, the newness of her body and the mysteries of its secrets were alluring and wonderful places to explore. Her innocence and inexperience reinforced my role as teacher. She was a willing student and the frequency of our meetings was driven as much by her desire for passion as mine. The heat and wetness of our bodies melded us into one.

But the peak of our passion was shaken to its core as the school was about to close for the month-long winter vacation.

"Kenny, I've missed my period."

Five words I had hoped I would never hear again.

The memory of the long train ride returned. I was so young then. How could I have been so stupid again?

We decided that she should go to the doctor in the town of Stockbridge to get a pregnancy test done. In 1962, getting a pregnancy test was an ordeal that took a week, sometimes longer, for the results to come in. It was an agonizing week and when the results came in, the rabbit test confirmed that Ellie was pregnant.

We both agreed that we did not want to have a baby. We were not in love, did not want to get married and she told me her family would disown her if she had a baby out of wedlock—let alone by a Negro. Having an abortion was the best thing for both of us, so I told her that I would somehow find the money to pay for it. But first, we had to find someone to do the abortion. There were no listings in the Yellow Pages or the newspapers because abortions were illegal.

I remembered a conversation I'd had while in college, with a New York friend who told me that she'd had an abortion—two, in fact. I called her. She gave me a name and a number. The rest was up to me.

Dr. Carparti was a fully trained doctor whose office was in a fashionable part of Lexington Avenue in New York City. When I called his office to make the appointment, I was told by the female voice on the other end that I should bring $600 in cash and come to the office on a particular day in early January.

Now I had to get the money. I had a little money saved, but not $600. The next call I made was to Dad. I told him I needed some money to get my car fixed. Five hundred dollars was a lot of money to spend on an old 1954 Buick, he said, but he agreed to lend me the money. Over the Christmas holidays, I went to Washington to see him and to get the money.

Everything was falling into place—the doctor, the appointment, the money—but there were so many things that could go wrong. Ellie could change her mind. Carparti could get arrested. He could want more money than I had. Ellie and I could get arrested. Ellie could die. As the days passed, the tension and anxiety grew, as did the pregnancy.

In early January, Ellie and I drove to New York and went to Dr. Carparti's office on Lexington Avenue. It was bitterly cold and snowing. The skies were gray. The snowflakes were white, but the mounds of snow on the ground in the city were dirty and covered in black soot. We entered the self-service elevator that took us upstairs to the eighth floor. When we entered the waiting room, there were six or seven other women already there. One or two were sitting with men, but most were alone.

Were they all there for abortions? Was this the only thing that Carparti did or was he a "regular" doctor who treated all kinds of problems?

I didn't really care. I just wanted it to be over. The fear and desperation was a feeling I hoped never to know again. I had promised myself that I would never be put in this position again. How could I have been so stupid? How could I have been so weak?

Sex is the most powerful of human drives. It makes men and women lie, steal, wage war, break the law, take risks and face death and disease in order to satisfy it. It brings men and women to their knees in weakness and in prayer. Vows of celibacy and chastity are broken in the pursuit of satisfying the sexual drive.

As we sat in the waiting room in silence, I worried and wondered. Did I have enough money? Would Carparti do it? Would the police raid the office, arrest Carparti and us? Finally, our time came and we were taken into a large room where there was the usual examining table with stirrups at the end. Off to the left of the table was a large, nearly life-sized bust of the Virgin Mary draped with Rosary beads. Dr. Carparti grunted something to us with a thick accent through his surgical mask. I gave the nurse the $600. Dr. Carparti asked Ellie to get on the table and the nurse took me to an adjacent small, windowless room to wait. I heard a few muffled moans from Ellie, but nothing more than that. A half-hour later, Carparti, still in his mask, came into my small prison and said that Ellie was further along than I had told him.

Oh, God, he is not going to be able to do it! She can't get the abortion! How could I be so stupid? I screamed to myself.

"Zis is going to take more zan one visit. I put somesing in ze mouth of her womb to open eet. Vhen you come back tomorrow, I finish."

Another delay! Oh God! One more day for something to go wrong! We had to get this done now.

Carparti left. A few minutes later, his nurse came in and told me to stay in the hotel next door, where I could get a room. Ellie was dressed. She looked pale, scared, in pain and pitiful. We made our way down to the street and got a room in the hotel. She complained of cramping in her stomach that got worse as evening descended on us. The next morning, we went back to Carparti's office. Everything was the same. The table, the Virgin Mary, the mask, Carparti's accent. I waited in the small room and heard Ellie's moans and whimpers. I heard the sound of clanging metal. I buried my face in my hands.

After what seemed like forever, the nurse came into the room where I was waiting and said that it was over and Ellie would be ready to go soon. She would need to rest and take some pills, which she handed to me. If there was a lot of bleeding, I should take Ellie to the emergency room of the nearby hospital. The nurse never told me what she meant by "a lot of bleeding."

We went back to the hotel next door and Ellie made it through the rest of the day and night without a problem. I lay in the bed next to her and held her close. It was the least I could do. In the morning, the cramping had eased, the bleeding had almost stopped and we did not get arrested. The police never came. The silent drive back to the Berkshire Mountains and Stockbridge School took a little more than three hours. I had just enough money left to buy gas for my car. After dropping her off, I drove across campus to my apartment and entered the afternoon coldness of the cinderblock walls. I dropped my bag and cried with relief. It was over.

———

I came to BCH knowing that I would perform abortions. Women were permitted by Massachusetts law and the policies of the hospital to have abortions if continuation of the pregnancy would be harmful to their physical or mental health. The case of each woman, however, had to be presented to the Abortion and Sterilization Committee. *The Committee* would then determine if the woman's request would be granted.

There were so many requests, and the process was so cumbersome, that sometimes a first trimester pregnancy progressed into the second trimester, when more complicated and riskier procedures were required to terminate the pregnancy. Several psychiatry residents agreed to see our patients on an emergency basis when they came in requesting abortions. They quickly wrote consultations simply saying that "continuation of the pregnancy would be detrimental to the woman's mental health," allowing us to get her case before *The Committee* within a week, and the abortions to be performed in the first trimester. It was an onerous process, but we made it work for the poor women of Boston.

During my residency at BCH, I learned to perform abortions in the first trimester—up to 12 weeks—by dilation and curettage. D&C consisted of dilating the cervix and scraping out the contents of the womb. It was the simplest and safest method.

For pregnancies from 16 to 20 weeks, I was taught how to do saline infusions, a procedure where a strong solution of salt in water was injected through the abdomen and into the amniotic sac through a long, thin needle. After several hours, the woman would begin to have contractions, and within 24 hours, would usually expel a dead fetus.

I also assisted one of the third-year residents when he performed hysterotomies. It was major surgery, rarely used, that required general anesthesia and an incision into the abdomen and womb to remove the fetus and the placenta. I learned the technique from watching him and from reading textbooks. Eventually, I was allowed to be the surgeon on hysterotomies, and the senior resident was my assistant.

These were emotionally difficult operations to perform, but for some women, it was their only choice. For us, it was always the last choice. I hated them.

As I learned to do abortions, I learned that they were never easy for me or for any of the residents who did them, but I understood the impact that an unwanted pregnancy could have. I believed that the decision to have or not have an abortion should be left up to each woman. I believed even more strongly that poor, black women should have that choice, too. I knew that abortion could save the life of a woman who had severe hypertension, diabetes, heart disease, kidney disease or cancer. I knew that abortion could help restore the lives of young girls who were pregnant as the result of rape, incest or because they fell prey to smooth-talking older men. I knew that abortion could help poor women who already had more children than they could afford to take care of. I knew that abortion could change the lives of women trapped by men who abused and controlled them with sex and pregnancy. I knew that abortion could give teenage girls the chance to finish high school and make something of their lives. I believed that a girl or a woman should not be forced to have a child as punishment for a mistake that she and so many of us have made. I also knew, as did my patients, that we were not only terminating the pregnancy, but the life of the embryo or fetus.

When I first arrived in Boston, many women went to New York for abortions, which had already liberalized its laws. Unfortunately, most black women could not scrape together enough money to travel to New York and pay for their abortions. A few did, but if they had complications when they returned home, they would come to BCH and we would have to clean up somebody else's mess.

Most of Boston's poor and black women did not have the option to go to New York, however. They came to BCH for their abortions.

No one made performing the abortions easy. There were a couple of nurses, a scrub tech or two and an anesthesiologist who would volunteer to help us, but all the other department staff—doctors and nurses alike—did not want to be involved in providing abortions for the women who came to BCH. For residents, there was little training value in providing abortions. A D&C was a D&C. Abortions were scheduled after the regular operating room cases were completed. The few of us who did perform them often did so in the late afternoons or on Saturday mornings, with a reduced operating crew of volunteers.

I wrote to the hospital administration and asked them to establish an ambulatory unit for first trimester abortions so that the service we were providing could be carried out under better conditions for the patients, in a more organized fashion.

A first-year resident writing to the hospital administration—unheard of! They refused my request. Nobody was going to make this easier for the patients or for us.

CHAPTER 10

SEE ONE, DO ONE, TEACH ONE:
THE STORY OF JIM LLOYD

In addition to the battles in the streets of Boston over the integration of public schools and the police and fire departments, there was an equally intense war being waged within the walls of BCH itself. The three medical schools at BCH were always on the alert for any opportunity to get more turf in the hospital and they fiercely guarded the territory they already had. Each school wanted to be at BCH.

Tufts had affiliations with New England Medical Center, the Floating Hospital for Children and various Catholic hospitals in Boston, but it wanted to stay at BCH because of its importance to their teaching and research programs.

Boston University was next door to BCH and had few other options for teaching its students and residents. University Hospital, its other next-door neighbor, was too small and too private. Boston University desperately needed the BCH affiliation. Otherwise, its medical program might die.

Harvard had established the famed Thorndike and Channing Research Laboratories at BCH. It was not about to leave. Although Harvard had other hospitals, like Massachusetts General, Peter Bent Brigham and Beth Israel, where some teaching could take place, it was BCH that provided the extreme cases—poor patients who waited too long to seek medical attention, the desperate who could not pay their hospital bills and would therefore agree to take an experimental route. Teaching and research opportunities were readily provided at City Hospital. Harvard did not want to lose that. The three schools were constantly at odds with each other to preserve their place at BCH.

The constant chaos, confusion and competition at BCH meant

that taking care of patients was never easy. There were always hurdles and obstacles which had to be overcome. But if it was hard for me, it was awful for the patients.

In addition to taking care of patients in this maze of bureaucracy, we were also expected to teach medical students when they "rotated" on the OB/GYN service for six weeks during their third year of medical school. Most of the students came from Boston University, but a few came from Harvard or Tufts. Twelve students were assigned to us and would help take care of patients by drawing blood, fetching X-rays and tracking down the results of blood tests from the morass of the laboratory. They would take histories from the patients and do physical exams, which they wrote up as part of the patients' hospital charts. In addition to being on night call, they also attended rounds, daily conferences and lectures.

By seeing, listening and doing, the students learned the rudiments of OB/GYN, how to take care of women and, most importantly, how to do a pelvic exam. I enjoyed teaching the students OB/GYN—especially instructing them on how to care for a patient the way I thought it should be done.

Jim Lloyd was a third-year medical student from BU. He was a tall, skinny, long-haired, idealistic white kid who began his OB/GYN rotation at BCH in October of 1971, four months after I started my residency. He was eager to learn, but because he had heard gory stories from upperclassmen about "teaching hysterectomies" on the OB/GYN service at BCH, he decided to document instances of patient mistreatment. He came to the Department of OB/GYN at BCH with a notebook in one hand, a pen in the other and his eyes and ears open. He secretly wrote down what he thought were cases of patient exploitation and mistreatment. He asked other students to do the same.

In January of 1972, three months after he finished his OB/GYN rotation, Lloyd went to BU Medical School's dean and told him what he had seen during his six weeks on the OB/GYN service. He described what he thought was unnecessary surgery and a general insensitivity toward the patients' feelings. He summed up his observations by saying that he thought "women were being butchered."

The dean needed something in writing, however, so he asked Lloyd to put together what he had seen in as much detail as possible. Two days later, Lloyd handed in his observations.

After reading the cases, the dean agreed that the problems Lloyd described were very serious. "Are there other students willing to put their observations in writing?" he asked.

Determined to expose this atrocity, Lloyd found eight other students who submitted written statements describing what they had observed. Each story exposed a deeper secret:

A 36-year-old Spanish-speaking woman was admitted for sterilization. Immediately, a senior resident began to wonder if he could get a vaginal hysterectomy out of the case. He scribbled on her chart, "Procedure of first choice: vaginal hysterectomy; second choice: total abdominal hysterectomy. If neither of these is possible, then bilateral tubal ligation."

On rounds, a student noticed the notation and was puzzled by the order. "Why is tubal ligation the last choice?" he asked.

The resident responded in a condescending tone, "We want the teaching experience. She's 36 and doesn't need her uterus."

"Couldn't she have an adverse psychological reaction after a hysterectomy?" the student asked.

"No, she's 36."

Not satisfied, the student tried to talk to the patient, but couldn't. He didn't speak Spanish. Instead, he arranged for a Spanish-speaking chaplain to see her and convey his concerns. The patient reacted with surprise. She had not understood that the papers she signed authorized a hysterectomy and was adamant in not wanting one. Once she realized what the residents had planned for her, she signed herself out of the hospital before the planned hysterectomy could be performed.

After reading through the reports by Lloyd and other students, the dean met with Dr. David Charles and gave him copies of the reports. Dr. Charles was furious and demanded to meet with Lloyd as soon as possible. It was arranged for the next day.

When Lloyd arrived for the meeting, Dr. Charles and Dr. Santamarina attacked him. They challenged his academic competence, his knowledge of obstetrics and gynecology and his motives. Charles and Santa refused to deal with his main concern—that medical decisions were being made for teaching purposes rather than in the best interest of the patients. Without investigating further, Charles insisted that the correct decisions had been made in all the cases and made several references to "this population," insinuating that a different course of treatment was sometimes indicated for BCH's poor, uneducated, predominantly black and Hispanic patients. Lloyd, he said, did not have enough medical knowledge to question the residents' decisions.

Lloyd didn't flinch. His main concern, he said, was the residents' attitude toward patients. They were not sensitive to the patients' needs or feelings. After a lengthy debate, Charles finally conceded that there were problems with "a couple bad apples" among the resident staff, but stayed on the offensive.

"The thing is, several members of the department have heard about these allegations and have retained attorneys to clear their names in the courts," said Charles. "You had better find yourself a good lawyer, son, or you'll be in some serious trouble."

As the meeting ended, Charles said that he wanted another meeting with all the students involved to clear up the allegations once and for all. Dr. Charles asked me and several other residents to attend the meeting. That day, we all crowded into the conference room on MAT l. In addition to the residents and the dean, Drs. Charles, Santamarina, Rankin, Penza and Smith of the OB/GYN department were there. Lloyd arrived with five other students. A chair had been put in the front of the room for him to sit facing the crowd alongside Dr. Charles, the dean and Dr. Santamarina. The other students quietly took empty seats at the rear of the room. Dr. Charles asked Lloyd to outline the problems he and the other students had seen.

Lloyd chose to deal with the residents' *attitudes* toward the patients.

Lloyd decided to try and show that non-medical considerations—particularly the residents' desire for more surgery—were behind the decisions that were made. He wanted to show that the way the residents viewed the patients negatively impacted the care they were given. Even if the right decision had been made, it was made for the wrong reasons.

As Lloyd began reading the cases, he was interrupted by a "visit" who thought he was being referred to. Lloyd ignored him and continued to read. More interruptions challenged his facts, but Lloyd defiantly said that he intended to finish reading the cases. Despite continued outbursts, Lloyd read the remainder of the students' statements.

Dr. Jim Penza took up the issue of medical student teaching and said that having him or any student in the operating room was not good for patient care, since student teaching prolonged surgery, thereby increasing risks to patients.

"If there is no teaching, there would be no doctors," he said.

The dean joined in by saying that he had made mistakes while in training, but that this was the only way to train future surgeons. Lloyd fought back and tried to show that these explanations did not satisfy his concerns.

"I'm not talking about legitimate training in surgery. What we object to is an attitude which resulted in unnecessary surgery done mainly for teaching purposes."

There was plenty of shouting and a lot of accusations were made during the meeting. Finally, to snatch the upper hand away, Charles turned the discussion from patient care to Jim Lloyd.

"The thing is," Dr. Charles began, "your performance on OB/GYN was inferior and you frequently failed to be present on the wards, especially at night when you were supposed to be on call."

Then came the most powerful blow. In an angry outburst, several faculty members confronted the dean.

"We do not want to teach BU students anymore if this is the way we're going to be treated! We would prefer to teach only Harvard and Tufts. They are better students anyway."

Stung by that threat, the dean interrupted the shouting and declared, "After hearing what the faculty has to say, I am personally satisfied that they would not allow patients to be mistreated. I don't think that Lloyd has substantiated the charges he has made. Furthermore, I am now satisfied that they are *not* true. I apologize to the faculty. I have been misled, but when such charges are brought to me, it is my duty to investigate them. I apologize on behalf of the medical school, the students involved and on Lloyd's behalf."

In spite of the apology, several faculty members indicated that they were in the process of instituting legal action against Lloyd in the form of libel suits.

His voice quivering, but still determined, Lloyd said, "Since we seem unable to communicate constructively and since I am likely to have anything I say used against me in court, I am not going to participate in the meeting any longer without the benefit of a lawyer."

With that, he walked out of the room. He was beaten, his spirit broken and his career as a doctor doomed. I felt sorry for him, but said nothing.

As the meeting was breaking up, the dean asked the other students if they had anything to say. One student insisted that everything in her statement was true and that she would stand behind it. Another stated that he had thought everything in his statement was true, but now realized that he might have been mistaken. He apologized for his part in the allegations. The other students left the meeting in silence.

Although Lloyd and the other students had certainly misinterpreted some of the things they had seen, others were real and true. There were some residents—"bad apples," as Dr. Charles had put it—who performed more complicated operations on patients because it was better for their training. The more surgery they performed, they reasoned, the better surgeons they would become.

Later that afternoon, Lloyd went to the dean's office. He felt hurt and betrayed. Sitting in front of the dean with his face in his hands, Lloyd said, "I came to you for advice before taking any action and followed your directions to the letter, including involving other students. You publicly demeaned my motives and good faith." Lloyd, in tears, looked up from his hands. "Why?"

"The OB/GYN faculty is threatening to resign and there is a serious possibility that BU students will not be allowed in the OB/GYN department at BCH. Other faculties in other departments have heard about the students' accusations and are upset over the incident as well. The teaching students would receive throughout BCH has been jeopardized. Faculty members might become afraid to speak openly in front of students. I had no choice. I did what I had to do in order to protect my faculty from attacks such as the one you have brought against the OB/GYN department, and to protect students from the loss of teaching. Furthermore, I am going to write a letter to the chief of every department to inform him what you have done. The letter will warn them that you are likely to be taking notes or pictures to use against them."

"No, no. Please don't do that," Lloyd begged. "If you do, it will deprive me of teaching and bias any evaluations and recommendations from these departments."

"I have a medical school to protect," said the dean. "Unless the OB/GYN matter is properly handled, the consequences for BU will be disastrous. We could lose much of the OB/GYN faculty and maybe all teaching at BCH. BU could not successfully expand its class size if that happened."

Devastated, Lloyd left the dean's office a broken man.

The students' written allegations, however, had been widely circulated and eventually found their way into the hands of Carl Cobb, a reporter at the *Boston Globe*. Cobb set up a meeting with the dean and said he was planning to use the students' allegations in an article that would charge the OB/GYN department at BCH with racism. Over the next several weeks, Cobb met with Lloyd and some of the other students and, on April 29, 1972, the big black letters of the headline on the front page brought Lloyd's allegations to the public eye:

STUDENTS CHARGE BCH OBSTETRICS UNIT WITH EXCESSIVE SURGERY

The *Globe* article brought more turmoil to the medical school and BCH than ever before, and struck fear in the hearts of the predominantly black and Spanish-speaking women of Boston who used BCH as their hospital.

The *Globe* article reported the students' allegations that black women on the OB/GYN service at BCH underwent excessive and unnecessary surgery because interns and residents wanted to do surgery for "training purposes." Too often, the article said, when alternatives were possible, the more radical and dangerous treatment was used, not to benefit patients, but to benefit interns' and residents' surgical training. The article went on to say that often, medical records did not reflect what was actually being done to patients, and that patients often signed consent forms for surgery without fully understanding the procedure they were about to undergo. Underlying all of this was an "indifferent and callous attitude toward patients, resulting in unnecessary patient indignities and anguish." The students, Cobb wrote, also "expressed concern" that black and Spanish-speaking women were often sterilized by hysterectomy while white women were more likely to be sterilized by tubal ligation.

Boston racism, which permeated the public schools and the fire and police departments, was alive and well at BCH.

The Commissioner of Health and Hospitals formed a committee of physicians to investigate the charges. Harvard Medical School established its own panel of experts to look into the allegations, perhaps seeing this as a way to force BU out of BCH.

BCH was in crisis and the OB/GYN department was in turmoil. Many patients protested by going to other Boston hospitals, where they were often admitted to segregated wards after they had their babies or their surgery.

What was the truth? There were some residents who saw the patients as only teaching material and would try to convince them to have more radical procedures than they needed, but not all of the students' reports were accurate or contained all the facts.

For example, one of the cases reported on involved my care of the 40-year-old pregnant diabetic who was having her 13th child, her third by cesarean section. The student's allegation mentioned that she had 13 children, 12 pregnancies and a previous cesarean, but failed to report that the woman was diabetic and in tears, begging for a tubal ligation:

> A conversation took place between Dr. Edglan [sic] and Mrs. Jones [not her real name] concerning tubal ligation during the cesarean section, to which she agreed. However, during a telephone conversation with her husband, he forbade the procedure. During the cesarean section, at which myself, Dr. Edglan and Dr. Penza were present, tubal ligation was carried out and listed as appendectomy. To my knowledge, neither the patient nor her husband were ever informed of this procedure.

I had told the patient the next day that I had tied her tubes. Everyone in the operating room knew what had taken place. In this case, the student was completely off the mark. The procedure had been documented inaccurately to bypass the system—that much was true— but it was done for the sake of the patient, not my experience.

The real problem was that resident supervision was less than it should have been. Although a few tried to help, most of the staff physicians were volunteers and "visits." That is one of the dangers of a resident-teach-resident training program, where "see one, do one, teach one" is the rule.

———

A gloom came over the OB/GYN department as a result of *The Globe*'s story, but nobody got fired. Jim Lloyd was discredited, graduated a year later but had difficulty getting into a residency training program. In a final letter, he angrily wrote:

> The white male professionals who control Boston University School of Medicine, the City Hospital OB/GYN department and the administration of City Hospital avoided confronting and correcting the substantive problems. This is, in itself, the ultimate act of racism as it deprives poor women, white as well as black and Spanish-speaking women, of their right to health care that they can be sure will not violate their emotional and physical integrity as human beings. These high-paid bureaucrats continue to violate the basic rights of these women each day they fail to publicly disclose the results of any investigation and the corrective steps they are taking to resolve them now and prevent the recurrence of these violations. Until they take such action, the poor women of Boston will rightfully fear receiving services from the Department of Obstetrics and Gynecology at City Hospital.

CHAPTER 11

CONTROL

———

Two months after the *Globe* article appeared, I began my second year of training at BCH and was assigned to the gynecology service. Patients admitted to the gynecology ward at BCH had severe pelvic infections, abnormal bleeding, miscarriages, fibroid tumors, cancers and blocked tubes that required surgery if the woman was ever going to be able to get pregnant. There were also many women who requested abortions.

In the outpatient clinic, I took care of women with these conditions and more. We did plenty of Pap smears and detected early- and late-stage cervical cancer. Many of the women who came to the clinic wanted birth control. The pill and the intrauterine devices were very popular.

August 1972

A young, black woman, who I will call Ethel, came to the clinic concerned that she might not be able to get pregnant. She was from a small town in North Carolina and had come to Boston to further her education. Now in her last year of college, she had met a young man and they had fallen in love. They were living together and planned to get married. For the last six months, she explained, they had been having regular intercourse and had not been using any birth control.

I asked if she had ever had an infection in her womb or tubes. She said she had not. She told me that her periods were regular, indicating to me that she ovulated on a regular basis. Her boyfriend had a child with another woman, so I presumed that he did not have a problem with his sperm count, but I ordered one on him anyway.

During the woman's physical exam, I saw an ugly raised scar that ran from her navel to her pubic bone.

"What is this from?" I asked.

In a quiet, barely audible voice, she answered, "I had a baby when I was 14. It had to be delivered by cesarean. I…I gave the baby up for adoption."

As she choked on the word "adoption," tears appeared in the corners of her eyes. She tried to blink them away, but was too late to stop a few from spilling down her cheeks.

In my years as a doctor, I had met scores of women who had given babies up for adoption. More often than not, they carried the sorrow and pain of that decision with them for the rest of their lives. I had seen this pain many times before.

Other than the scars on her abdomen and in her soul, the exam was normal. She appeared to be perfectly healthy. I was mystified. Here was a young couple, having regular intercourse without using contraception, and each of them had "proven" their fertility in the past. Her periods were normal. What could the problem be?

I ordered the usual blood tests, took cultures from her cervix for gonorrhea and told her about the sperm count I wanted to get on her fiancé. "I also want to get a hysterosalpingogram on you—that's a special X-ray to look at the inside of your womb and tubes to make sure that they're open," I said. "A liquid that can be seen on X-ray will be injected into your cervix, up into the cavity of the womb. If all is well, it should be seen spilling from the ends of the tubes."

"Will the liquid do anything else?" she asked.

"No. It's perfectly safe. It just can be seen on the X-ray."

"Okay. Let's do that."

In Ethel's X-rays, the solution filled her normal-appearing womb, but did not spill from her tubes. In fact, the X-ray showed that her tubes were abnormally short and blocked—something had happened to them.

When she came back to the clinic to get the results of all of her tests, I dreaded telling her what I had discovered. She sat down at the wooden table, surrounded by a dozen or so other women waiting for exams, without any privacy whatsoever. She looked so hopeful—she wanted so badly for me to tell her how she could have a baby.

But I had to tell her what I had discovered.

"Your X-rays showed that your tubes are blocked," I said as quietly as I could. "From the looks of things, I suspect they were tied when you had the c-section when you were 14. I'm sorry."

Ethel wept. There was nothing I could do to console her. Cradling her head in her arms, she sobbed into the table, adding her tears to the collection that had soaked into the wood over the years. It took 10 minutes for her to calm herself down enough to stop sobbing. Silent tears flowed down her face, clinging to her chin before falling into her lap and onto the table.

"I had that c-section in a hospital in North Carolina," she said, her voice strained. "The white doctor who took care of me was so mean—he kept referring to me and my family as 'you people' and made snide remarks every chance he got. You know what he said to me when he examined me? 'Lie on your back so I can examine you—you know how to lie on your back, don't you?' I should have known he'd do something to me…I should have known…"

Ethel, like so many black and Hispanic women, had unknowingly and involuntarily been sterilized. She was the victim of a racist doctor who wanted to stop the reproduction of "you people." This doctor took control of Ethel's reproductive life and left her without the choice of having more children.

———

Poor black and Hispanic women who came to BCH wanted to be in control of their own lives, their own bodies and their own reproduction. The family planning clinic at BCH was always very busy. It was a place of liberation. By now, the pill had been available without restriction for 12 years and the poor women of Boston wanted it. The family planning counselors who worked in the clinic were passionate and driven in their desire to help poor women control their lives and their futures. For those women who could not or did not want to take the pill every day, we offered the IUD, diaphragms, contraceptive foam and condoms.

As a second-year resident, I was responsible for responding to calls to the emergency room. The tragedies of life came to the ER at BCH. I took care of women who had been raped, women having miscarriages and women who had acute PID—pelvic inflammatory disease—resulting from sexually transmitted bacteria. I delivered babies in the ER, in the back seat of the taxicabs that had brought the mothers to the emergency room, and sometimes I even delivered them in the tunnels on the way to the Maternity Building.

The hours I worked were long and the on-call schedule was exhausting. Meanwhile, my marriage continued to deteriorate. Ramona's position at Northeastern required her to travel and spend long hours away from home and our children, so we hired a young woman as a live-in babysitter. She loved the kids and made sure they were fed, clean and in bed on time (which they often were by the time Ramona and I came home), but our children were being raised by someone other than us, and it showed. The arguments that Ramona and I had about our schedules became more frequent, louder and more heated. Neither one of us would give in.

During my 30-minute drive home from Boston to Framingham, the tension, turmoil and anger inside of me would come to a boil so quickly that by the time I walked through the front door, I was in a rage whether Ramona was home or not. I did not realize how difficult it would be for me to overcome the views that had been drilled into my brain since early childhood. The traditional role of a woman as wife and mother was all I had ever known and it was not being fulfilled. Ramona and I saw little of each other and when we did, we argued or didn't speak at all. Our marriage was falling apart.

CHAPTER 12

THE YEAR OF *ROE*

January 22, 1973

The Supreme Court of the United States declared that American women had a legal right to abortions. Their ruling in *Roe v. Wade* and *Doe v. Bolton* stated that women had a right to privacy and during the first 12 weeks of pregnancy, they could terminate it without any interference from the state. During the second trimester, the state could only intervene to say where the abortion could take place, for the safety of the woman. During the last third of the pregnancy, when the fetus became increasingly viable and was able to live outside of the womb— even with the help of respirators and other machines—the state might have an interest in the potential for life of the fetus, and may regulate the performance of the abortion. Women, however, still had the right to terminate the pregnancy in the third trimester.

The *Roe* decision was like a door being blown open. It hit like a bombshell. It threw out all restrictive laws against abortion in every state in the country, including Massachusetts. Women were now free to make their own decisions about terminating a pregnancy in private and in safety.

With *Roe*, illegal abortionists were driven out of business and along with them, the humiliation, abuse, maiming and killing of women— particularly poor women. Clinics staffed by well-trained doctors and skilled nurses opened up to provide women with the choice to terminate unwanted pregnancies safely. Doctors stopped going to jail and women stopped dying.

Shortly after *Roe* was handed down, I was invited to debate the impact of the decision at a conference for medical students being held in Boston. My opponent was Dr. Mildred Jefferson, a black woman surgeon who was a member of the faculty at Boston University School of Medicine.

In preparing for the debate, I knew that my presentation would have to be based on facts and how this Supreme Court decision would impact the lives of black women, their health and their options in life. These were medical students and they wanted facts. My research confirmed what I already knew—that women had been seeking to terminate unwanted pregnancies for almost as long as women had been on this earth; that they were willing to put their lives and health on the line to do it; and that the women who suffered most when abortion was illegal were poor women and black women. During the days of illegal abortions, women hemorrhaged, became infected and had hysterectomies as last-resort, life-saving measures. And black women suffered and died in disproportionate numbers from these poorly performed, illegal abortions.

On the day of the debate, I arrived early and spent some time talking to the students. Eventually, Dr. Jefferson walked into the room and all eyes turned in her direction. She was not an unattractive woman, but there was a cold rigidity about her that was unyielding and ugly. Her skin was very dark and she wore her hair in bangs and tightly pulled back in a bun. She wore a yellow construction helmet and in each hand, she carried pictures, some of fetuses that she claimed had been aborted and others of babies resembling those found on baby food jars.

Although Mildred Jefferson and I were in the same room and in the same space, we did not acknowledge each other. She insisted to the moderator that I go first.

By then, the room was full. All the chairs were taken and more students were standing in the back and sides of the room, leaning against the walls. The moderator framed the debate and then introduced us to the audience. The debate began.

My argument was about women's lives.

Her argument was about the life of the "baby," which, she said, began at conception.

My argument was about women making choices about their lives.

Her argument was about the "baby" having no choice.

My goal was to emphasize the tragedy of the women who were hurt by illegal abortions.

Her goal was to humanize the fetus.

It was an argument in images and words and I think I won. She left the meeting right after the debate and I hoped never to see her again. I'm sure she thought she won. I promised myself that I would never again debate "right to lifers." Their position was too rigid and absolute. For them, life was black and white. For me, there were always shades of gray.

———

As a result of the *Roe* decision, BCH did away with *The Committee* and we struggled to make abortion part of the routine services provided to our patients, but there was resistance at every turn.

We set up a second trimester abortion unit, which allowed us to perform three saline infusions per week. There were nurses who chose to work in the unit, staying with the women during the entire procedure, comforting them, supporting them and teaching them. They taught them about their bodies, about relationships with men and about contraception. It was their goal to keep women from having to come back to the unit again. It was their goal to empower these women to take control of their lives.

Spring 1973

My marriage continued to fall apart. I finally gave Ramona an ultimatum: either her schedule changed, or I would leave. Ramona's schedule did not change. Now I had to tell my two small children that I was leaving. It was the hardest thing I ever had to do, but I believed that it was better for all of us if I left, rather than living through the incessant arguments.

The three of us were riding in my car, with six-year-old Kenny sitting in the passenger's seat and three-year-old Kim sitting on the armrest between us.

"I'm moving out of the house to live somewhere else," I told them.

"I want to go with you, Daddy," said Kenny. Kim, not knowing what to say, just mimicked her big brother's words. I felt the lump form in my throat. I didn't want to leave, but it was for the best. My children, I reminded myself, should not have to witness their parents arguing every time they were together.

"No…you guys are going to stay with Mommy in the house and I'll see you on the weekends and whenever else I can," I managed to say.

Kenny and Kim both sat in silence for a moment. Then, starting with Kenny and moving immediately to Kim, they began to cry.

In April of 1973, I left. I left our home, I left my wife and I left my two children. My marriage had failed. I had failed. Our marriage had come to cause us both great pain. Leaving provided relief from that pain, but it was replaced by a pain of a different kind.

I found myself an apartment near the hospital that had a second bedroom where Kenny and Kim could sleep whenever they came to visit. They stayed with me every other weekend and I would try to pick them up during the week when I was not on call or moonlighting.

It was a time of great personal anguish and a time of professional joy.

David Charles announced that I was to become the new Chief Resident beginning in July of 1973. With my personal life crumbling, I poured my energy into my job, my patients and, as best I could, my children. I developed a program that I believed would improve the patients' care and assure that the residents received good training with more supervision. I presented my plan to Dr. Charles and asked him to provide more attending coverage. He said he would try.

June 1973

One month before I was to become Chief Resident, an article was published in *The New England Journal of Medicine* entitled "Transplacental Passage of Erythromycin and Clindamycin." It gave the details of the fetal research project carried out by Drs. Charles, Sabath and Philipson.

The research was carried out on 33 pregnant women who presented themselves for abortions at City Hospital between 1971 and 1972, and the results concluded that both erythromycin and clindamycin, antibiotics often used as substitutes when the patient is allergic to penicillin, reached the fetus at high enough levels to be effective when multiple doses were given to the pregnant women.

The New England Journal of Medicine is the most respected of all medical journals published in the world. It was a major achievement for David Charles and his two Harvard colleagues to have the results of their research published between its covers. The results of the research were significant, but the political impact of the article would far outweigh its scientific contribution.

CHAPTER 13

CHIEF RESIDENT

July 2, 1973

The ringing pierced my unconscious mind like an arrow through my brain and for a moment, I didn't know where I was. Like Pavlov's dog, my hand reached for the phone. At the sound of the nurse's voice, a surge of adrenaline coursed through my body.

"Ken!"

Prying my tongue from the roof of my mouth, I groaned, "Yeah."

"It's LaShana in bed three. The fetal heart just dropped down to 60."

"Okay, I'll be right there."

I lay motionless with my eyes closed to collect myself. Then, as if struck by a bolt of lightening, I sat upright in the small, dark, windowless sleep room that the senior residents used when we were on call at night. I felt for my scrub cap—it was only half on my head—stood up and reached for the door. We always slept in our scrubs. They were comfortable and sleeping in them saved time.

As I emerged from my stupor and the tiny room in the far corner of MAT 4, the bare florescent lights shocked my eyes and completed the waking process. Stopping briefly at the receptionist's desk, I glanced at the large clock on the wall. It was 3:30 in the morning.

"I'm glad I went to bed when I did."

The secretary behind the desk smiled, waved her fingers and continued talking on the phone.

I pushed open the double doors that separated the reception area from the delivery rooms and entered the long, dingy corridor that led to where LaShana was in labor. I walked past the newly renovated delivery

52

rooms and emergency operating room that opened off either side of this wide passageway, using these few seconds to consider all the possible reasons why this baby's heart rate was dropping and what I would do in response to each. By the time I reached the entrance to the labor room, the emotional mix of anticipation and challenge were churning inside me. I was alert, wide awake and my head was clear. I was ready.

In the newly renovated labor room, there were six labor beds parallel to one another, lined up against the far wall. Each bed was separated from the next by a shoulder-high plastic partition, making the room look like a barn with rows of stalls. Each stall contained a bed, a small table and a monitor for keeping track of the baby's heartbeat during labor. Crowded into the corners of the stall were an IV pole and other paraphernalia. Protruding from the wall at the head of each bed were oxygen nozzles and a light. There were no frills; the stalls were designed to be functional. This was BCH.

There were two women in labor, but nearly everybody was crowded in and around stall three, where LaShana Howard panted and groaned with labor pains. Two nurses were adjusting the patient's IV, the oxygen mask on her face and the monitor straps around her massive abdomen. A couple of cherub-faced medical and nursing students watched with wide-eyed wonderment and terror, looking frightened and useless. I could not see past the crowd to glance at the monitor.

"What's the story?" I asked of one of the nurses.

"She was doing fine until a minute ago, when all of a sudden the bottom dropped out of the fetal heart. It had been at 120 all night, but without warning, it dropped down to 60. I put the oxygen mask on her and called you. I was afraid to try and have her turn on her side. Can you imagine if she fell out of the bed? The fetal heart is back up to 120 now."

LaShana was possibly the biggest woman I had ever taken care of. She weighed at least 500 pounds when I first met her in the clinic back in February—and at that point, she was only four months pregnant. It was impossible to examine her in the clinic because her massive body did not fit on the examining table. The clinic staff had to take her to a bed in the emergency room. Her abdomen was so large that I could barely feel her pregnant uterus when I examined her and her humongous thighs guarded the opening of her vagina like giant boulders at the portal of a secret cave. We all wondered how she got pregnant.

"Where there's a will, there's a way," someone had quipped.

"I'd like to see Will, and especially his way," one of the nurses had muttered under her breath.

The nurses had to use an extra large cuff to take her blood pressure, and the only way she could be weighed was in the hospital kitchen on the industrial meat scales.

LaShana came to the clinic only that one time. Now, five months later, she was back and in labor.

Since her arrival, her contractions had become more frequent, lasted longer and become more intense. The difficult internal examination initially revealed that the mouth of her womb was opening slowly. Not much else could be felt. At BCH, in 1973, we didn't have an ultrasound machine and she was too fat to X-ray. I had to rely on my hands and fingers.

After examining the fetal heart tracing, I looked at LaShana again. The pale green oxygen mask was puny on her moon-shaped face. The elastic band holding it in place creased her cheeks and jowls. Her body filled the entire bed, and her glistening black skin stood out against the white, rumpled sheets.

"Can somebody get me a glove, please?" I asked. "When was the last time she was examined?"

"Not since you did at midnight."

Approaching the side of the bed, I gently but firmly held LaShana's hand. Touching was important; it established and reinforced the humanity between us. I was going to need her help and cooperation, and she was going to have to trust me and follow my instructions. Looking into her face and wiping the sweat from her forehead with a small towel, I spoke to her in a low, reassuring voice.

"How ya doin', LaShana?"

"It hurts. It hurts real bad. I can't take any more of this pain. Can't you do something? Is the baby all right? Can't you take it now?"

"Baby's fine. Heartbeat went down a little bit, but it's fine now. I need to examine you, okay?"

LaShana nodded, squeezing my hand even tighter as the next labor pain began. The nurses began their mantra to ease her through the contraction.

"Breeeeeeathe, slooooow deeeeeeeep breaths. That's gooooood. In deeeeeep. Now blooooow it ooooooout. Goooooooood. Real slooooooow. That's gooooooood. See your breath and the pain go out of your body. Breeeeeeathe for your baby."

The contraction approached its crescendo and the nurses repeated their incantations more rapidly, synchronizing their chants with LaShana's breaths, which were escalating from moans to cries. She was beginning to lose control. My eyes went back to the monitor where the staccato tracing of the fetal heartbeat was being recorded on graph paper scrolling continuously out of the machine and onto the floor. The heart rate dropped down to 60 again and stayed there for the duration of the contraction. As it eased, the heart rate slowly climbed back to 120.

I withdrew my hand from LaShana's tight grip and placed it on her knee, maintaining contact. As I moved down toward the foot of the bed, she became more and more frightened.

"Don't leave me."

"I'm right here, LaShana. I won't leave. I want to examine you before the next contraction comes."

Without being prompted, one of the nurses closed the curtain to the stall and pulled the sheets down from LaShana's massive body. Then, together, we flexed her hips and knees and put the soles of her feet together. The "frog leg" position was supposed to make the internal examination easier. With LaShana, it didn't do much good.

"I need your help, LaShana. I want to do an exam to see if the baby's coming down. Let's do this before the next contraction comes."

LaShana knew what to do. She reached down with both hands and grasped the inside of her massive thighs, pulling the pendulous flab up and back, barely revealing the entrance to her vagina. As the fat-laden flesh was lifted up and away, I sat on the side of the bed and inserted one, then two, lubricated, gloved fingers into her vagina. Shifting my weight so that I was practically in the bed with her, I advanced my fingers cautiously along the moist, fleshy walls of her vagina. I could feel the nurses' eyes on me as they watched my face for clues. I pushed harder to get in deeper. I had to know everything and I didn't have much time before the next contraction began.

Then, I felt it. Instead of the smooth, round firmness of the baby's head, my fingers met the irregularity of the baby's buttocks. Its thighs and legs disappeared up into the womb. Sweeping my fingers around the baby's back and thighs, I felt for the remaining rim of cervix. There was none. Along the side of the baby, I felt what I dreaded most: the smooth, twisted, rubbery umbilical cord.

"It's a breech, at a plus two station. I can't feel cervix, but I can feel a loop of cord. The pulsations are strong, but that explains the drop in heart rate."

I felt the weight of the nurses' stare as they listened for my next audible thought. I looked up at LaShana. I strained to look over her massive abdomen into her tiny eyes.

"The baby is butt-first, and is down pretty far in the birth canal, which is good. It's hard for me to tell if the mouth of your womb is fully open, but I think it is. Part of the cord is also down in the birth canal and when you have a contraction, the pressure of the baby's butt is squeezing the cord and cutting off its oxygen. That's why his heart rate slows down. We're going to have to get him out of there soon. I'm pretty sure we can get him out naturally—it's either that or a c-section. But I think we can deliver him through the birth canal. You're gonna have to help me, though. You and me together, LaShana."

As I talked, I continued the exam to make sure I hadn't missed anything. My arm, wrist and shoulder began to ache from my contortions.

LaShana's eyes widened. "It's a boy?"

"That's what it feels like to me." I smiled and ended the exam, slowly unfolding from the position I was in. As I stood up, another contraction began and the fetal heart again dropped down to 60 where it stayed well beyond the end of the contraction, recovering back to 110 very slowly. Things were getting worse. I squeezed LaShana's hand again as we all breathed through the contraction. She was crying out louder now and digging her nails into the back of my hand.

Her baby was being forced into the birth canal buttocks first. He was a breech. His buttocks, scrotum, penis, thighs, legs, feet, abdomen, chest, arms and shoulders would come out with ease. The baby's head, however, not having the chance to be molded to his mother's pelvis by the forces of hours of labor, would come last and it might not fit through the tightest parts of this narrow passageway. Breeches were the most difficult and challenging of obstetrical deliveries. They required a series of choreographed maneuvers that all had to be performed at the right time and in the right way, quickly and harmlessly in less than two minutes. The vagina would cover his mouth and nose while the compression of his own body against the cord would prevent him from receiving the oxygen he so desperately needed. The cervix—the mouth of the womb—which had fully opened and merged with the vagina to allow the baby's body to pass through, could constrict down on the baby's neck, trapping his head inside its mother's womb, further squeezing the umbilical cord in the process. The baby could die or be born with severe brain damage.

The challenge of obstetrics is that we care for two patients simultaneously—the pregnant woman and her yet-to-be-born baby. What we do for one affects the other. LaShana and her son brought this into sharp focus. It was risky to attempt a vaginal breech delivery, but it was even riskier to perform a c-section on this massively obese, pregnant woman. The biggest risk to LaShana would be anesthesia, and the obstetrical anesthesia service at BCH was not very good. Risking general anesthesia in this high-risk patient and performing major surgery by cutting through mounds and mountains of fat would surely result in a seriously ill patient—perhaps even a dead one. Those were my choices. Those were LaShana's choices. I discussed the risks with LaShana briefly and she agreed to try the vaginal delivery.

The labor nurses at City Hospital were the best. As soon as the decision was made, they knew exactly what to do. The nurses on the night shift and I had worked together many times before and I could not have been happier with the staff I was working with that night.

"Could somebody call the 'visit' for me and ask him to come in? I need his help."

After writing a brief note on LaShana's chart, I turned my attention back to her.

"Well, LaShana, you ready to have this baby?"

The fear was apparent in her eyes. She barely nodded.

"Let's go, then!"

With that signal, the nurses disconnected the oxygen tubing from the wall, freeing LaShana from all attachments to the tiny stall. I strained to pull the bed toward the door of the labor room as the nurses pushed from the head of the bed. We struggled to move the bed up the hall. I directed the nurses on where to push, steering LaShana toward the OR.

"You're gonna do this in the OR?" one of the nurses asked.

"The delivery rooms are too small for the bed. Somebody move the OR table out. We're going to deliver her in the bed."

The OR was also the only room big enough to hold the bed and the crowd that would assemble—pediatricians, anesthesiologists, nurses and students, some coming to do their jobs and others just to watch the spectacle of this large woman having her baby. As the OR table went out one door, we wheeled the bed through the other and into the center of the room, right under the large lights hanging from the ceiling. Position was critical. The bed had to be in the right spot. Everything had to be exactly right.

"Lock the wheels of the bed," I ordered.

The beds that were used in the labor room were specially made to convert to delivery beds. The footboard could be removed and two candy-cane-shaped stirrups inserted in their place. After adjusting their angle and securing them, I went to the head of the bed, gently removed the oxygen mask from LaShana's face and took hold of her hand again. I had to prepare her for what was going to happen. Without her help, this could be a disaster.

"This is what we're going to do. In a few seconds, I'm going to ask you to move down to the bottom of the bed so that your butt is right on the edge. We're going to put your feet into the stirrups and then I'm going to go wash up. I'll be back in a minute to wash you off and cover you with sterile sheets. You're going to have to help by keeping real still, with your butt down on the bed and pushing as hard as you can when I tell you to. Whatever you do, don't rise up off the bed. That'll make it harder to get the baby out. I'll give you a local anesthetic so you won't feel anything, but I might have to make a small cut down there to give him some more room. Everything's gonna be okay. You with me?"

LaShana nodded, tears streaming down her massive cheeks. Placing the oxygen mask back on her face, I gave her hand one last squeeze and then moved back toward the foot of the bed.

"Okay, move down toward me."

I put my hands under LaShana's massive buttocks in a futile attempt to lift her. My hands were really more for guidance and reassurance than anything else. She was going to have to do this by herself. The nurses on either side of the bed struggled to help as much as they could. Inch by tiny inch, like a giant walrus lumbering on a rocky beach, she moved toward the end of the bed. Suddenly she stopped.

"Wait! I'm having another pain!" she screamed.

The nurses encouraged her to breathe through the pain, but she was losing control. The fetal heartbeat dropped down to 50 and stayed there well beyond the end of the contraction, then slowly recovered to 100 beats per minute.

With more urgency, I pleaded, "Move down toward the end of the bed, LaShana. Just a few inches more. Hurry! Before the next contraction—you're almost there."

With one more move, she was at the edge of the bed. As she put her buttocks down for the last time, the bed became a seesaw and the head tipped up, nearly spilling her on the floor right in front of me. As I pushed back on this huge mass, the nurses instinctively put their full weight on the head of the bed, forcing its upper wheels back to the floor.

"Somebody's gonna have to stay up there!" I yelled.

One of the nurses climbed on top of the headboard and perched there like my guardian angel, keeping the bed grounded. It took four of us to lift LaShana's legs and put her ankles into the canvas straps that hung from the top of the stirrups. Her rolls of fatty flesh spread across the disheveled sheets like mounds of sagging dough and her enormous breasts hung off either side of her body like saddlebags. Having her feet separated and suspended by canvas straps didn't prevent her thighs from converging and hiding the opening to her vagina.

I left the room, putting the OR mask over my nose and mouth. My heart was pounding and all of my senses intensified. At the scrub sink, I began the customary short, perfunctory scrub for a delivery—quick, small circular motions with a plastic brush, from my fingertips to my elbows. As the antiseptic lathered, I stared at the foam and lost myself in the vision of what I was about to do. In the minute it took me to scrub, I saw every move, every hazard, every possibility in my mind's eye—everything but the finale. I could not be sure if the baby was going to make it.

As I backed through the double doors to the operating room with my arms and hands dripping with water, LaShana was having another contraction. Falling into the nurses' rhythms, I joined their incantations.

"Breathe, LaShana. It's almost over. We're almost there. Breathe through the pain."

"Fetal heart is down around 50," one of the nurses reported.

I quickly prepped LaShana's inner thighs with Betadine, but I still could not see the vaginal opening because of the massive folds of fat. With one gloved hand, I pulled the flesh back from the left thigh. I barely saw the opening. I placed the sterile sheets over her legs and turned to the two medical students in the room.

"I need you to hold back her thighs. Get a stool to stand on, put your hands under the sheets and pull back her thighs like this." I demonstrated with my gloved hands. As a bonus, I added, "You'll be in the best position to see everything." I needed instant cooperation.

As they scurried to get the stools and to get into position, I readied things on the sterile instrument table behind me. Everything was there—Novocaine, scissors, forceps, sutures and so on.

"LaShana, I'm going to examine you now. We're getting ready to deliver the baby. How're you doin' up there?"

She managed to whisper a faint "okay" through fear and the oxygen mask.

As the two medical students struggled to hold the fat of her thighs back, I gently inserted two gloved fingers into the vaginal opening. The baby's hard buttocks were right there.

"The baby's butt has come down further and I can still feel the cord pulsating," I said aloud.

After giving a small injection of Novocaine into the lower part of the vagina, I made a small incision to enlarge the tiny opening. I sat down on a low, metal stool, which put me face to face with her vaginal opening. Inserting a finger from each hand in, I placed them on either side of the baby's buttocks, found the groove where his hips were flexed against his abdomen and gently pulled the baby toward me. It came easily and I was able to deliver the baby's buttocks and thighs, quickly followed by the rest of his legs and feet. Next came the abdomen with the pulsating umbilical cord attached and the baby's chest. With a sweep of my fingers across the baby's shoulders, the right and then left arm emerged from the vagina. Not even a minute had passed and the body of the baby had been delivered, his arms and legs straddling my right forearm as I supported his abdomen and chest. So far, so good. But I had less than a minute to deliver the baby's head. The cord was being compressed even more as it went from the baby's abdomen, up across its chest and through the cervix, toward the placenta. The baby's lifeline was being cut off by the process of its own birth.

As the students struggled to prevent the boulders of fat from crashing down, I dropped down on one knee and ran my fingers along the back of the baby's neck, still inside the vagina. My horror was instantaneous. The cervix, which only seconds before had permitted the body of the baby to escape easily from his mother's body, was tightening around the baby's neck. Not only was it trapping the baby's head inside, but it was strangling the umbilical cord.

Kneeling, I gently pulled down on the baby's body as I struggled to push the vise-like cervix up and over the back of his head. Rising to a standing position, I raised the baby's torso. With that motion, his mouth and nose appeared at the opening of LaShana's vagina. One more downward motion, then up again, and he was free!

There, in my arms, was LaShana's son, arms and legs extended and a grimace on his face. I suctioned the mucus from the baby's nose and mouth with a bulb syringe to clear his passages. He inhaled deeply and let out a loud cry. LaShana's son had completed his journey into the world.

The crowd in the room broke out in tears and applause. After clamping and cutting the cord, I held the baby up. His cry grew stronger.

"Look, LaShana, you have a beautiful son. He's perfect."

"A boy! I got my boy!" LaShana cried.

The grin on her massive face made her glow.

CHAPTER 14

THE BOSTON CITY COUNCIL

———

A natural high always followed a difficult, triumphant night. It was a mixture of pride, confidence and euphoria, knowing that I made the absolute correct decisions and pursued those decisions to a great outcome. I loved what I did. I loved the sense of accomplishment. I was able to bring the best to the least. The high would last for the rest of the day; it energized me.

In the shower, I let the hot water massage my face, shoulders and back as my mind's eye replayed the last four hours. The sound and feel of the warm water, the solitude, the smoothness of the soap on my body. All of my nerve endings were releasing their heat and I was warm, inside and out.

Maybe I'll call Carol, I thought.

Carol and I worked together on the GYN service. We had flirted off and on for a while and finally hooked up at Liver Rounds a month before. She was on the rebound from one of the other OB/GYN residents, whom she had been dating until she found out he was married.

Although still legally married, I was separated and lived alone in an apartment near the hospital. It didn't take long for Carol and me to find each other. I took special vindictive pleasure in leaving with her that first Friday night after Liver Rounds because Enrique, her recently dumped boyfriend and a perpetual thorn in my side, saw us leave. When I glanced over at him, I could see it in his eyes: he was pissed. From then on, Carol and I saw each other whenever our schedules would allow.

I put on a fresh scrub suit and my short, white jacket and headed downstairs to make rounds. I always went to the Newborn Intensive Care Unit first, so that I would have the latest information on the sickest babies before I saw their moms. There were babies in the NICU who had been born prematurely or were having seizures because their mothers had used cocaine or heroin while pregnant. Both mother and baby went through withdrawal.

BCH cared for the people that most Bostonians didn't see or care about—the drug addicts, the abused women who lived in terror and poverty with little to do but shoot dope and make love. For many it was the only love they knew. Some of the women who delivered at BCH never came to the clinic for prenatal care. They were too busy trying to survive in this city by the Charles River, in the shadows of the world's greatest universities, to worry about being pregnant and the baby they were carrying. Many didn't want to be pregnant in the first place; too often, babies would be born unwanted and unloved.

After rounds, the rest of my day was spent in the prenatal clinic, seeing pregnant patients—15 in the morning and 15 in the afternoon. Hardly any were routine. Many of the pregnancies were complicated by medical conditions, and a lot of time was spent on the phone, trying to track down blood tests and X-ray results, trying to find housing for the homeless and food for those without any, and getting cab vouchers to help those without transportation to get home. It was a typical day at BCH, but the reservoir of adrenaline that had been filled with the success of LaShana's delivery was still pumping through my system.

That evening, Carol came over. She was an attractive, full-bodied blond, a good friend and a great lover. She was fun, and we provided each other with what we both needed to get relief from the stress of work. We had dinner, sipped wine, gave each other massages and made love. Our evenings and nights were full, wonderful and passionate. We were good for and to each other. Enrique hated seeing us steal glances at each other during rounds.

Dr. Enrique Gimenez-Jimeno was an unbelievably handsome man from Mexico. Tall and haughty, his features were a blend of European and Native American nobility. Born into a wealthy family, his father was a prominent obstetrician in Mexico City. Enrique had gone to medical school in Mexico, but had come to Boston and done his internship at Carney Hospital, one of Boston's Catholic hospitals. In July of 1972, as I was starting my second year of residency, he came to BCH as a first-year resident and immediately became a pain in the ass.

He was lazy. If asked to see patients at night when he was on call, he would take his time showing up, if he showed up at all. Dr. Charles received complaints from nurses, other residents (including me) and patients about Enrique's apathy and attitude. After issuing many warnings, Dr. Charles gave Enrique his final chance in January of 1973: one more complaint and he would be ejected from the program.

That one complaint came in May of 1973. Dr. Charles fired him. However, by this time, it had been announced that I was going to be the next chief resident. With one less resident, I would not be able to carry out my plans for revamping patient care at BCH, so I asked Dr. Charles to rescind his firing. I promised Dr. Charles that as chief resident, I would make Enrique my personal responsibility. He reluctantly agreed and rehired Enrique. He started his second year of residency in July of 1973.

I thought being fired would scare Enrique straight, but it did nothing of the sort. Enrique was Enrique. He resisted the new clinic schedule I devised and often would not show up when he was scheduled to be there. Sometimes, he could not be found at night, when he was on call and supposed to be covering the emergency room. When he and I were on call on the same night, the emergency room nurses would frequently call me in frustration, after paging Enrique for nearly an hour. I would go see the rape victims, the patients with PID and the women with ruptured ectopic pregnancies or ovarian cysts. Enrique was nowhere to be found. As Chief Resident, it was my responsibility to make sure that the residents were where they were supposed to be. Enrique and I clashed nearly all the time. He felt that his experience working in his father's office in Mexico City made him a better doctor than the other residents in the program—especially me. He hated the fact that I was his Chief Resident. He hated the fact that Carol was now with me. He continually refused to respond to my orders that he carry out his responsibilities as a second-year resident.

So I reported him to Dr. Charles and Dr. Penza.

They already knew that he hadn't changed, and told me that a security guard had found him with one of the nurses in the back seat of his car in the hospital parking lot. He was my most troublesome resident. He didn't like me and I didn't like him.

———

As September rolled around, I began to work in a prenatal clinic for pregnant teenagers at the Florence Crittenden Home in Boston. Originally a residential facility for middle-class pregnant white girls who were putting their babies up for adoption, the Crit had just started a "day program" for black teenage girls from Boston's inner city. Each day, a school bus would bring 12 to 15 pregnant, inner city teenage girls to the Crit, where they had their school classes and where I would go one afternoon each week to give them prenatal care and to teach them about their bodies, pregnancy and what to expect when they went into labor. At the end of each afternoon, the bus would take them back to Boston's black neighborhoods. When the girls went into labor, they would come to BCH and I was called to deliver them, whether I was on call or not.

I developed a special relationship with each of the teenagers at the Crit and became godfather to many of their children. I went to baptisms and held the babies that I had helped bring into this world as the preacher poured holy water over their heads, blessed them and gave them back to their young mothers to continue the cycle of poverty and lost love.

Several abortion clinics opened in Boston after the Supreme Court's ruling. The New England Women's Services (NEWS) was opened by a Hungarian entrepreneur from New York. Several of the attending physicians from BCH worked there, including Dr. Charles and Dr. Santamarina. I moonlighted there on Wednesday nights, running a family planning clinic. The extra money was helpful, since I was now responsible for maintaining two households.

I also moonlighted one or two evenings a week at neighborhood health centers scattered throughout Boston, providing prenatal care to pregnant women and family planning services to others. When many of the pregnant patients came in to BCH in labor, they carried my card and asked if I was around to deliver their babies.

Doctors who worked in neighborhood health centers were not allowed to take care of their patients once they were admitted to BCH. Dr. Charles didn't think they were good enough. Plus, he wanted his residents to get the experience of doing the deliveries.

There were women who came to the evening clinics who wanted abortions. If they had insurance, I referred them to one of the abortion clinics in Boston, but if they had no insurance, I referred them to BCH. I was able to provide continuity of care for those women as well.

I loved being able to provide care for women from the neighborhoods of Boston, and I took pride in reorganizing the way we ran things at BCH.

Working in the neighborhood clinics of Boston made me realize how important it would be to strengthen the ties between the clinics and BCH, to create a network of quality patient care throughout the city.

That same thought had also occurred to Dr. Leon White, the Commissioner of Health and Hospitals for the city of Boston. In a meeting held in his office, he asked if I would consider staying on the staff at BCH after I finished my residency, to help develop this network. I was set on going to Atlanta to join a practice there, but White's offer was an intriguing one. I enjoyed what I was doing and the changes that were being made. I told him I would think it over.

My typical day was long. I would come to the hospital and make rounds at 6:00 a.m., reviewing the progress of 20 to 30 patients during their hospital stay. As Chief Resident, it was my responsibility to make sure all the patients had been seen and that all the progress notes and orders had been written.

Each patient who was admitted and discharged from the hospital had to have a discharge summary dictated—a synopsis of the patient's hospital stay, including laboratory tests, procedures and operations, which also had to be dictated.

The mounting paperwork so often interfered with patient care that I frequently neglected and avoided dictating hospital discharge summaries and operative notes in favor of doing something that I deemed useful. The patient records at BCH were a jumbled mess. Laboratory results were often missing, progress notes were frequently unreadable and pathology reports were nowhere to be found. Each record would take hours of reconstruction in order to dictate an accurate summary of the patient's hospital stay. I was so busy running the department, working in the clinic, in the operating room doing surgery, going to the Crit and working at NEWS and neighborhood health centers in the evenings, that I did not dictate operative notes immediately after the case, but would merely scribble a brief, handwritten description of the operation in the chart, fully intending to go back later that day to dictate a complete operative note. I hardly ever did. I always had shelves of patients' records to dictate and was often scolded by Dr. Charles because of my incomplete medical records. When that didn't work, Dr. White, the commissioner, threatened to withhold my paycheck until I had dictated all of my outstanding records.

One day, I received a message to call Dr. White. I assumed he wanted to talk to me about the many incomplete medical records that

I had accumulated. This time, however, the purpose of his phone call was different. The Boston City Council was going to hold hearings on abortion practices at BCH.

After the publication of Dr. Charles' research in *The New England Journal of Medicine*, the Boston City Council received several outraged letters about abortion and fetal experimentation from anti-abortion activists. One in particular was written by a young state representative, Raymond Flynn, who would later become the mayor of Boston. He was in the tradition of the long line of Boston Irish politicians.

Dear Councilor O'Neil,

It has been brought to my attention that certain inhumane procedures are being practiced at Boston City Hospital and other city medical institutions, both public and private, following the Supreme Court decision permitting abortions on demand.

I refer to *The New England Journal of Medicine*, Drs. Philipson, Sabath and Charles at Boston City Hospital, June 7, 1973, which cites the results of some practices at our own Boston City Hospital.

I share your views and the views of all right-thinking people that abortions should not be permitted under any circumstances, despite the decision of the United States Supreme Court.

I know you are supporting our efforts to pass a constitutional amendment prohibiting abortions and striking down the high court's ruling. However, the decision has created a situation where there are no regulations on abortion procedures and practices of physicians and hospital administrators.

I am requesting the filing of an order to require the Committee on Health and Hospitals to conduct an investigation and to hold public hearings with a view toward drafting suitable legislation for the city of Boston and model legislation for the entire Commonwealth.

Sincerely yours,
Raymond L. Flynn

Dapper O'Neil, another of Boston's old-line politicians, was a member of the City Council and chair of the Committee on Health and Hospitals. Dapper was crusty, old, irritable and the champion of his people in South Boston. He had never married, had a sharp tongue and an acidic wit. The people of "Southie" were, as he was always quick to point out, *his* people and he stuck up for them. BCH, he claimed, was his hospital. Some said he was a racist, and angry at the changing complexion of Bostonians and the patients who came to his BCH. He didn't like the new doctors and nurses who were now working there. He called us all "outsiders" for not being part of his notion of what Boston should be. Boston was changing right before his eyes, and he hated it.

Dapper's Catholicism made him strongly opposed to abortion. After he received Flynn's letter, he announced his intention to hold hearings to investigate the horrors of abortion at his beloved BCH.

Leon White had planned to attend the City Council hearings and he suggested that as chief resident, I should also attend. I agreed.

September 18, 1973

The council chambers at City Hall were cavernous, concrete, cold and often a place of comedy. This time, when the curmudgeonly Dapper O'Neil gaveled the hearings to order, it was a theatre of the absurd. I sat with Commissioner White and his assistant in the stadium-like seats and watched the proceedings unfold.

Dapper opened the hearings by reading Ray Flynn's letter, followed by a long, rambling speech about how he had publicized the date and purpose of the hearing by notifying all of the newspapers, radio and TV stations. He also said he had sent notices to all of the residents in the Department of Obstetrics and Gynecology at BCH, but when he read the list, I noticed it included everyone's name but mine. A curious omission, but I didn't know what to make of it.

He then called on Monsignor Paul Harrington to testify. He was representing "his eminence, Cardinal Medeiros," the leader of the Boston Archdiocese. Monsignor Harrington, naturally, was against the abortions and fetal experimentation he said was going on at BCH, and praised the "great physicians" who had been a part of the hospital's past.

"These giants of the medical world," he said, "were not concerned with solving the personal, social, economic and political problems of their day. These concerns were never meant to be a part of the practice of medicine."

I thought about the child in Nashville who had died of lead poisoning on my first day in pediatrics as a medical student. I thought about the young woman I had seen die as the result of an illegal abortion when I had been assigned to the OB/GYN service. I thought about the poor families I had cared for in Mississippi. I thought about the hundreds of women I had taken care of during my short career in medicine, who had suffered because of their living circumstances, their poverty, their poor diets and their abusive relationships, which caused injury and sometimes death. I thought about the open wards at BCH, the lack of privacy in the clinics, the former injustice of *The Committee* and all of the changes I sought to make at BCH—changes that would improve patient care. Was I not supposed to be concerned about the social and economic problems of my patients? Where were the giants who were responsible for the flawed, heartless system already in place? I did not understand how someone championing love, compassion and morality could call for such an unfeeling attitude toward these women and their predicaments.

I thought about my own experience. One week before I'd boarded the Greyhound bus to Nashville and medical school, I'd attended The March on Washington. The message I'd received while standing on the Mall in front of the Lincoln Memorial on that hot August day in 1963 was that not only *should* I get involved in the lives of my patients, but I *must* get involved in them.

We were from two different worlds.

The Monsignor went on to say that there were no medical reasons to perform abortions. Seriously ill pregnant women, he claimed, could be carried through to term by the skill and work of those "giants of medicine." Abortions were never performed at City Hospital back then, he said. There was never a need.

His nostalgic and inaccurate testimony seemed to go on forever as his rhetoric echoed his Church's opposition to abortion. He decried fetal experimentation and ended his testimony, at last, by saying that he hoped the Boston City Council would enact some sort of legislation that "maintained the role of the doctor as the practitioner of the art and science of curative and preventive medicine" rather than "the architect and technician of solving personal, social, economic and political problems."

The hypocrisy of his pro-life testimony was thrown into the light many years later, when some of the priests from his archdiocese were exposed for sexually abusing young children, especially young boys. Violating their vows of abstinence and the bodies of children, they not only broke the laws of man, but the laws of God. In his testimony, Harrington chastised physicians who performed abortions for violating the Hippocratic Oath, while he belonged to a faith of men who violated their oaths to God.

Dapper O'Neil and the other members of the City Council thanked the monsignor for his testimony. Dapper then read another letter, this time from Sister Sheila, who also wrote to the City Council about abortions at BCH. He invited her to speak. She identified herself as the administrator of the Laboure Center in South Boston, a Catholic social service agency. In her testimony, she repeated much of what the Cardinal had to say, but also distributed color photographs of the stages of fetal development. They became a part of the record of the Council hearings.

Dapper then called on Ray Flynn, the ambitious young politician who represented South Boston in the state legislature. Flynn urged the council to join with the Massachusetts Citizens for Life to push for legislation within both the city and the state that would restrict women's access to legal abortion. He also described a larger, nationwide effort to pass a Human Life Amendment to the US Constitution, which would overturn *Roe*. Finally, he asked the City Council to send the minutes of the hearings to the Suffolk County district attorney's office for possible criminal action. Dapper O'Neil assured Flynn he would do just that.

"On the information I have so far, I will be at the district attorney's office myself tomorrow morning and get an investigation started," Dapper promised.

The next three anti-choice speakers made up a panel before the council. The first to speak was Dr. Mildred Jefferson. She introduced herself as a surgeon and vice president of the board of directors of the Massachusetts Citizens for Life, which she described as being affiliated with the National Right to Life Committee. Her voice was crisp, clipped, frigid, rigid and precise. She described the political purpose of the Massachusetts Citizens for Life and their beliefs about when life begins.

"I was called by a house officer at Boston City Hospital. One of the things occurring at the moment is the pressure on various interns and residents in the obstetrical services who do not participate in abortion. The particular resident who called me wanted his identity kept secret to assure that some other plans for completing his training may be made if he was fired for appearing here before you."

Who is that? I wondered. Residents were not put under any pressure to perform abortions. In fact, it was an individual decision for each resident to make. It was unnerving that one of the residents was in contact with members of the Massachusetts Citizens for Life. The policies of City Hospital, even though they were cumbersome, permitted us to provide abortions, even before the decision in *Roe* came down in January. Since then, of course, every restrictive law against abortion had been made null and void.

Mildred Jefferson then turned to the second member of the panel, Dr. Joseph Stanton, also a member of the MCFL. His task was to explain the research which had been published in *The New England Journal of Medicine*.

After summarizing the research, Stanton proceeded to describe, in great detail, the process of abortion by hysterotomy, calling it a "miniature cesarean section where the baby is always alive when it is lifted from its mother's womb, unless it has been killed by prior unsuccessful saline injection."

He concluded his long, rambling testimony by saying that while the research may have yielded scientifically important results, the means of obtaining these results were not justified. When he finished his testimony, the members of the Massachusetts Citizens for Life—who had now filled the city council chambers—broke into applause.

Next on the panel was Professor James W. Smith, a professor of law at Boston College, the Jesuit University in Boston. He presented the council with model legislation which would outlaw fetal experimentation and require life-saving equipment to be present when an abortion was carried out, if there was a chance that the fetus could survive outside of the woman's womb.

By the time Monsignor Harrington, Sister Sheila, Ray Flynn, Mildred Jefferson, Joseph Stanton and James Smith had finished their testimonies, it was early afternoon. Their speeches and the grandstanding of Dapper O'Neil made it very clear that they wanted to stop abortions and fetal experimentation at BCH altogether.

Another panel was called, consisting of officials from the Department of Health and Hospitals, including the chairman of the board, Herb Gleason. They assured the City Council that the research had been approved by the Committee on Human Experimentation at BCH and that as far as they knew, all of the abortions performed were legal and requested by the women involved. No experimentation, they asserted, was performed on living fetuses. They told the City Council that no one was forced to have an abortion nor were any employees pressured to provide abortion services.

Immediately following the second panel was the final right to life testimony. Members of the Massachusetts Youth for Life, the Value of Life Committees and the Massachusetts Citizens for Life made it clear that there was a concerted effort by a group of activists outside of BCH, working with sympathetic employees inside the hospital, to learn about abortions at BCH in hopes of putting a stop to them.

Judging by the information they already had, it was clear that their claim was not a bluff. At least one of the residents from the OB/GYN department was feeding them information that should have remained private and confidential—a list of residents who performed abortions and the names of their patients. They even had a copy of the letter I had written to the hospital administration, threatening to stop performing abortions unless the hospital agreed to improve the conditions under which we were forced to work. They also described a new abortion research project headed by Dr. Hugh Holtrop, of the Outpatient OB/GYN Clinic.

The second pro-life panel stated that their information was from a source they could not divulge, "but the source is available by means of subpoena and by means of putting the witness under oath."

At the end of their testimonies, these anti-abortion activists requested that "the district attorney make a sweeping investigation of the OB/GYN service, so that the saving, rather than the destruction, of human lives may be reinstated at City Hospital." They wanted the DA to investigate the possibility of a criminal conspiracy by Dr. David Charles to obstruct the detection of felonies committed at BCH.

The final witness was Edna Smith, a courageous black nurse and director of the Boston Family Planning Project, which provided the counselors in our family planning clinic at BCH. She took her seat at the witness table—alone. Quietly, regally, but forcefully, she spoke directly to Dapper O'Neil:

"I sat here all day and I am concerned that I am only now being given the opportunity to speak, when there are only two members of the council left to hear my testimony. I am also concerned that the presentations you have heard today have been pretty much one-sided. This issue warrants greater participation from both sides.

"You have mixed up two very different issues here today. I don't think that we should have been discussing whether or not abortion is right. It is the law. The Supreme Court has made that decision. It is the law! It is my right under the Supreme Court decision to have an abortion if I choose to have one. I think the only issue that should have been presented before the council should have been the issue of fetal experimentation. It is not your prerogative to decide whether a woman has the right to have an abortion. I am here to defend my right to have an abortion without the interference of people who have different morals or religious persuasions than my own.

"A lot of the issues surrounding abortion would not be necessary if we could get people concerned about prevention. Many of the same people who spoke before you today against abortion are also against family planning. If you fight family planning, if you fight the use of the pill, if you fight the use of anything that helps a woman plan and determine her destiny, then you leave her with nothing left but to have an abortion. And she is going to have one whether you like it or not. She is going to have one whether we have a Supreme Court decision or not."

Elegantly, with a firm use of words, Edna Smith presented her opinion and that of countless others who were not called to testify before the City Council. The remaining City Councilors had no questions for her. She and her testimony were dismissed.

Dapper O'Neil stood up and, ignoring the words of Edna Smith, waved the written testimony of his witnesses and shouted, "I am going to go to the district attorney. I want him to assign a couple of men to me, and I am going through that hospital with a fine-toothed comb to find out the truth. This hearing is adjourned."

CHAPTER 15

EVONNE

It was a warm, mid-afternoon in May in the Roxbury section of Boston. As Evonne climbed the stairs and stepped onto the wooden porch, she reached for the key hanging from a string around her neck. As she had done many times before, she put the key first in the top lock, turned it, heard the click of the bolt being released, then, hands trembling, inserted it into the second lock, listening for the same sound. The twin emotions of fear and anticipation rose in her chest. She was aware of every heartbeat as she slowly turned the doorknob and entered the house. Stepping inside, she froze and listened. Nothing. Leaving the door slightly ajar, she walked in quietly and carefully, heading for the base of the stairs. She stopped and listened again. Still nothing.

"Hello? Anybody home?" she asked. Her crisp, West Indian accent traveled from the hallway into the living room, through to the kitchen. "Mommy? Daddy?" she called up the stairs. Nothing. She followed her voice into the living room, on through the dining room and into the kitchen. No one! She quickly ran up the stairs, looking in each bedroom. Empty! Gently, she closed each door as she had found them. Except hers.

She ran down the stairs and eased through the open front door of the house. Standing on the porch, she looked down the street. She could just see him at the end of the block, his body partially hidden by trees. They made eye contact—touched and spoke to each other with a glance. Her head nodded once as she slipped back through the open front door, retreating to the base of the stairs. It seemed like forever. What was taking so long? Finally, unaccompanied by sound, he slipped through the front door and closed it behind himself. She walked to him, reached around and turned the latches on both locks. That'll give us a few seconds more, she thought.

They embraced and kissed, full of the feelings that only teenagers knew. The newness. The stimulated nerve endings. The untapped passion that lay deep inside them. The exploration. The discovery. She grasped his hand and led him up the stairs and into her room.

She quietly closed the door to her bedroom and turned to him. Again, they kissed as they shed their clothes. In a moment they were on the bed. The heat of that moment and the late May afternoon covered their bodies in glistening sweat as their hands, fingers and tongues explored each other, finding new places, feeling new sensations, tasting each other's newness over and over and over again. The passion and heat rose until he was on top of her, slipping slowly inside. With eyes closed, lips joined and tongues searching, they melded into one, moving against each other as the intensity rose. He thrusted deeper and faster, the sensations moving from their lips to their chests, down to their gut and settling in their groins, moving, pushing, giving, receiving, harder, faster, more and more, on and on…until the explosion came.

"Ugghhhhhhhhhh!"

The sound rose in both their throats at the same time as their backs arched and their muscles contracted, relaxed and pulsed, pushing the air and sound out along with juices from deep inside. Fast and hard at first, and then quietly and gently. Lingering, slowly fading, with a flood of warmth that started in their groins and radiated out from this epicenter of convulsions to the rest of their bodies.

And then it was over. They went limp in each other's arms.

"I love you, Vonnie."

"I love you."

September 1973

I first met Evonne in the OB/GYN clinic at BCH. Doctor Hugh Holtrop, the director of the clinic, asked me to come into one of the small examining rooms one afternoon to meet her. Standing in one corner was Evonne's mother. A big woman, her face was grim, her eyes saddened and silent. Lying on her back on the old examining table in the sparsely furnished room was a frightened little girl.

"This is Dr. Edelin," Holtrop offered to both of them. "He's the Chief Resident and will take care of Evonne when she comes into the hospital."

I nodded to the woman standing next to the young, brown-skinned girl lying on the examining table. As I did, Dr. Holtrop proceeded to explain to me that this 17-year-old girl was about 16 weeks pregnant and had decided to terminate her pregnancy. He had convinced both the girl and her mother to participate in a research project that he and a Harvard colleague were carrying out at BCH to see if they could find an "anti-hormone" that would counteract the effects of the pregnancy hormone, progesterone. If such a thing could be found, they would try to find a way to cause a woman to abort by giving her the anti-hormone; they hoped to develop an abortion pill.

Holtrop wanted to give Evonne a drug and then measure her progesterone levels for 48 hours, to see if the amount in her blood would drop, indicating that the anti-hormone was working. After they finished drawing their blood samples, I would perform the abortion.

"Can you admit her to the Saline Unit?" he asked.

The Saline Unit had been set up by a group of nurses and me at BCH to provide abortions to patients who were too far along for a D&C—more than 14 weeks pregnant. Many of the women who came in for second trimester abortions were teenagers, often trying to hide their pregnancies until it was too late. Many were alone, lonely and with nowhere else to turn. There was little or no hope that the men who got them pregnant would either be fathers to or providers for the children they made.

The nurses in the Saline Unit were determined to provide support and education as they helped these pitiful souls get through the abortions. They taught them how to prevent future unwanted pregnancies. They talked about sex and taught them about birth control. They discussed women's relationships with men and boundaries that should not be crossed.

Three nurses were scheduled so that there would be a nurse with the patients throughout their stay in the hospital, explaining every procedure and providing support and comfort. There was no other place in Boston like the Saline Unit at BCH. In other hospitals, women undergoing saline abortions would be placed in the labor and delivery units, next to women who were having and keeping their babies.

The Saline Unit was named for the procedure used to perform the abortion. A concentrated solution of salt and water was injected through a long needle which had been inserted through the abdomen and into the fluid-filled sac surrounding the fetus. At BCH, it was the most common way second trimester abortions were performed. It was very effective, but there were dangers to the woman. If the concentrated salt solution was inadvertently injected into the woman's blood stream, it would cause seizures, coma and death. Even when the solution was injected into the amniotic sac, there was a risk that the woman could develop a bleeding disorder so that her blood would not clot, resulting in uncontrollable hemorrhage. Then, of course, there was always the risk of infection.

Nevertheless, saline abortions were common and safe when performed carefully and with safeguards. Most women aborted within 24 hours and were discharged within a day or two.

"There's a patient of Dr. Charles coming in on Sunday for a saline," I said. "I think the other bed in the unit is open. I'll check. If it is, I'll book her for Monday."

"Great. Why don't you fill out the paper work to admit her and I'll write a note in her chart?" Holtrop said.

I turned to Evonne. She was lying on the table, wearing a blouse, her naked abdomen and legs covered by a frayed and wrinkled white sheet.

"Hi. I'm Dr. Edelin. How ya doin'?"

She didn't respond. She kept her eyes lowered—almost closed, as if she were not there.

"Can I examine your tummy?"

Her face was expressionless. Her eyes never met mine. She stared down into her lap, as if she wanted to shut out the whole world.

"When was your last period?" I asked as I folded the sheet down from her abdomen.

"I don't know. Maybe April or May," she whispered.

As I examined her abdomen, it became obvious that she was well into the second trimester of her pregnancy. Though the top of her uterus was below her belly button, indicating to me that she was less than 20 weeks, I measured her uterus as a double-check. The pregnant uterus grows at about a centimeter a week. Evonne's fundal height was 17 centimeters, confirming my estimate that she was 17 or 18 weeks pregnant.

As I went through these measurements and calculations, the quiet, frightened little girl lay on the table in silence. I wanted to make this as easy for her as possible.

"We're going to admit you to the hospital on Saturday and after we draw some blood tests, I will perform a saline infusion on Monday."

I explained what that was to Evonne and her mother, trying my best to calm their fears. I told them I thought she would be home by Wednesday and back to school by Thursday. After asking them if they had any questions, I began the paperwork to allow her to be admitted to the Saline Unit that coming weekend.

I understood all too well the fear and terror she must have been feeling—finding herself pregnant when she did not want to be. Feeling trapped. BCH would provide her with an escape. BCH would free her from her dilemma and let her get on with her life.

There were two patients admitted to BCH for second trimester abortions that weekend. Each had different reasons for requesting the procedure and each had been admitted under the name of an attending physician in the Department of Obstetrics and Gynecology.

One was a 38-year-old, married white woman from New Hampshire who had undergone a D&C abortion by Dr. Charles at NEWS in June. Unbeknownst to him and her, the procedure failed, the pregnancy was missed and she traveled back to New Hampshire still pregnant. Nearly three months later, she returned to NEWS, outraged. She was now 17 weeks pregnant. Dr. Charles was out of town and could not be reached. The head nurse from NEWS called me and asked what to do. I told her to send the woman over to the hospital and I would take care of everything. As the chief resident, I had to get Dr. Charles out of the jam that he didn't even know he was in.

The other patient was Evonne. Her mother, once again, was with her. Since Evonne and her mother had agreed to participate in Dr. Holtrop's research project, she was admitted to the hospital the day before her 38-year-old roommate.

October 2, 1973

I went to the Saline Unit, where each patient waited in bed; one nervous and frightened, the other full of anger. I examined each in turn and judged them both to be less than 20 weeks pregnant. This was well within hospital guidelines, my personal guidelines and the law. In fact, there were no laws in Massachusetts restricting abortion since the *Roe* ruling.

I decided to perform the saline infusion on Evonne first because she was the most nervous.

I had performed saline infusions countless times before. After prepping her abdomen with an antiseptic solution, I injected a local anesthetic into its midline. I waited a minute or so for the anesthetic to take, then inserted the thin, three-inch long needle down through her skin, fat, abdominal muscles and into what I believed to be the uterine cavity. As I removed the thin wire stylet from the inside of the needle, I waited to see clear amniotic fluid drip out of the hub of needle.

I waited. Waited...

Slowly, at the hub of the needle, a bubble of bright red blood appeared. The possibilities raced through my mind. Was it Evonne's blood or that of the fetus? Had I punctured the placenta? Or did I just cause bleeding to begin, hidden deep inside her womb, away from my view? Was Evonne in danger? Where was the blood coming from?

I had no way of knowing. Withdrawing the needle an inch or so, I pushed it in at a different angle, but again, only blood returned. I tried again. There was still blood. Again. Blood. The minutes passed. More insertions. Feeling my frustration rise and Evonne's anxiety grow, I stopped.

Instead, I decided to perform the saline infusion on the other patient in the room and return to Evonne later that day. My time was running out and I had a clinic full of patients to see. I explained everything to Evonne and her mother and assured them that I would be back after morning clinic—around noon.

I re-examined the abdomen of the other patient and went through my routine—washing the abdomen with Betadine, anesthetizing the area and inserting the three-inch needle into the skin and down into the uterine cavity. Immediately, clear amniotic fluid came from the hub of the needle when I removed the stylet. I then injected the concentrated salt solution. The patient tolerated the procedure well. As the nurse and I cleaned her up, I told the patient that I would continue to try to find Dr. Charles and would be by to check on her later that day.

I went to the clinic to see patients assigned to me that morning. There were infertility patients, women complaining of vaginal discharges and itching, women returning for follow-ups of abnormal pap smears, women seeking birth control, women with heavy periods, women with fibroids, women seeking abortions—it was a typical gynecology clinic at BCH.

At noon, I returned to the Saline Unit to repeat the procedure on Evonne. Despite more attempts in different locations, at different angles, the procedure still produced blood from the hub of the needle. After several tries, I explained the difficulty I was having to both Evonne and her mother. I could see the fear overtaking their faces; I hoped it didn't show on mine.

I could not simply assume that it was the fetus' blood. If the hypertonic saline was mistakenly injected into Evonne's circulation, she could die. If I decided to do nothing and sent her home—which neither Evonne nor her mother wanted—there was the risk that all of the needle sticks into her uterus could have introduced some bacteria and result in an infection. Who knew what the repeated penetrations had done to her, her uterus or the fetus?

I reassured Evonne and her mother again and left to explain the trouble I was having to an attending physician, Dr. James Penza.

Jim Penza was an excellent doctor, surgeon and teacher. He had a gentle way with patients and seemed to be genuinely concerned with the plight of the poor women who came to BCH. I explained Evonne's desperate situation, that both she and her mother insisted that the pregnancy be terminated, and told him that I was worried about the repeated bloody taps.

"I think this might be causing her to slowly bleed internally. And even if it's not, it could cause an infection," I said.

Jim Penza nodded in agreement. I asked him to perform the saline injection; maybe he would have different results.

"Ken, you probably are as good at this as I am and if you can't do it, I doubt that I will be able to," Penza said.

He thought about it for a brief moment and laid out a plan. He wanted me to put Evonne on the operating room schedule for the next morning. He would attempt the saline infusion in the OR, and if he couldn't do it, I would have to perform a hysterotomy. It would be the only way left to terminate Evonne's pregnancy. Before returning to the clinic to see my afternoon patients, I added Evonne's name to the OR schedule for October 3rd.

Back upstairs in the Saline Unit, I explained Jim Penza's decision to Evonne and her mother and laid their limited options out before them.

Evonne and her mother looked at each other, their faces weary and worried. Evonne's eyes glistened with tears.

"All right," Evonne's mother said. "That okay with you, Vonnie?"

Evonne nodded. Her mother looked up at me. "See, Dr. Edelin, we just don't want her father to find out. He's…well, he has a temper. If he knew she was pregnant, the least he would do is throw her out of the house. I just…I don't want him to hurt her."

I had heard similar stories before. A surgery would be harder to lie about than a saline injection. But, recognizing Jim Penza's decision as the only safe option, Evonne's mother signed the consent form for the hysterotomy.

———

October 3, 1973 was a crisp, early fall day in Boston. The sky was clear and the trees already had patches of brilliant red, yellow and orange. It was a day like many others, but for me, it would turn out to be a day like no other. It was a day that would change many lives—Evonne's, her mother's and, most unexpectedly, mine.

When Jim Penza entered the operating room that morning, Evonne was already positioned on the operating table. The OR table was narrow, with many interconnected moving parts. It could be moved up or down by pumping a pedal, or tilted from side to side by turning a crank. Arm boards projected out from each side. Evonne lay there, her brown skin standing out against the white sheet covering her body. She wore the typical hospital johnny and her arms were outstretched on arm boards, her legs crossed at the ankles. She stared straight up at the ceiling, hiding her fear in an unblinking, trancelike gaze.

Jim greeted her with an understanding smile, a gentle grasp of her hand and reassuring words. Pulling back the sheet that covered her abdomen, he used his hands to gently outline the shape and size of her uterus. Talking to Evonne all the while, he put on his sterile gloves, prepped her abdomen with the antiseptic Betadine solution and numbed a small area of Evonne's skin, midway to the top of her uterus. Then, inserting the point of the three-inch needle into the pain-free area, he skillfully, purposefully and slowly pressed it down through her skin until it met the wall of her uterus. Pushing past the expected resistance, he guided the point of the needle as it sought the sac containing fluid, placenta and the tiny fetus. I watched in anticipation as he removed the thin wire stylet from the inside the needle, hoping to see the clear fluid. There was nothing. Nothing, nothing…

Slowly, a drop of dark red blood appeared at the hub of the needle and eventually dripped onto the sterile, green towel draped over

Evonne's abdomen. Once again, droplet after droplet of blood appeared, and the stain on the towel grew. Penza advanced the needle. The blood continued. He changed the angle of its trajectory. The blood continued. Two, three, four attempts. Still, the blood continued.

"That's it, Ken," he said as he removed the needle for the last time. "You'll have to do the hysterotomy."

As Jim and I left the operating room, he went to the locker room to change out of his scrubs. I took off my mask and walked out to the hallway where Evonne's mother was pacing.

"Dr. Penza couldn't do the saline, either," I told her.

She took a deep, shaking breath and, in a voice mixed with sadness and desperation, responded as I knew she would. "Go ahead. Do what you have to do. I can't take her home pregnant."

She had told me as such numerous times already. "I can't take her home pregnant. Vonnie can't come home pregnant. She can't continue this pregnancy. Her father can't know about this, Dr. Edelin." I couldn't imagine the fear that the two of them felt. My heart went out to them both.

Evonne was a 17-year-old high school senior. She wanted to go on to college and her mother supported her in that decision. She wanted to finish college, have a career and have children sometime in the future. Just not now.

She and her mother had asked the hospital, and now me, to help them. She was determined to have the abortion and would have had one whether *Roe* had permitted them to or not. Evonne, unlike countless other teenagers before her, was fortunate enough to have become pregnant when she did, and not years earlier. They were able to come to BCH and I was able to help give Evonne back her life and hope.

I had only a hint of what they were feeling. I remembered how trapped I felt, once in New York and again in Stockbridge. I remembered the knot in my stomach. I remembered the desperation I had felt. A doctor had helped me then. Now it was my turn to help Evonne.

"Dr. Edelin, Vonnie can't go home pregnant," Evonne's mother repeated. "She just can't."

That was all I needed to know.

I made arrangements to proceed with the hysterotomy. Jim Penza changed out of his scrubs and went downstairs to his office.

There is a routine in getting the team ready for surgery. I notified the nurse in charge of the operating room of the decision to perform the hysterotomy. She already knew and had notified other nurses and technicians.

I told the anesthesiologist what we were planning to do, then went back to the OR to talk to Evonne. I started to tell her everything that was about to happen, but she, too, already knew. In her silence and through her fear, she had heard and understood everything.

The OR staff started to set up the room for major surgery and the anesthesiologist prepared to put Evonne to sleep.

I was going to need an assistant for the hysterotomy, but the residents who would have volunteered were busy elsewhere. I asked a group of third-year medical students from BU if one of them would assist me. I got one volunteer.

While the setup was taking place, my medical student assistant and I left the OR to scrub. As the surge of adrenaline began to course through my veins, all my senses became acute. Lights, colors and objects became brighter and more easily seen. Sound was pushed down to a lower place with vision and touch taking over.

In my mind's eye, I pictured what I was going to do. I slipped into that place where the only things I could see were Evonne, her need and the operation I was about to perform. I visualized the incision I would make. I could see what I was going to find, what I was going to do.

I backed through the doorway into the operating room, my clean, dripping hands raised up and extended away from the rest of my body. My senses were at their peak. I could see everything in the room with sharp clarity. While drying my hands with a sterile towel, I looked at the setup of the operating room. People and things were almost all in place. Evonne was on the table, asleep and intubated. Her arms were still extended out from her sides at shoulder length to give the anesthesiologist access to veins in either arm. The room was quiet except for the metallic sound of the surgical instruments being arranged. The mood was somber and serious.

Irene, the scrub tech, organized the instruments on a sterile table. Without a word, I washed Evonne's abdomen with Betadine and covered her with sterile towels and sheets, leaving only a small area of skin visible just above her pubic hairline. After donning new sterile gloves and a gown, I stood close to Evonne's left side. Across from me was my medical student assistant. Irene stood to my left, wearing an OR hat with a flowery design.

The circulating nurse brought sponges and sterile wrapped

instruments into the operating room—clamps, scalpels, retractors, syringes and long, tweezer-like instruments called "pick ups." Each instrument had to be counted before and after surgery, and that count had to be recorded: the number of instruments, the type of instruments, as well as the number of sponges and their types. Everything had to be accounted for and documented, including the name of each person in the operating room.

To me, this operation represented failure. I failed her because the saline infusion had failed and I was going to have to subject her to major surgery in order to terminate her pregnancy. She and her boyfriend had failed each other by not using birth control, or if they did, it had failed them. She failed herself and her parents' dreams for her. Now we were boxed into a corner. I could not fail her again. This had to be perfect.

Silently, Irene handed me the scalpel. I looked over the cloth screen that separated me from the anesthesiologist and Evonne's face. "Ready?" I asked. "Can I start?"

The anesthesiologist nodded and I began the operation. I had decided to make an incision low in her abdomen, just above the pubic hairline—the so-called "bikini scar." Even though it would reduce my ability to see once I reached her uterus, when it healed, the scar would be covered by her pubic hair as it grew back, and go unnoticed.

Each time I cut through human flesh, adrenaline surged. Surgery is full of risks and dangers, and from that moment, Evonne's life was in my hands. She was totally defenseless and completely dependent on my assistants and me. There was no room for self-doubt.

On the surface of her uterus were the puncture marks made by the multiple saline attempts. They were surrounded by tiny areas of hemorrhage. I inserted my hand into her abdomen and gently felt her uterus from the narrow, low portion up to the rounded top—like a large, inverted pear.

Now, I faced another critical decision.

What kind of incision would I make into Evonne's uterus? Which type would be best for her? Which type would be easiest for me? Which type was likely to have more complications, now or in the future?

I could have made a long, vertical incision in the front of her uterus, from the broad part of the pear down to its narrowest segment, through the thick muscle, cutting it nearly in half. This would have made the procedure easier for me because it would be bigger and I would be able to remove the fetus, placenta and sac together. But if I made that kind of incision, she would run the risk of rupturing her uterus in subsequent pregnancies. She would always have to have a cesarean section.

So instead, I decided to make the incision in the lower part of her uterus—the neck of the pear. I wouldn't have as much room to operate, but the danger to Evonne now and in the future would be much less. Though it would make the surgery more difficult, I knew I could do it. I was good at surgery. Nurses and residents alike often said that I had "gifted hands," especially in difficult and unusual circumstances.

I asked one of the circulating nurses to get Dr. Charles. A few minutes later, he came into the room holding a surgical mask over his nose and mouth. I gave him a brief summary of the case and the type of incision I was making and why. He looked at the surgical field framed by the green towels.

"Okay," he said, and left the operating room.

I made the incision into the lower portion of her womb and the sac containing the amniotic fluid began to bulge through the tiny opening. Inserting one finger through, careful not to rupture the sac, I explored the inside of Evonne's uterus and found, as I expected, the placenta attached to its anterior wall. It was best to try to remove the entire contents of her womb intact and together—the sac, the placenta and the fetus—so that's what I started to do. I separated the placenta from its attachment to the uterine wall with my fingers and as the uterus contracted, the sac began to bulge through the incision. Suddenly it broke, spilling the bloody amniotic fluid onto the sheets and towels draped over Evonne's body.

I had to move with deliberate speed. I began the difficult (both surgically and emotionally) procedure of removing the fetus and placenta from the uterine cavity. I felt no resistance as I extracted the fetus. It fit into the palm of my hand, was pale and mottled in appearance, limp, with no signs of life. It did not move. It did not gasp. It did not breathe. I placed my fingers on its tiny translucent chest. It did not have a heartbeat. The amniotic fluid in which it floated was wine-colored. The fetus had been dead for many hours.

I placed it into the stainless steel bowl that Irene held out for me. She looked at it briefly and then placed the bowl on the corner of her instrument table, covering it with a sterile, green towel.

I removed the placenta and began to sew up the incisions—uterus, peritoneum, fascia, fat and skin—layer by layer. Evonne had been asleep for an hour and a half. Her blood loss had been was minimal. She had survived the operation and should have no complications. She would be able to go home in two or three days without her father suspecting anything.

I visited Evonne each day after the operation and saw the relief on her face as she healed. The fear was nearly gone from her mother's face—nearly, but not completely. She and Evonne still had to concoct a story to tell her father, a believable lie explaining where she had been for the last four days. Evonne recovered from her surgery and was discharged three days later.

It is impossible to do a hysterotomy without feeling the full impact of the operation. It is the one abortion procedure that is most likely to produce a fetus with signs of life—gasping, movement, a heartbeat, albeit a feeble one. I had seen it before. This time, however, the fetus showed no signs of life. It had already died in Evonne's womb.

CHAPTER 16

THE GRAND JURY

It was a busy and beautiful fall. The fiery burst of color in a Massachusetts mid-October is second only to the colors of birth and growth—the intense greens of the buds and the sounds of the birds in the spring. In the fall, the New England sky is an intense blue and the outlines of the wispy clouds are sharp and clear. As the months go by, darkness expands, extending its reach to late morning and earlier in the afternoon.

That particular fall, Kenny, Kim and I explored the color-filled hills of New Hampshire and Vermont, picking apples and pumpkins for Halloween. In a tradition taught to me by my mother, I scooped out the pumpkin seeds and roasted them in the oven while we carved the happy face on the jack-o-lantern.

Carol and I saw each other whenever either of us needed to, though I spent most of my time at BCH. The clinics were busier, and the continuity of the care program I set up was working well, with only a few glitches popping up from time to time. Our family planning clinic was very busy and our family planning counselors were the best in the city.

The operating rooms and the delivery rooms were busier, too. Though most of the women had normal pregnancies, deliveries and healthy babies, there were some who had the most horrendous complications, threatening the lives of both mother and child. There were premature separations of the placenta, which deprived the fetuses of oxygen and caused the women to hemorrhage. There were women in early labor that we were helpless to stop, so many of the babies born at BCH were small and premature. There were pregnant women with rapidly growing fibroids. There were women who wanted to get pregnant, but couldn't. And, of course, there were women who were pregnant and didn't want to be. They all came to BCH.

Ramona and I were legally separated, moving toward divorce, and I made monthly child support payments to her. Working at NEWS helped me do that, and I really enjoyed my weekly trips to the Crit to see the pregnant, black teenagers in their "day program." I began to think more about where I was going to practice once I finished my residency at City Hospital in eight months. Atlanta still called to me because of the number and power of black people there. I had enjoyed living in the south for four years when I'd attended medical school at Meharry in Nashville, and looked forward to the slower pace of Southern life again. I visited Atlanta in the fall to consider my options and to talk to friends about how life would be in the city for a single, black obstetrician. My only hesitation was that I would be separated from my two children.

My life in Boston was busy and full, but I began to plan for the next phase of it.

December 1973

I got a call from Commissioner Leon White. He asked me to come to his office in the Administration Building to look over some medical records. When I arrived, he showed me to a room where, in the middle of a long conference table, there were piles of patients' charts.

Dapper O'Neil had kept his promise and the district attorney of Suffolk County had subpoenaed 88 records of patients who had been treated in the OB/GYN department. Leon White and Frank Guiney, the hospital administrator, wanted me to go through all the records and let them know if there was anything in them that could cause BCH or its doctors any trouble.

Most of the records were of women who had come to BCH seeking abortions—mainly the poor, black patients who used BCH for all of their health care needs and those who were part of Dr. Charles' research project involving antibiotics. Nearly all had come through our Saline Unit or had hysterotomies.

Among the records were those of the two patients I had taken care of in the Saline Unit at the beginning of October. Since Evonne's records did not have a dictated operative note in it, the commissioner told me to dictate the summary then and there—two months after the operation had taken place—so it could be included in the record before it was sent to the DA's office.

Busy as I was, I did not think much about those records after I finished looking through them and completed the dictation. I had other things on my mind. In six more months, I would be finished with my residency, would take my specialty qualifying exam, leave Boston and begin my practice as an obstetrician-gynecologist. Only six more months. Life was on track.

Christmas came and went. As the calendar changed from 1973 to 1974, so did everything in my life.

January 1974

Three weeks into the New Year, a sheriff came to the hospital and handed me a subpoena to appear before a grand jury convened by the district attorney. Over the next several days, all of the residents, some of the attending physicians, a few nurses and a handful of other hospital employees received subpoenas as well.

All I could think was: *Dapper O'Neil. Must be an investigation into fetal experimentation.*

I was concerned, but not overly so. I had never appeared before a grand jury before and didn't really understand what its function was. I called Sam Hoar, a Boston lawyer who was handling my divorce. I told him what I thought was happening and asked him what I should do. He said that I should testify fully, openly and truthfully, because from what I had told him, I had done nothing illegal or outside of the law. I felt better. I had enough to worry about at work.

As much as I still loved my job, it was a very stressful environment, where the slightest distraction could put a patient—and possibly her unborn child—in serious jeopardy. On top of that, as Chief Resident, I often had to deal with problems with the other residents. Nothing caused me more difficulty than the complaints I received about the behavior of Enrique Gimenez-Jimeno.

February 2, 1974

At 4:30 in the morning, Enrique was called to the emergency room to see a patient who had just been discharged from the hospital after having a baby a few days before. She was complaining of a lot of pain in the vaginal area and could not sit down. She was running a fever, was generally miserable and unable to take care of her new baby. Enrique refused to go to the emergency room to see her.

After repeated calls from the ER, he finally showed up, only to send the patient home after a cursory examination. The ER staff was outraged. The chief of the emergency room, along with a nurse on duty that night, reported the incident to Dr. Charles.

When I learned about Enrique's behavior, I was livid. He was more than just a pain in the ass. He was cruel. And in a heated argument we had the next day, I told him so. The tension that had always existed between us was now palpable.

I told Dr. Charles that Enrique should not be allowed to finish his residency at BCH, and should be fired at the end of the year. Dr. Charles told me he would think about it. I didn't hold my breath.

February 14, 1974: Valentine's Day

I went to the Suffolk County Courthouse to appear before the grand jury. I had been in the courthouse before, testifying as an expert witness in rape cases, so the surroundings were familiar, but that day, they seemed different. Imposing. Oppressive.

I waited in the hallway outside the grand jury room, talking with other residents who had also been subpoenaed to testify. I was sure— and reassured by my lawyer—that I had done nothing illegal. I had followed the law and the policies of the hospital. Even so, I could not seem to quell the butterflies in my stomach.

Finally, my name was called and I was ushered inside. The grand jury room was dark and cramped, with wood paneling and the stark, utilitarian furniture found in virtually all government buildings.

I was shown to a hard, wooden chair behind a rail, facing two men seated at a table. To my right, a dozen or so people were seated with their backs against the wall. Before I could sit down, a man in a uniform asked me to raise my right hand.

"Do you swear to tell the truth, the whole truth and nothing but the truth?"

"Yes," I said.

"Please sit down."

As I did, one of the two men seated behind the well-worn table in front of me rose and approached the railing. He was short, had a cherub-like face, a head full of well-groomed, graying hair and wore a flowery necktie, which he positioned inside of his jacket as he faced me. He had piercing, steel blue eyes, menacing front teeth and, unsurprisingly, a thick, Boston Irish accent.

"Would you identify yoahself?"

I told him my name, and when asked, where I lived and worked, feeling more uncomfortable by the minute.

"Docktah," he said, leaning on the railing, "befoah I ask you any questions, I want to advise you of yoah legal rights. We have been investigating a series of mattahs concehning questionable criminal activities at City Hospital ovah the last few yeahs. With that in mind, I'm going to advise you that you do not have to testify heah. Anything you say heah, if you decide to testify, can be used against you at a latah date." Looking down at a card he held in his hand, he read, "The Fifth Amendment of the United States Constitution states that no pehson shall be compelled in any criminal case to be a witness against himself. Do you undahstand what I just read to you?"

My mind raced forward, backward and in every other direction. What could I have done? I followed policy. Nothing against the law. I didn't violate my own laws.

This investigation cannot be about me! I thought. Before I began to panic, I remembered Sam Hoar's advice.

"Yes," I said. "I understand."

The little man with the flowery tie showed me Evonne's hospital record and fired question after question after question at me.

"Do you have a lawyah?"

"Yes."

"Do you perfoahm hysterotomies?"

"Yes."

"Do you know Dr. Holtrop?"

"Yes."

"Did you operate on Evonne?"

"Yes."

"Was she in a study?"

"I think so," I said.

"Why did you do a hysterotomy on Evonne?" he asked. His condescending tone was getting on my nerves.

"Because the saline infusions had failed," I answered.

"How old was the fetus?"

"Twenty weeks." Where was this going? Why was he asking so many questions about the procedure itself if this was an investigation into experimentation?

The squat little man lifted his double chin and looked down his nose at me. "Suppose I told you that the medical examinah did an autopsy and detahmined that the fetus was twenty-fouah weeks. What would you say to that?"

I looked him straight in the eye, unflinching. "It would depend on the criteria he used to come to that conclusion."

He frowned. "Who else was in the operating room?"

"I don't remember."

"How many othah people were in the operating room?"

"I don't remember." What did it matter?

"Was the fetus alive when you stahted the hysterotomy?"

"I don't think so. During the saline infusion, I kept hitting a blood vessel which was probably one of the large vessels going to the placenta."

"Was it alive when you removed it?"

"No. I have never delivered a live fetus by hysterotomy."

"You say it was dead befoah it came out?"

"Yes."

"Did you file a death ceahtificate on the fetus?"

"No. This was an abortion."

The little man with the flowery tie smirked. "Thank you," He said. Then he turned to the grand jurors. "Any questions?"

A woman sitting in the front row asked, "Did the patient request this operation?"

"This was a young lady who requested a termination of her pregnancy," I said.

"Did her case go to the Abortion Committee of the hospital?" a man two seats away from her asked.

"We don't have to do that anymore."

Hearing no further questions, the little man with the flowery tie said, "You ah excused."

That was it. Confused and probably showing it, I stood up and started to leave the grand jury room. Just as I made it through the door, I felt a hand on my shoulder. I turned around to find myself looking up at the other man who sat behind the table. He glared down at me with his stony eyes.

"This is a secret proceeding," he said. "You shouldn't discuss what you have testified to with anyone except for your lawyer. And if you don't have one, I advise you to get one."

With that and nothing else, he turned and disappeared back through the doors of the grand jury room.

For the first time, I felt fear. I had thought that this was a hearing to investigate the fetal experimentation, but the longer I stayed at the courthouse, the more I became convinced that it was an investigation into abortions.

I called Sam Hoar and he reassured me again that it would all be okay. "You're protected by *Roe*," he said. "Don't worry."

Over the next several weeks, the other residents went to the grand jury to testify, along with David Charles, Leon Sabath, Jim Penza and Bob Holtrop. Dr. Philipson had gone back to Sweden and avoided the subpoena.

Shortly after he testified, David Charles announced that he was resigning his position at BCH and would be taking a similar one in Newfoundland, Canada. A couple of the residents were going to join him there in July. He was running. And taking some of the staff with him.

Jim Penza and Joel Rankin were appointed co-directors of the department. Therefore, when Charles left, we would have one less attending physician to supervise, and in July, they would lose two residents. The strain on the department was already overwhelming, and more of the day-to-day running of it fell into my lap.

———

Life at BCH was busy—the GYN Clinic, the Prenatal Clinic, the Family Planning Clinic and the request for abortions. My specialty board exam, which I had to take at the end of my residency, was coming up in just five months, so I had to squeeze studying into my already full schedule. This exam, along with another one given two years after finishing residency, were required for me to be certified as a specialist in obstetrics and gynecology. Preparing for it was just one more thing I had to do.

April 1974

A psychiatrist on staff at BCH told me that he suspected that alcohol abuse among our pregnant patients was being missed. He told me about a new condition, Fetal Alcohol Syndrome (FAS), which came about when women drank during pregnancy. He wanted to investigate the prevalence of alcohol abuse during pregnancy and the impact on the newborns. On the 11th, we had a noontime meeting with nurses from the clinic, wherein the psychiatrist outlined his proposed study of FAS and alcohol use amongst our pregnant patients. He had developed a simple, five-question survey that he wanted to ask of our patients to determine the extent of their alcohol use. I insisted that in exchange for having access to our patients, he or his assistant must be present in our prenatal clinic to counsel women against using alcohol during pregnancy. He agreed, and we worked out the details of how he would do that.

As we wrapped up the meeting, the secretary from the clinic came into the room and told me that the district attorney was on the phone and wanted to talk to me.

Finally, I thought. After nearly four months, this was all about to be over.

"Docktah." The little man with the flowery tie. Even after months free from his questioning, his voice made me cringe. "This is Newman Flanagan. I'm calling to tell you that the grand jury has indicted you for manslaughtah. I'm calling you to let you know befoah you heah it on the news tonight. I'm not sending the police around to arrest you because of yoah position at the hospital. I just wanted you to know."

My mind and body went numb. I have no memory of what happened next. I must have walked out of the clinic because the next thing I knew, I was in my apartment, dazed, dumbfounded and consumed by disbelief. This couldn't be happening to me. I had worked so hard. I was nearly finished. My future was ahead of me. I had never had any trouble with the law. Not me...not me.

I sat on the couch in my living room and replayed Newman Flanagan's words over and over again in my head. *The grand jury has indicted you for manslaughter.* As I sank deeper into the couch, I sank deeper into depression. This wasn't happening. My future was in front of me but drifting further away by the second. I tried to force myself to wake up from this nightmare.

I picked up the phone and called my sister. As I filled her in, I could hear her quietly sobbing, trying to control her breathing so I didn't know. She didn't talk. She just cried. When I finished telling her everything, she took two slow, shaky breaths. "Do you—" she croaked. She paused and cleared her throat. "Do you want me to come to Boston? What are you going to do?"

I didn't know what I was going to do. My world had been turned upside-down by a grand jury and a little man in a flowery tie.

"No...not yet," I told my sister. "Let me see how this pans out. I might need you to later, though."

"Of course," my sister said, her voice cracking again.

Her words were reassuring, but the instant we hung up, that hollow feeling returned to the pit of my stomach. Elbows resting on my knees, I held my head in my hands and asked, aloud, to anyone or anything that could hear me, "How could this happen?"

Later that afternoon, my indictment was all over the news. I could not turn on the television without hearing my name or seeing footage of BCH. Four other physicians—Drs. Charles, Sabath, Nathenson and Berman, who were all involved in fetal research—were also indicted on charges of "grave robbing" under a 19th century Massachusetts statute. I felt sick.

As I watched news stories, I was interrupted again and again by phone calls. Ramona called. Patients called. Friends offering advice, lawyers who wanted to take the case, abortion rights activists who wanted to make my indictment a cause—everybody called. Everybody had suggestions. Everybody wanted to help.

Someone called to offer me a job working in a clinic on an island in the Caribbean—he must have thought I wanted to escape the country and the charges brought against me. I turned it down. I couldn't run.

When my phone stopped ringing for a few seconds, I dialed Sam Hoar and arranged to meet him in his office the next morning.

I sat back on the couch to continue watching the news when the phone started ringing again. Jim Penza called to tell me that the hospital administration had suspended me from my residency. In announcing my suspension, Frank Guiney, the hospital administrator, said that "if such actions occurred, they are against hospital policy. They have always been forbidden, and they continue to be so."

Such actions? What, exactly, were they trying to say I did? Manslaughter? I had performed an abortion—*after* the *Roe v. Wade* decision. What had I done against hospital policy?

I had two months left in my training and it was coming to a screeching halt. All the work. All the plans. The new programs I had introduced. It was all drifting further away. I had no future.

Riiiiiing!

I didn't want to pick up the phone. If it was a friend, I didn't want to relay my side yet again. If it was someone from the hospital, I didn't want to know what else was being taken from me.

Riiiiiing!

Sighing, I picked up the phone.

"Hello?"

"Dr. Edelin?"

"Yes."

"Hello, doctor. My name is Bert Lee. A friend gave me your number and I just wanted to let you know that there are a lot of us out here who are behind you. We appreciate what you have been doing at BCH."

Bert Lee went on to describe the political landscape in Boston, its history and some of the "movers and shakers" in the city. He seemed to know everybody who was anybody, both black and white, and he liberally sprinkled names of important people throughout our brief conversation—including those of several lawyers for me to consider. As with everyone else who called with such recommendations, I wrote down every name. I brought the list with me to my meeting with Sam Hoar the next morning.

Though Sam and I had talked on the phone several times, we had only met once before—we never needed to sit face to face. He was handling my divorce, which was far more civil than many others I had heard of. Now, however, I needed legal help in fighting a manslaughter charge, but wasn't sure if he could help me.

"Our firm can handle the case," Sam said. "But I want you to be aware that this case is bigger than you and the other doctors indicted. There are so many other issues involved—other forces. Irish Catholic Boston is angry about the Supreme Court decision and is looking to make an example out of anyone to find ways around it. Your trial is likely to attract national attention."

I wasn't interested in that. I was only interested in the charges brought against me. I wanted to finish my residency training. I wanted to practice my profession. I pulled out my list of recommended lawyers and asked Sam about each of them. For one reason or another, he advised against most of them. There was, however, one lawyer on the list he seemed to like.

"William Homans," he said, tapping his finger against the hand-written name. "He's good. Give him a call."

Back in my apartment later that afternoon, I called William Homans' office. A secretary picked up. I asked to speak directly to Mr. Homans, was put on hold for a moment, then a deep but pleasant voice spoke on the other end.

"Bill Homans."

"Mr. Homans, my name is Ken Edelin. I've been indicted for manslaughter in the death of a fetus during an abortion. I'd like to talk to you about it."

"Oh yes," he said. "I think I've heard something about that. Why don't you come to my office tomorrow morning?"

CHAPTER 17

WILLIAM PERKINS HOMANS

April 13, 1974

My life was like a shattered bowl and I needed help putting it back together. The little man in the flowery tie had told me I'd broken the law, and he had managed to convince a grand jury to indict me for manslaughter. *Manslaughter*—not some archaic crime left over from centuries ago. He'd said I'd killed a person. What was more, BCH did not stand behind me. Afraid my indictment would make the hospital look bad, they had suspended me from my residency, and the Board of Registration in Medicine was considering revoking my license.

Everyone said that William Homans was the attorney I needed. His name had appeared on everybody's lists. He was well known as a brilliant lawyer for the underdog, for those in our society who were being victimized by the system.

Homans came from a long line of important Brahmins in Boston's history. His ancestors were abolitionists, Civil Rights activists and politicians. His cousin, Endicott Peabody, had been governor of Massachusetts. His mother, Edith Walcott Parkman Homans, had been an early advocate of birth control and had worked to overturn Chapter 272. William Homans himself had gone to Harvard. After graduation, he'd attempted to join the Navy, but at six-foot-four, he was too tall, so he'd enlisted as a lieutenant in the British Navy. Later, he'd been able to transfer to the US Navy, where he'd served as an officer until the end of World War II.

He'd returned home to attend Harvard Law School and graduated in 1948. Like many in his family, he'd thought his future was in politics and eventually had gotten himself elected to the Massachusetts state legislature. However, he'd only stayed there for one term. It was impossible to practice law, which he loved, and be in the legislature at the same time.

He represented an eclectic mix of clients—those called before the House Un-American Activities Committee for being suspected Communists, people who had been arrested for protesting the war in Vietnam, those who had been charged with murder and still others who somehow ended up on Nixon's enemies list. Many of his clients were poor, however, and his propensity to work for little or no pay nearly destroyed his personal and professional lives, both of which were in constant turmoil.

I walked through the door of his office in the ornate Old City Hall, just before nine in the morning. His secretary was seated a short distance from the entrance. Judi Bernstein was a small but attractive woman with long, dark hair, a soothing, comforting voice and a welcoming smile. She looked like she was used to working on Saturdays. She took my coat and gestured to a seat opposite her desk. Behind her, I caught a glimpse of the man countless people had said should represent me.

He was sitting at his desk in shirtsleeves, talking to someone on the phone and smoking. Books and papers littered his desk, along with stacks of pink telephone messages, overflowing ashtrays and empty Styrofoam coffee cups.

Homans hung up the phone and came around from behind his desk. He was a big man—he had a big frame, big hair and a reputation for having a big heart. Part of his wrinkled, white shirt was being untucked by the massive belly that hung over his belt. He looked to be in his early 50s, with thick, dark hair tinged with white at the sides, piercing dark eyes, and a deeply lined, big-featured face. Tucked under his left arm was a yellow legal pad. As he extended his right hand to me, he gave me a sudden, engaging smile.

"Hi. I'm Bill Homans," he said. "Let's go into the conference room. My office is a mess." His rich, baritone voice added dimension to his size; he was imposing, comforting and protective all at once.

As we passed by one of the open office doors, he motioned to a young woman sitting at her desk, working.

"This is Jeanne Baker. She's one of my associates and I would like her to join us."

Good, I thought. It was important to have a woman lawyer involved in my defense. She would understand.

We sat at a large table in the conference room and finished up the small talk. Bill then cleared his throat and leaned back in his chair, his hands folded and resting on his round belly. "Tell me what this is all about. I want to hear the whole story."

I began my story with the day Dr. Holtrop had called me in to introduce me to Evonne. Bill Homans wrote down every detail of the events of my life over the course of the last seven months. I talked. He wrote. He asked questions and wrote some more. Pages and pages of words. Pages and pages of facts. Pages and pages of ink.

When I came to the grand jury hearing, Bill Homans held up his finger to interrupt me. "Do you remember the name of the district attorney who questioned you?"

I didn't, but before I even finished describing the little man with the cherub-like face, Bill asked, "Did he have on a bright, flowery tie?"

"Yes."

"Newman Flanagan."

The words came out syllable by syllable and carried a whole new weight into my case. Newman Flanagan and Bill Homans had apparently met many times in the courtroom. When Flanagan went after poor, black and other disenfranchised people, Bill defended them.

"Flanagan's family has been involved in Boston politics for generations. He's been an assistant district attorney for more than a decade, and is a confidant of District Attorney Garrett Byrne."

The more Bill Homans told me about Newman Flanagan, the less confident I felt. I did not know the ins and outs of Boston politics, but I knew enough about them from working at BCH to realize that Flanagan was a powerhouse of influence.

Like his father, Flanagan was active in the Knights of Columbus and involved in their right to life activities. The Knights, the world's largest lay organization in the Catholic Church, have often been called "the strong right arm of the Church." Cardinals and Popes alike have praised the Knights for their support of Church programs and Catholic education.

Flanagan was 44 and lived with his wife and seven children in what Bill Homans called the Lace Curtain Irish section of Boston: West Roxbury. West Roxbury was considered a step up from South Boston—a neighborhood for the upwardly mobile Irish. Flanagan was known for his aggressive prosecutions, his flashy style, his sarcasm and his steady stream of quips and jokes. He could play a Boston jury like a master musician.

Bill flipped over yellow page after yellow page in his legal pad, writing furiously, pausing only to ask questions and grab himself another pen. When my story was complete, Bill skimmed over his notes and said, "I don't see what their case is. You're protected by *Roe v. Wade* and the laws of Massachusetts."

He began to quote legal cases, citing the various laws that resulted from them. He knew the law and its precedents, but could not understand why Flanagan wanted this indictment.

"It doesn't make sense. By the law, they have virtually no case." Bill paused, tapping his pen on the legal pad. "I wonder if Garret Byrne is getting ready for retirement..."

If that were the case, then it all made sickening sense. At my expense, Newman Flanagan was setting himself up to run for the DA's job. What better way to do it than with a high-profile case?

That was what Bill figured. Jeanne Baker also agreed that there must have been a hidden motive. She thought that there was something bigger behind all this than just politics.

All I knew was that he had me indicted for manslaughter.

I was, however, reassured to hear that they thought the case against me was weak. I liked Bill's ability to quote cases and the law. He was amiable, warm and smart. He was methodical and he listened. He was an intellectual, but his experiences defending poor people had made him real and down to earth.

After hours of conversation, I asked Bill to represent me. He agreed and gave me an idea of what lay ahead. I would be arraigned, which meant I would have to go to court, hear the reading of the charges against me and enter my not guilty plea. He wanted to get that scheduled right away. He also wanted to get copies of everything Newman Flanagan had—hospital records, grand jury testimony transcripts, everything—so he could understand Flanagan's theory of the case and how he managed to get the grand jury to indict me for manslaughter. Because it was the weekend, he would not be able to find out anything until that Monday, so he asked me to come back to his office then. We never discussed money. I didn't know how much his fee was, nor did I have any idea how I was going to pay for any of this.

I shook Bill Homans' hand and thanked him. Just as I was getting up to leave, he said in a hesitant, subdued and somewhat apologetic voice, "I just lost a case to Newman Flanagan."

I sat back down.

"I just thought you should know. He's good. Knows how to manip-
ulate a jury." Bill sighed. He ran a hand through his hair and told me
the story of Ella Mae Ellison.

In 1973, three young black men—all armed with handguns and all
needing money to feed their heroin addictions—entered a pawnshop
and began scooping jewelry from the display case. A Boston police
detective wearing civilian clothes was present in the shop. He was shot
and killed during the struggle with the robbers.

The three addicts were apprehended within a day. After they were
locked up and denied their "fix," two of the robbers tried to bribe
Flanagan with the only thing they could: another conviction. They
offered to testify against a supposed accomplice who, they said, had
driven the getaway car. Flanagan agreed and allowed them to plead
guilty to second-degree murder after they identified Ella Ellison.

Although Ella knew the defendants, she had not participated in the
robbery in any way. The only evidence against her was the junkies'
testimony. They had accused her so they could get a reduced sentence.

Ellison, the mother of two young children, was convicted of first-
degree murder and armed robbery and sentenced to two life terms. Bill
had defended Ella and he, along with nearly everyone else who knew
the details of the case, was outraged by the tactics used by Flanagan to
get the testimony against her.

Ella Mae Ellison's story stunned me and raised plenty of questions
in my mind. Was Flanagan so low that he would allow an innocent
person to be sentenced to life in prison? If he was that vicious, what
would he do to me? How could he have won such a case? Was he better
than Bill? I wondered what their record of convictions and acquittals
was and, for a brief moment, reconsidered taking Bill on as my lawyer.
I dismissed the notion almost immediately. Wasn't Bill recommended
by nearly everyone who'd offered me advice?

*Flanagan can't win two cases in a row against Bill. No way. The odds
are against it,* I told myself.

Despite my self-reassurance, I was sobered by this news. I left Bill's
office more shaken than when I'd come in.

I hardly remember my drive through the narrow streets of Boston,
back to my apartment in the South End of the city. Though I felt
relieved that Bill Homans, too, thought that the charge against me was
bogus, I was stunned to learn how low Flanagan would stoop to get a

conviction. If he had it in for me, there was little chance of simply getting the case dismissed.

My apartment was a mess, with dirty clothes and dishes everywhere, beer bottles scattered on the tables and the floor, and the TV still on. I hadn't really slept for two days, so I was exhausted. My telephone answering service had collected another dozen or so calls while I'd been in Bill Homans' office. There were more suggestions of lawyers—many from lawyers themselves, offering to help. Bert Lee called again and left a message saying that he had spoken to Mayor Kevin White about the indictment. The mayor, apparently, thought the whole thing was "a dumb move" on the DA's part.

When I called Bert back, I told him I had just hired Bill Homans.

"Good choice. Good choice. Listen, I'm going to get a group of friends together to help raise money for your legal bills—they're going to be enormous." He then began to rattle off the names of several people, some of whom I had never even heard of.

I thanked Bert Lee several times. I hadn't really thought about how I would pay my legal bills, but others apparently had. People called to tell me about individuals and organizations, with vested interests in the issues of family planning and abortion, who might be potential sources of money, including Planned Parenthood, the American Civil Liberties Union, John D. Rockefeller III, the National Abortion Rights Action League and the Sunnen Foundation.

Dean Friedman of Boston University School of Medicine called to say he was looking into the possibility of having the University's lawyers represent me and assume the cost of my defense. There were messages from other residents and calls from the head of the House Officers Association at City Hospital. They were putting pressure on the hospital to reinstate me so I could finish my residency. After all, they argued, I had not been convicted of a crime, just charged with one. I was innocent until proven guilty.

The phone rang and rang and rang. Since I was not working, it became my lifeline and connection to the outside world. I took copious notes so I wouldn't forget suggestions, names and any other details of my phone conversations. I was comforted by the suggestions and offers of help, but the shame and fear I felt drove me deeper into the depths of despair.

I fell asleep on the couch. The phone calls resumed early Sunday morning and lasted throughout the day. There was more news about the indictments in the Sunday papers and on the TV. My picture was everywhere. It was one of the longest days of my life.

When Monday morning finally dawned, I went back to Bill Homans' office and spent the entire day there, going over my case detail by detail. Even though everything was slammed in my face, being in Bill's office was calming. I was out and about, *doing* something about my life, rather than sitting at home, wallowing in shame and misery.

By early afternoon, he was able to finally get a copy of the indictment. As I read the brutal accusation that Flanagan was able to get the grand jury to hand down, my blood ran cold and my depression deepened.

At the SUPERIOR COURT, begun and holden at the City of Boston, within and for the County of Suffolk, for the transaction of Criminal Business, on the first Monday of April, in the year of our Lord one thousand nine hundred and seventy-four.

THE JURORS for the COMMONWEALTH OF MASSACHUSETTS on their oath present that
KENNETH EDELIN
on the third day of October, in the year of our Lord one thousand nine hundred and seventy-three, did assault and beat a certain person, to wit: a male child described to the said JURORS as Baby Boy Gilbert and by such assault and beating did kill the said person.
A TRUE BILL

Assault and beat. Baby Boy Gilbert. Did kill said person. The language of the indictment described something that I never did and something that I could never do—beat a child to death. Jeanne Baker said it was just the arcane language of the courts. That didn't help. The image the indictment would conjure up in the mind of the public was exactly what Flanagan wanted. The words were cutting and wrong, but they were the first words that Flanagan used to paint his public picture of me. I was angry, and his tactics frightened me.

Bill the Brahmin didn't show emotion. He studied the indictment, then pointed out something that I, in my distress, had not noticed: in its brevity, the indictment gave no specifics of the charges. What did I do? Assault and beat? Certainly not. It was just language, he assured me, but he needed to know the specific acts Flanagan was charging me with.

Bill was angry about something else, too.

"Flanagan has her name in the indictment," he said in disgust. In blatant disregard for Evonne's privacy, Flanagan revealed her last name in a document that was about to become public.

Once the indictment was made public, it would be easy for reporters to discover her identity and descend upon her for interviews and stories, also revealing the abortion to her father which she, her mother and I tried so carefully to keep secret. Evonne's privacy would be invaded. Evonne's safety could be at risk. But the little man in the flowery tie didn't understand that, nor did he care.

How do you fight someone who doesn't fight fair? We were engaged in a battle representing our different Americas. We had different views of life, death and everything in between. He would do anything to win. He would do anything to convict me of homicide. His ideals, his America, had to be right.

Bill tried to reassure me and looked for other explanations. "It probably was an innocent mistake. He just overlooked it. Somebody else drew up the indictment and Flanagan never saw it." I didn't believe any of that and I doubted Bill the Brahmin did either. We both had come face to face with Flanagan. He didn't care. His fanaticism blinded him.

I left Bill's office late that afternoon and went back to my apartment and the ringing telephone. I ignored it. I didn't want to talk to anybody. I sank into the couch and the blackness of gloom. How was I going to get through this?

The phone continued to ring and I continued to sink. As the sun went down, the darkness consumed me. How do you fight someone who doesn't fight fair?

CHAPTER 18

The Kenneth Edelin Defense Fund

April 16, 1974

I had to get reinstated at BCH to finish my residency. When I was suspended five days earlier, so was my pay. I needed to live. I needed to pay child support. I had to continue working.

To help get my suspension reversed, Bill called his Brahmin buddy, Herb Gleason, the chairman of the board of trustees of City Hospital.

"It is unfair to suspend Dr. Edelin," Bill insisted. "The trustees should immediately reverse Guiney's decision to suspend him. Put it to a vote."

Bill contacted the organization of interns and residents both locally and nationally and asked them to continue to put pressure on the city officials. If the suspension were allowed to stand, he argued, every house officer in every training program in the country who was following the orders of an attending physician could be vulnerable to suspension and criminal indictment for carrying out medical procedures. It was a precedent, he argued, they could not let stand.

In addition to Bill's efforts, Mayor Kevin White again expressed his opinion to Leon White, the commissioner of health and hospitals, that Flanagan had made a mistake in bringing the indictment.

That afternoon, in the midst of our struggle to get my suspension revoked, we received word that my arraignment was scheduled for the next morning in the Suffolk County Courthouse.

106

April 17, 1974

The morning dawned bright and clear, lifting my mood a little. The cool spring air felt good against my face as Bill, Jeanne and I walked to the Suffolk County Courthouse. We walked around corners, through archways, up and down stairs and across a wide open plaza before reaching the front door of the courthouse, over which was its promise chiseled in stone: *Justice for All.* I hoped they meant it.

The outside of the building was pink marble. Sturdy, double glass doors led into an ornate, grand lobby where the floors, ceilings and walls were also made of marble. Beyond the lobby was a bank of eight art deco elevators. There were four on each side with fluted brass doors, each spotless and fully functional. The polished luxury of the criminal justice system was a far cry from the dingy disrepair of BCH. I asked myself for the hundredth time that morning, *Why am I here?* All I wanted to do was be a doctor and take care of patients.

Bill led the way out of the elevator on the ninth floor and I followed closely behind. Flashbulbs and the bright, continuous lights of the television cameras blinded me before I even heard the commotion of clicking cameras and shouted questions. I could not even find my voice to say, "No comment."

I was led through the heavy, wooden double doors to Courtroom 906—to the inner sanctum of Boston justice. The room had a very high ceiling with four paneled glass windows stretching the full height of the room. Directly in front of me was the judge's bench, elevated to give it a position of power and authority. In front of that, but lower, a grim-faced blond man sat in the clerk's box, helping the judge manage the flow of paper and information. To the right was the witness stand and down from it, along the wall, was the 16-chaired jury box. The oak rail in front of it was worn from years of lawyers' hands rubbing it as they walked back and forth, making their arguments, asking their questions and pleading their cases.

The room had a dark gloom about it. As I looked around, taking it all in, my eyes landed on Newman Flanagan. At the same moment, he looked up and our gazes caught one another. Locked. I stood a little taller. I was not about to let this little man intimidate me.

The randomly chosen judge arrived and my arraignment began.

Bill stood up. "Your honor, before we proceed," he said, "my client would like to move to have the last name of the patient removed from the indictment. Her name and the date of the operation is an invasion of her privacy."

After a minor debate, Flanagan and the judge ultimately agreed, and the judge impounded the date of the procedure and Evonne's last name.

With that out of the way, the court clerk then turned to me and said, "Kenneth Edelin, on April 11, 1974, the grand jury returned an indictment. Do you waive the formal reading of this indictment?"

Assault. Beat. Baby Boy. I didn't want to hear it again. Bill and I agreed that we would waive the reading of the indictment and deny Flanagan another stroke of his word brush as he tried to paint this horrific portrait of me.

"Yes," I responded.

He continued.

"Kenneth Edelin, on indictment number 81823, charging you with manslaughter, how do you plead?"

"Not guilty."

Not guilty of anything!

"Kenneth Edelin, the court recognizes you personally without surety in the sum of one thousand dollars."

That was it. The first step was taken and we were done. Bill had a trial in another courtroom that morning, so he asked one of his partners to go with me to police headquarters, to get my mugshots and fingerprints taken.

We pushed our way through the crowd of reporters and flashbulbs, making no comment along the way, made it to the elevators and headed down to the lobby. The ride to police headquarters was quick, but the process of having my picture and fingerprints taken was not.

Boston Police Headquarters was a nondescript, red brick building, marked by perfectly placed windows and the blue Boston Police logo hanging over the front door. Boston Irish police officers and their patrol cars were everywhere, as if they had been waiting for my arrival. Eyes followed me as I stepped out of the car and walked up to the station doors.

Once inside, we were taken to a window so I could have my first police record made. Behind the window was a fat, red-cheeked sergeant in a blue uniform—which might have fit him several years ago, but was now far too small. His belly hung over his belt and the buttons on his shirt strained to stay closed. He began to enter information on the official booking form, using an old, manual typewriter. The keys got stuck with every stroke.

"Damn!" the fat cop swore as he unjammed the N again.

"I hope Boston justice works better than that typewriter," I blurted out with a nervous laugh.

The fat cop in the tight, blue uniform did not think my joke was very funny. He shot his blue eyes at me and sneered, the red from his cheeks spreading out to the rest of his face and up his receding hairline. He continued to type one letter at a time, unjamming each key as he went along.

When the paperwork was completely filled out, he took me to a room with a large camera and a white backdrop, where he again struggled as he fished around in a container filled with white plastic letters, so he could spell my name. He pushed the letters onto the background of a framed, black box. Underneath, he pressed in a series of numbers. I felt humiliated, holding my name and number as he took his mugshots.

"Smile," he said.

"Smile?"

Are you crazy? I thought. *Smile about what?*

He then took me to a tall table, where he rolled each of my fingers on an inkpad, then into little boxes on the bottom of the sheet he had typed up.

"You're done. You can go."

He turned and waddled back to his window, the tight, too-short pants of his blue uniform threatening to burst at the seams with every step.

Boston justice.

I could not believe this was happening to me. The indictment. Police headquarters. Fingerprints. Mugshots. Was I a criminal? A murderer, as they had said? How did this happen?

I'd come to Boston to become an obstetrician and gynecologist because Boston was the Mecca of medical care and education. What I hadn't known was that Boston was also the hell of fierce racial and religious struggles, a place where white men and Catholicism ruled nearly every aspect of life in the city, particularly the right to life, and led the charge in the fight against birth control, abortion and a woman's right to control her own life. Boston was a city where black people were denied not only power, but all access to that power. It was a city where whites tried to overturn buses and laws intended to help black children. I'd become a doctor because I'd wanted to help those children be wanted, wellborn and healthy. But here I was, indicted for manslaughter so the city could make an example out of me.

We took a cab back to Bill's office, but I only stayed there for a short while. Bill was still at the courthouse on another trial. There was really nothing for me to do.

That afternoon, there was a rally being held on the front steps of the hospital, to pressure the administration to reverse my suspension. I couldn't go to the rally, so I waited in my apartment, near the phone— my lifeline.

Hundreds of interns, residents, nurses and hospital workers showed up for the rally. In a speech, Steve Saltzman, head of the House Officers Association at BCH, said that it was clear I was being "scapegoated" by anti-abortion forces.

"Dr. Edelin was performing his duties in accordance with accepted gynecological practices throughout Boston and the country, and within the recent US Supreme Court guidelines. Dr. Edelin is an able, compassionate and conscientious physician and we are certain that he will be cleared when the facts are known. His suspension from his training program without pay is ill-advised and inappropriate."

The phone calls, the messages, the offers of help, the letters and the rally infused me with hope and energy. It was now time for me to take charge of my own fate and my own future. I could not sit around my apartment feeling depressed and sorry for myself. I could not be afraid of the little man in the flowery tie.

My apartment was still a mess. The pile of dirty clothes had grown, the dirty dishes had multiplied and empty beer bottles had found new places to hide. With a new burst of energy and confidence, I set about cleaning the sty. As I straightened and reorganized my apartment, I began to straighten and reorganize my life.

The phone rang shortly after five p.m. It was Jim Penza.

"Ken, we are going to meet with the trustees of the hospital tomorrow. Is there anything I should know that I don't already?"

Jim's memory of the case was fuzzy and incomplete, so I went over the facts with him. I also told him that there were others working to get me reinstated and that both the mayor and the chairman of the BCH Board of Trustees, Herb Gleason, had been contacted on my behalf.

"And Jim?"

"Hmm?"

"Thanks again for standing with me."

"No problem, Ken. We know you were operating within the law. This'll all sort itself out."

I hoped so. I really hoped so.

Jim and I wished each other luck and ended the call. As soon as I hung up the phone, it rang again.

Bert Lee called and told me about the political efforts that he had put into play in order to get me reinstated. He asked me to come to his house in Roxbury the next morning for breakfast, so we could finally meet and talk about ideas and strategy he had.

I had my daily conversation with my sister. She noticed the change in my voice and spirit and said she felt better about how I was doing. She then turned the conversation to our families, and she asked about Ramona, Kenny, Jr. and Kim She always gave the best advice and knew how to lighten up a conversation. She would not let me forget my family.

I tried to talk to my children every day. Ramona was outraged at the system as only Ramona could be. She made sure that I remembered the racial context that my indictment and arraignment represented, and she made sure Kenny understood as well. Kimi, however, was too young to know what was going on. Ramona's mother wrote a letter to the editor of the *Boston Globe*, vividly describing the impact that my indictment was having on my children—her grandchildren. The support from Ramona and her family, despite the differences between us, gave me new courage.

The next morning, I went to meet with Bert Lee. Bert and his wife, Edith, lived in a grand house on Hutchings Street, in what had come to be called the Black Roxbury section of Boston. He was a black businessman operating in a turbulent America. He and one of his best friends were partners in a consulting business. Their relationship, like their business, was as tumultuous as it was successful.

Originally from Virginia, Bert had backpacked throughout Europe after college, wearing sandals, shorts, a big Afro and a beard—the uniform of the '60s radical. He'd visited both Western and Eastern Europe, spending time in several Communist countries.

Bert was short, had mahogany-brown skin and a full-toothed,

disarming smile. He knew everybody and was able to weave the names of prominent, powerful people into a conversation. His voice was deep and had a melodious quality about it. He always spoke in calm, even tones—I never heard him shout or snap.

Bert introduced me to his wife and their two daughters and cooked breakfast for all of us that Thursday morning. The meeting began a friendship that remained strong for years to come.

Bert simply said that he wanted to help. His friend, Vivian Pinn, a respected black physician and pathologist on staff at Tufts Medical School, had asked him to do what he could for me. Vivian, and many other black women physicians I had met, felt very strongly about the issue of privacy and abortion. She and Bert wanted to set up a legal defense fund on my behalf, which could be headquartered in his office in downtown Boston and run by a committee of supporters. They would help me raise funds for my legal expenses—which, Bert reminded me, were certainly going to be huge.

"The committee members could also act as advisors," Bert said as he scooped a fluffy omelet onto my plate. "And a clearing house for requests that I'm sure will come for you to speak to groups of supporters or give interviews to the press."

Those calls had already started to come in. It all sounded like a good idea to me.

"I'd like the committee to be separate from Bill Homans' law office," he continued, "but I think it would be beneficial for both you and Bill to attend the meetings."

Bert and Vivian had drawn up a list of possible committee members. It was a mix of dedicated and concerned Bostonians, both black and white. As I skimmed the list, I recognized many of the names.

Hazelle Furgeson. Among the first black women to graduate from the BCH School of Nursing, she was smart and sophisticated. As a nurse at BCH before *Roe*, she had taken care of women who were sick and dying from illegal abortions.

Henry Morgan. He was a professor at MIT and, I found out, one of Bert's business associates. Henry knew a lot of wealthy people and had a fair amount of money himself.

Peter Tishler. A physician, geneticist and Harvard professor who was adamant in his belief that safe abortion should be available to women, especially those who carried fetuses with severe congenital defects. He had seen the tragedy brought about by babies born with severe deformities and early death.

Vivian Pinn. Naturally, she would be a member of the defense fund. Aside from her other impressive credentials, she had attended the debate I'd had with Mildred Jefferson back in 1973, right after the *Roe v. Wade* ruling. As a professor of pathology at Tufts and an expert in kidney diseases, she was an example for young women to follow of a smart, black woman making it in the man's world of medicine while maintaining her femininity.

Josh Young. He was a friend of Vivian's and lived in the South End of Boston—a neighborhood where 19th century elegance had given way to rooming houses and winos. It was now being gentrified by young, progressive, white couples and families who were moving back into Boston.

"Well?" Bert said. "Any suggestions?"

I thought for a moment. "Dr. Stanley Robbins."

He was a professor of pathology at BCH and the author of the most famous textbook on pathology—the one that I and thousands of other medical students had used to learn about human diseases. He was the chairman of the search committee that was looking for David Charles' replacement as chairman of the OB/GYN department. In addition, Stanley Robbins had been among the first to call me immediately after I'd been indicted. He was Jewish and determined not to let Catholicism impose its view of life and abortion on the rest of America. He had national prominence, and had told me that he wanted to do whatever he could to be helpful.

"Having him on the committee gives it instant credibility in the world of doctors," I said. "In all honesty, he should probably be chairman, if he's interested."

"Great," said Bert. "Anyone else?"

"Dr. Robert Stepto. He's a professor and the chairman of OB/GYN at Cook County Hospital in Chicago. And he was the first black man to be chief of obstetrics and gynecology at a white hospital."

When I'd been on the search committee to find Dr. Charles' replacement, we had interviewed Dr. Stepto and I'd been impressed with his class, insight and smarts. Bert agreed and jotted his name down on the list.

Finally, I suggested Pam Lowry, who was the head of MORAL: the

Massachusetts Organization to Repeal Abortion Laws. She was an activist and had worked as a family planning counselor at BCH when contraception was available only to married women.

My meeting with Bert lasted a few hours. We had finished breakfast long ago and were on our fourth cup of coffee when we finally wrapped things up. Bert grabbed the dirty dishes from the table and put them in the sink, then gathered up his list of potential committee members.

"All right. So I'll call each of these people and ask them to join." He tucked the papers under his arm and extended his right hand. "It was very nice to finally meet you, Ken."

I shook it. "Same to you." I bade his wife and daughters a quick farewell, then went back to my apartment.

Each of the nine people Bert and I discussed agreed to help, and formed the Kenneth Edelin Defense Fund. From day one, they were a source of strength, guidance and wisdom for me as I embarked on this legal journey, which was certain to have many dimensions and last a long time.

Each of them had their own reasons for supporting a woman's right to legal abortion, and each of them had their own reasons for believing in me. I was able to depend on them for sound advice and knew I could trust them to help me raise and protect the money I needed to defend myself.

More good news came at noon, when Jim Penza called. The board of trustees at BCH had voted unanimously to reinstate me in my position at the hospital. I could continue in my training program—I had my future back.

Jim said that there had been many speakers on my behalf at the trustees' meeting. It not only included the head of the House Officers Association, but nurses, other residents from the OB/GYN department and even some of my patients. Though Jim had arranged and coordinated the entire presentation to the trustees, Bill Homans and Bert Lee had done their work behind the scenes.

Better still was the statement the trustees released to the press when they announced their decision to reverse my suspension:

> We found nothing in this case to indicate that anything occurred which could be considered illegal. Dr. Edelin did nothing inconsistent with his duties or with established hospital

policies applicable to Supreme Court rulings and accepted medical practice. There is no evidence that any abortion was performed except in accordance with the guidelines laid down by the US Supreme Court. Dr. Edelin has an outstanding record of service to City Hospital over the last three years, and enjoys a fine reputation among the senior staff, as evidenced by the fact that prior to this situation, he was invited to join the hospital as a full-time junior staff member next July.

I exhaled. The week I was suspended gave me the time I needed to hire a lawyer and establish the KEDF—the Kenneth Edelin Defense Fund—but now, at last, I could get back to work. I could start studying again to prepare to take the written examination in two months. Already, my mind was kicking back into gear. I had programs to put together and patients to take care of. Those were the things I loved to do.

Still looming over me, however, was the State Board of Medical Examiners' threat to revoke my license to practice medicine, which would make the trustees' decision to reinstate me moot.

All of these thoughts raced through my mind as I listened to Jim Penza's account of the meeting. I thanked him again for all his help and told him I would be back to work on Monday morning.

Just before we hung up, he said, "One more thing, Ken. The administration would still like you to join the medical staff in July after you finish your residency. Their offer for you to become director of ambulatory services of the Department of Obstetrics and Gynecology still stands."

Relief flooded over me. That solved another problem. I now had a job. Atlanta still was an allure, but I wasn't going to be able to leave Boston any time soon, with the manslaughter indictment and a trial due to take place within the next few months.

Appearing before the grand jury, being indicted, being arraigned, fingerprinted and photographed had made me more determined to fight. I knew that everything I had done for all of my patients was in their best interest. All the women and girls I had come to know in the clinics at City Hospital, NEWS, the Crit and the neighborhood health centers were standing in my corner. All of the nameless, faceless women I had never known, who had been fighting for the right to control their lives, drove me forward. I summoned my strength and will from all of them. The little man in the flowery tie was not going to intimidate me. I was determined to beat him and those who had helped him indict me in court and on the stage of public opinion. He could not impose his narrow views on me—or my patients.

I spent all of the next day lost in my textbooks and medical journals. I had less than two months to prepare for my specialty exam and, starting Monday, I would be back to seeing patients at City Hospital, taking care of the pregnant teenagers at the Crit, spending time with my children, helping Bill Homans prepare for my trial and raising money for my legal bills. My life was back on track.

CHAPTER 19

SMOKING OUT THE FOX

April 20, 1974

Bill and I met in his office around mid-morning, ready to roll up our sleeves and get to work. The indictment gave us very little information about the specifics of Flanagan's case against me, and when Bill asked him privately for more information, he refused to give it up. We would have to go to court to force him.

News of my indictment spread from Boston out to the entire country. Bill and I discovered that there had been other attempts in other cities to indict or bring charges against doctors and nurses who provided second trimester abortions, but none of them were successful. "The Edelin Case" was the first and only one that resulted in an indictment. Boston was the only city where white, Catholic men wielded enough power to ignore the Supreme Court decision. It was seen as the test case for those who were for and against a woman's right to a legal abortion.

More offers of help began to pour into Bill's office. Lawyers from around the country offered their opinions on how to fight the charge of manslaughter. Many, like Cyril Means, Harriette Pilpel and Roy Lucus, had been involved in the long fight to legalize abortion. They knew all the usual legal arguments surrounding the issue. Their perspectives and experiences were enormously helpful.

Philosophers, anthropologists, historians and scores of others also called with advice. Physicians offered their expert medical testimonies—they knew that this was not just a case against me, but a case against all physicians who performed legal abortions, acting in the best interest of their patients. In a very short time, Bill's office became the epicenter of legal, medical and philosophical thinking about abortion in America.

One of the doctors who contacted us was Kurt Benirschke from California, the world's foremost expert in fetal pathology. He offered to review the autopsy report performed by the state medical examiner, Dr. George Curtis. Curtis had recently come under fire because of the inaccurate and inadequate autopsies he had performed in previous criminal cases, so we hoped that Dr. Benirschke's analysis would further discredit him. Flanagan, however, refused to give us the autopsy report, so Bill filed a motion to force him to send us and Dr. Benirschke copies of the report and the microscopic slides.

April 22, 1974

I was finally back at work and seeing patients at BCH. I still moonlighted in a neighborhood health center one evening a week and continued to give prenatal care to the teenagers at the Crit, but my Saturdays and many of my evenings were spent with Bill Homans or, whenever I could, with Kenny and Kimi. Any and all free time was spent either with them or studying for my boards. My life was jammed and moving fast. April melded into May. Busy, the month passed in a spring blur.

June, 1974

What an event-filled month! I took the three-hour written examination in obstetrics and gynecology—and passed it. June also marked Kimi's fourth birthday, so I made sure I was available to attend the party Ramona threw for her. Privately, it was a double celebration for me. The first step in becoming certified as a specialist was complete.

When formally asked, I accepted BCH's offer to join the staff as the director of ambulatory services for the Department of Obstetrics and Gynecology. At the end of the month, I graduated from my residency and began my new job, all the while continuing to meet with Bill Homans on Saturdays to plan the fight for my freedom.

In the middle of the month, we received word that the chief justice of the Superior Court of Massachusetts had assigned James P. McGuire to be the judge in my case.

Who was James McGuire? Bill didn't know much about him, so he sent a private investigator to find out what he could about him. What he found did not look promising.

James McGuire was a 1930 graduate of Catholic University in Washington, DC, where he later received an honorary degree and the school's prestigious Judiciary Award in 1973. He received his law degree from Boston University in 1933 and began his law practice as both a civil and criminal trial lawyer. He was corporation counsel for his hometown of Fall River, and later Boston, under Mayor Kevin H. White. He was appointed to the bench of the Superior Court of Massachusetts not long before he was assigned to my case. He was active in the Catholic Charities Appeal, the United Way and, like Flanagan, was a member of the Knights of Columbus. He attended church regularly at St. Joseph's. To me, McGuire was very much like Flanagan, Mulligan and the other Boston politicians I had encountered since the beginning of this ordeal.

June was also when Bill formally filed our motion for a Bill of Particulars, since Flanagan refused his private requests for information. In the motion he pointed out that both the Constitution of the United States and that of Massachusetts said that I could not be "held to answer for any crime or offence, until the crime is fully and plainly, substantially and formally described." We all have the right, our Constitution said, "to be informed of the nature and cause of an accusation." Neither Flanagan, the grand jury nor the indictment had fully explained what it was I had done.

Bill was determined to get the information from Flanagan so we could, as he put it, "smoke out" Flanagan's theory of his case against me. The indictment was so brief, so vague and so contrary to existing law that it gave us no information to help us prepare for our defense. We had to get Flanagan's theory of the case out into the open so we could mark it and destroy it.

Bill's motion contained more than 30 questions and requests for information. Was Flanagan charging me with voluntary or involuntary manslaughter? Why did Flanagan describe the fetus as a "person" in the indictment? What specific act did I do to cause the death of the "person" he described in the indictment? Flanagan had stated repeatedly in the press that this was not a case against abortion. What part of the procedure I performed was not an abortion and what part was? What part of the operation did Flanagan claim caused "death?" Was he claiming the "death" occurred in the womb or afterwards? If inside, when? If afterward, when? What duty did I have to the fetus immediately following its removal from the womb?

Bill's written brief to support his motion for the particulars was brilliant. He knew the law—both the statutes on the books and the case law—because he had established many of them in the cases he had handled. He quoted from British Common Law, the US Constitution, the Massachusetts Constitution and from established precedents in prior Massachusetts cases. He concluded his brief by declaring that without answers to the questions, it would be impossible to prepare an adequate defense.

Predictably, Flanagan argued against having to provide the information, but Bill pushed on, filing additional briefs and memoranda to counter Flanagan's refusals.

The process was long, tedious and frustrating. Flanagan did not give up information easily. Over the next several weeks, Bill filed multiple motions and made numerous oral arguments before Judge McGuire to get the list of witnesses who testified before the grand jury, a transcript of their testimonies, the transcript of my own testimony, Evonne's hospital record, the operating room logbook, the autopsy report and the answers to the Bill of Particulars.

Finally, McGuire ruled that Flanagan did not have to release the grand jury testimony of the witnesses until two weeks before the beginning of the trial, whenever that might be. He also said that Flanagan did not have to answer all of the questions in our Bill of Particulars. He did, however, order Flanagan to release copies of the autopsy report and agreed that copies of it and the slides could be sent to Dr. Benirschke in California.

Even after McGuire's order, it took Flanagan weeks to release the report and the slides. He was not going to make this easy.

Finally, on July 24th—nearly six weeks after our request—Flanagan answered some of our questions in a document that was absurdly brief. He said I'd committed manslaughter by cutting off the blood supply to the fetus and waiting three to five minutes before I removed it from the patient. According to him, this act constituted manslaughter and was not part of a legal abortion. He said that this 24- to 28-week "baby boy" would have remained alive had it not been for my actions.

In a rare show of emotion, Bill the Brahmin was livid! Compounding the ruling by McGuire that Flanagan did not have to respond to most of our questions, the few questions he did answer gave us hardly any new information. And since McGuire didn't require it, Flanagan did not tell us whether he was charging me with involuntary or voluntary manslaughter.

Nevertheless, with the meager information we had, Bill filed a motion to have the charges against me dismissed. McGuire, Bill and Flanagan agreed that oral arguments on the motion would be made at the end of August—we had about a month.

That gnawing fear about Flanagan's tactics continued to grow. Bill, forever the optimist, believed in the judicial system and its fairness. He believed that Judge McGuire, in spite of his upbringing and his Catholicism, could be fair and impartial in his handling of my case if we ever went to trial. Bill always saw the positive, believed that good would always triumph and always saw our legal system in its best possible light. I was less trusting. Those lining up against me were all beginning to look frighteningly the same.

Boston was a conservative city and much of it was still under the control of the Catholic Church, as it had been for most of the century. Priests preached from their pulpits against abortion and a woman's right to choose. *The Pilot*, the official newspaper of the Boston Archdiocese, wrote a scathing editorial against the *Roe v. Wade* decision after it was handed down, and another after my indictment in April of 1973. Could I get a fair trial in Boston? In Suffolk County? I wasn't sure. We needed to do a poll.

We hired Irwin "Tubby" Harrison, a seasoned pollster and opinion sampler, to survey residents of Suffolk County who could potentially sit on my jury. We needed information on their views regarding abortion, in case we wanted to make the argument for a change in venue. If the trial was held in Suffolk County as scheduled, then the results of the poll would at least help us to select a jury.

Meanwhile, my life at BCH was very busy. I continued to organize programs, recruiting OB/GYNs to work in both the outpatient department of the hospital and the neighborhood health centers. Under the old system, the OB/GYNs who worked in the health centers had no contact with their patients once they were admitted to BCH. Babies were delivered by whichever resident or medical student was on call and all surgeries were performed by the resident assigned to the case. I was determined to change this, to make sure patients received as much personal service as possible, to increase the humanity and the continuity of care.

Meanwhile, I had started my private practice in the Doctors' Office Building—the DOB—of University Hospital. At first, I had office hours one afternoon a week, but quickly found that it was not enough. There were many black women in Boston who preferred a black OB/GYN to take care of them. Other women came to me because they had seen my name and picture in the papers nearly everyday. I attracted young, middle class, well-educated black and white women, as well as poor women with no insurance—not even Medicaid—because they knew me from BCH. In no time, my private practice became so busy that I had to expand my office hours to two afternoons each week while still working in the OB/GYN clinic at BCH, the neighborhood health centers and taking care of the pregnant teenagers at the Crit.

My first private patient delivered in mid-summer. She was a young, single Puerto Rican woman on Medicaid who was having her first baby. I stayed with her in the hospital as she went through labor and then helped her deliver a healthy baby girl after 15 hours of labor. It was an emotional time for both the new mom and me. I had arrived at the place I had dreamed of—a specialist taking care of women when they were at one of the most important and special moments of their lives. There was no experience in any other part of medicine that could rival the sense of accomplishment when assisting a woman giving birth.

In the midst of all this, I still had to spend weekends preparing for my trial, which included meeting and working with the defense fund. Requests came into Bert Lee's office from around the country for me to speak to various groups and to give interviews to the press, and we decided that I should begin to accept some of them as a means of raising money through donations. People offered to host house parties and other events to raise money. Stanley Robbins suggested that we run an ad in *The New York Times* to reach a larger audience. As the idea evolved, he decided that the appeal should be signed by doctors on the Boston University Medical School faculty to show their support for me, since I was now one of them.

Over a hundred physicians responded, sent in money and agreed to lend their names to the ad. Faculty members from Harvard and Tufts Medical Schools began organizing their own ad.

It was decided that the BU quarter-page ad would run in the Sunday *New York Times* first. Several weeks later, a similar ad would run, signed and paid for by physicians from Tufts and Harvard Medical Schools.

I spent a lot of time with Bill, mapping out our legal strategy and teaching him about medicine in general—obstetrics and gynecology in particular. He had to understand the subtleties and intricacies of obstetrics, gynecology and abortion so that he would be able to communicate with the many experts willing to come to Boston to testify on my behalf. Even as we prepared for a trial, Bill was confident that he would be able to get the charges against me dismissed.

Summer wore on. At the end of August, we went back to court to try to get more information from Flanagan. McGuire was no help and Flanagan still refused to give any more than he already had. Bill, the smart lawyer that he was, used these court appearances to listen to Flanagan's arguments to try to get inside his head. The more Flanagan talked, the more Bill was able to learn and surmise. By the same token, Flanagan was learning about our defense. It was a game of hide and seek, cat and mouse, hound and fox—except it was not a game. Flanagan was toying with my freedom and future.

Crucial to our defense was to know where Flanagan said the fetus was located at the time of death and what specific act he was claiming I carried out to cause its death. After weeks of motions and oral arguments in court, Flanagan finally answered that I either used my hand to separate the placenta, or squeezed the umbilical cord for three to five minutes, thereby causing the death of the fetus.

Bill shot back. "Or? *Or?* I cannot recall another time when I have *ever* seen or heard that word used in an indictment or bill of particulars! The Commonwealth is saying, 'Well, if I can't prove this, then I will prove that.'"

Flanagan admitted that he did not have any evidence that I squeezed the umbilical cord, so he withdrew that ridiculous assertion.

The oral arguments to dismiss the charges against me were postponed from August to October. McGuire's ruling on this motion would be the ultimate test of his objectivity and Flanagan's strength.

October 10, 1974

My palms were sweaty. I was back in a courtroom, already too familiar with the surroundings, waiting for the oral arguments to begin once again. Newman Flanagan and I caught each other's eye several times, but I refused to let him see my fear. I sat perfectly still, keeping my facial features relaxed and under control.

Bill began.

"The motion to dismiss is based on two grounds. First, the indictment as it was originally filed does not sufficiently inform Dr. Edelin of the crime with which he is charged. Second, the indictment does not constitute a crime because Dr. Edelin is protected by the holdings in *Roe v. Wade*. There was no law that penalized him or gave notice that he *could* be penalized for the type of conduct that Mr. Flanagan has reluctantly outlined in his Bill of Particulars. Mr. Flanagan has put his own imprint, his own interpretation upon the manslaughter statute. Dr. Edelin is being prosecuted in violation of his right not to have an *ex post facto* interpretation of the law applied to him."

Bill then produced several textbooks, showing that the surgical procedure I had used to perform the abortion was a standard procedure.

"Hysterotomy," Bill argued, "is a recognized procedure for performing an abortion, contrary to what Mr. Flanagan says. Furthermore, at the time of the hysterotomy, on October 3, 1973, the legislature had not passed any laws restricting abortion since the ruling in *Roe v. Wade*. With this indictment, Mr. Flanagan is putting himself in the position of the state legislature.

"There is not a single legal case in which a fetus, while still within its mother's body—particularly the uterus—is described as a person. Nevertheless, Mr. Flanagan insists that the fetus was a person. The only way that could be true is if the fetus was alive outside its mother's body. Then it *might* be a person."

Flanagan shot back in his heavy Boston accent. "Pregnancy is not the issue heah. Abortion is not the issue heah. The manslaughtah was not during the course of an abortion, not aftah an abortion, nor does it have anything to do with the abortion itself. The victim in this case was a baby boy and he would have lived except foah the fact that the defendant committed the act of detaching it from the mothah and allowing it to remain for a peahriod of three to five minutes on its own *in the mothah*. Those acts are the killing that resulted in the charge of manslaughtah. The baby boy would have lived but foah the fact that the defendant, with his hand, committed an act which subsequently led to its death. The victim in this case was a viable child and was not a paht of the mothah. As a result of the defendant's actions, its life was terminated."

Bill countered that there was no evidence that the fetus was alive inside or outside the womb at the time of the abortion. To substantiate his contention, Bill produced an affidavit from Dr. Kurt Benirschke, our expert fetal pathologist who had examined the autopsy slides. Dr. Benirschke had concluded that there was no evidence the fetus ever breathed.

Flanagan disputed Benirschke's findings. Who was this Dr. Benirschke, he wanted to know? Just because he submitted an affidavit, it didn't make his findings true. He wanted the opportunity to cross-examine him to see if the findings he made by examining slides in California would stand up under his questioning here in Boston. Then, Flanagan slapped Bill across the face with his own words.

"Mr. Homans has stated that theah were no laws on the books that prevented the defendant from doing what he did. Well, your honah, I respectfully submit that manslaughtah laws were on the books long befoah anyone in this legislature evah lived and long befoah anyone in this pahticulah coahtroom ever lived. I presented evidence to a grand jury and they indicted him for the crime of manslaughtah. The defendant killed an individual who was on his own—and if that isn't manslaughtah, I would like to know what is. The defendant's actions are not protected by *Roe v. Wade*. I respectfully submit that the motion to dismiss should be denied."

Judge McGuire sat quietly listening and didn't ask either lawyer any questions. "I'll take all this under advisement," he said.

We had finally smoked out the fox! Flanagan's arguments opposing our motion to dismiss revealed it all. His legal theory was that once the placenta had been separated, the fetus was born and became a person, even though it was still inside the womb. It was a new definition of birth and personhood. But would McGuire accept it and deny our motion to dismiss the indictment?

He ordered us back to court on October 31, 1974. Halloween. Trick or treat?

There were no Halloween treats for me when we went back to

court. Without explanation, McGuire denied our motion to dismiss the charges.

Flanagan should have been elated that our motion to dismiss was denied. Instead, he was furious about the television and newspaper interviews I had given. He said I was trying to taint the jury pool.

I did want to get the issues of my case before the public, but I knew my limitations and always checked with Bill before giving an interview. I had not discussed my case directly in any of them. I talked about a woman's right to choose and the Supreme Court ruling in *Roe*. Bill assured McGuire of this, but I knew that in the future, I would have to watch what I said even more so, or Flanagan would pounce.

I was not about to keep quiet, though, and become some obscure manslaughter case in Boston. I wanted to be sure that my trial was carried out in the light of day and in full public view. Let the entire country see the level to which Flanagan would stoop to impose his beliefs on people.

Flanagan then objected to the ad that had appeared in the Sunday *New York Times* on October 27th—the one Dr. Stanley Robbins had organized. More than 125 physicians had put their names on the ad. It opened with a large headline:

AN AWESOME INDICTMENT

It then went on to give the details of my indictment, followed by declarations of support from Boston City Hospital and Boston University executive committees. The ad ended with a request for donations to the defense fund:

> We whose names are listed below are concerned that our colleague is being harassed for medical practice consonant with the recent Supreme Court decision. We ask for public support for the adequate preparation and presentation of the legal defense of Dr. Kenneth Edelin. What is at stake is not only Dr. Edelin's reputation and his ability to pursue the practice of medicine, but also the freedom of *every* physician.

Flanagan was beside himself. "I read the ad yestahday," he said. "I think it was unwahranted and unfaiah and I think it would prejudice the Commonwealth."

For that reason, he wanted to delay the trial until January to put some distance between the interviews, the ad and the trial. However, I was not about to stop trying to bring public scrutiny to his actions just because he was angry. We had just begun.

After venting some more of his anger, Flanagan finally suggested that the trial start on January 6, 1975. Bill checked his calendar and agreed. Now that that was settled, Bill wanted to know when he could finally get the copies of the grand jury testimonies. Flanagan referred to his own calendar and his face lit up. He seized another opportunity to jab. "I couldn't think of a better date than Friday, the 13th of Decembah." He chuckled. "Friday the 13th!"

Nobody but Flanagan thought that was funny.

Flanagan cleared his throat and pushed on. He wanted a special jury pool called for this case and he wanted the jurors sequestered for the duration of the trial—isolated from the media coverage of the trial and the tremendous support I was receiving from the public and the press. McGuire agreed to both of Flanagan's requests.

The New York Times ad produced overwhelming results. Hundreds of letters came pouring in from across the country with checks made out to the KEDF. Most were small $5 and $10 donations, but every little bit helped. In their letters, women described the horrors they had gone through to obtain illegal abortions. Other donations were sent in memory of friends, daughters, aunts, sisters, cousins and even mothers who had died as a result of illegal abortions. These expressions of financial and emotional support boosted my morale and strengthened my resolve even more.

In early November, we received a letter from the Sunnen Foundation, a charity organization in St. Louis, Missouri. They offered a $10,000 contribution to my defense fund, the largest donation we had received. They wanted it to be delivered personally by a lawyer named Frank Susman, so we arranged for him to come to Boston to meet with Bill, the members of the KEDF and me.

Frank Susman arrived in Bill's office on the last Saturday of November, right after Thanksgiving. He was a thin, white man, around six feet tall—my height—with a red, bushy near-Afro. He wore large, tinted eyeglasses, had a well-groomed mustache and was immaculately dressed in an obviously expensive suit. In his flat, Midwestern accent, Susman explained that the Sunnen Products Company manufactured machine tools, as well as EMKO Foam, a very popular contraceptive. Bob Sunnen, the president of the company, had formed a charitable foundation so he could support efforts to legalize abortion and further contraceptive research. Susman presented me with a check for $10,000, but there was one stipulation: Susman had to become part of our legal team.

Bob Sunnen had financed many of the legal challenges to the restrictive abortion laws in Missouri. Frank Susman had been the lawyer on those cases and argued them in both the lower and Supreme courts of Missouri.

Frank was a dry Midwesterner who spoke in an often humorous way. He was passionate about individual rights and had belonged to some civil rights organizations in college. He spoke slowly, often understating things. I liked him. I liked his passion for women's rights, Civil Rights and the experience he had in the fight against restrictive abortion laws. Bill and I both agreed to bring him on as a member of the team, but Bill made it clear to me that he was still my chief counsel and would make all final decisions. I assured him that he was in charge of the case—I preferred to have someone familiar with the intricacies of Boston politics in that position—and made sure that Frank Susman understood he would be working for him. I insisted, however, that all final decisions, legal and otherwise, were not Bill's, but mine. This was my life, my case, my career and my freedom at stake. It was the first time that I asserted my control over the situation. Bill swallowed hard, but agreed. Frank Susman joined our team.

December 8, 1974

The Harvard and Tufts ad appeared in *The New York Times*:
WE AGREE
An Awesome Indictment

The ad went on to recount the details of my indictment and stated that the abortion I'd performed was approved by the executive committees of Boston City Hospital and Boston University School of Medicine as being "completely ethical, legal and consistent with the best medical and scientific practices." The ad was signed by over 200 physicians from

Harvard and Tufts and ended with their own plea: "We join our colleagues from Boston University School of Medicine to ask for your financial support for the defense of this dedicated and highly regarded young physician."

This ad generated more donations and more letters of painful memories. Reading about these experiences brought a gruesome collage of life before *Roe* into focus—the desperation, depression and dangerous places where women had found themselves when trying to terminate unwanted pregnancies. The pictures these letters painted were both graphic and familiar.

In the meantime, the portrait of the people who were going to make up my jury was also becoming clearer. Tubby Harrison was just completing his poll of attitudes in Suffolk County, particularly in Boston, about abortion. The results revealed that there might be a significant number of people called to sit on my jury who were opposed to abortion in all circumstances.

Bill did not think that the preliminary results were strong enough to get McGuire to agree to a change in venue, but before a final decision was made on whether to ask or not, we had to wait for Tubby's full analysis. Even if we couldn't get a change in venue, perhaps the poll would give us information that would help us select a jury. Tubby went back to crunching the numbers.

Friday, December 13, 1974

We finally received the transcripts of the grand jury testimonies. Most of the testimony had been supportive. The operating room nurses, the medical student who assisted me, the scrub techs and the nurse anesthetist all gave testimony indicating that I had done nothing wrong. Dr. Jim Penza was not only supportive, but combative under Flanagan's questioning.

I was disappointed to discover that Dr. Hugh Holtrop, who I admired, who had introduced me to Evonne and who had admitted her under his name, took the Fifth Amendment against self-incrimination. He was saving his ass and sacrificing mine. The only person whose actions were more shameful was Dr. David Charles, who also took the Fifth Amendment and then fled back to Newfoundland, Canada, to avoid prosecution.

There was only one person who testified against me: Enrique Gimenez.

I was not surprised. During the two years I had known him, I had tried to get him fired, intervened once to keep him *from* getting fired, had numerous run-ins with him because of his failure to carry out his responsibilities as a resident, and taken Carol from him. He had a grudge against me and was now getting his revenge.

CHAPTER 20

A New Year

Under the separation agreement I had with Ramona, Kenny and Kimi spent alternating holidays with me. It was my turn to have them for Christmas of 1974. On Christmas Eve, the three of us drove three hours to my sister's house in upstate New York for the holidays.

For that time, I was neither doctor nor defendant. I was Ken. I was Daddy. I was Santa Claus. It was comforting to be with family. It felt great to get away from Boston and the pressures of preparing for the trial, but it still loomed over me like the promise of nighttime looms over a bright sunny day.

On the evening drive back to Boston, with the kids asleep in the tiny back seat of my car, I sped east into the darkness of the turnpike and back into my future.

1974 became 1975.

Mom, Dad and me.

Dad and me on H Street.
Washington, D.C.

Brothers Milton, Bobby, Sister Norma & me.

Graduation from sixth grade.

Graduation from medical school.

ObGyn Residents, BCH. Me, back row, second from Left.
In the middle, David Charles and Bernardo Santamarina (with cigar).

The tub room at Boston City Hospital.

The tunnels at Boston City Hospital.

Form 115C 2M-1-71   (Bring this summons with you)

Commonwealth of Massachusetts

Suffolk, to wit:

L. S.

To the Sheriff of our County of Suffolk, or his Deputy, or any Court Officer of said County, or either of the Constables or Police Officers of any city or town within said County, or any District Police Officer of said Commonwealth,

GREETING:

We command you that you summon *Dr. Kenneth Edelin*

No. *78949*

(if they may be found in your precinct) to appear before the GRAND JURORS attending the Superior Court for the transaction of Criminal Business, at the Court House in Pemberton Square, in Boston, aforesaid

ON *THURSDAY FEB. 14 1974* AT *9³⁰* O'CLOCK IN THE FORENOON,

and from day to day until discharged, then and there to give evidence of what they know in the case of the Commonwealth against

John Doe

HEREOF fail not and make due return of this writ with your doings thereon into the said court.

Witness, Walter H. McLaughlin, ESQUIRE, Chief Justice and the seal of said Court at Boston,

aforesaid, *FEB. 7 1974*

EDWARD V. KEATING,

Clerk of the said Superior Court.

Officer of Court,
Deputy Sheriff,
Police Officer.

A true copy.
Attest:

Summons to Grand Jury.

Bill Homans and me.

Me and Bill Homans in court.

Courtroom sketch of me testifying in my defense.

CHAPTER 21

THE JURY POOL

January 6, 1975

Ten months after I had been indicted for manslaughter, Bill Homans, Frank Susman and I left the Old City Hall and made the now familiar 10-minute walk to the Suffolk County Courthouse. Reporters and cameramen followed our every step and even more were gathered in front of the courthouse as we walked up the stairs, across the plaza and into the marble lobby. Our every move, my every facial expression, was recorded until the brass doors of the elevator closed to take us up to the sixth floor.

Outside of the courtroom, there was a crowd of people. As Bill, Frank and I pushed our way past them, I tried not to look like a deer in headlights. More cameras flashed, voices called out all at once, some in support, others already convicting me of murder.

"Good Luck!"

"Baby killer!"

"Go get 'em, Bill!"

"God bless Newman Flanagan!"

The courtroom was plain and cold, despite the crowd of people already in it. Every seat in the spectators' section was filled, as was the special section that had been reserved for reporters. We walked through the gate to the other side of the rail that separated the court from the spectators. It was then that I saw Flanagan and his gang around their table near the front of the room. Newman Flanagan, the little man with the flowery tie and his assistant, Joe Mulligan, the large, imposing man with the big hair, looked in our direction as we came through the gate. With them was Charles Dunn, another assistant district attorney, and a special member of their team, Donald Brennan, a lawyer who was added because he was an expert in medical malpractice.

Flanagan, Mulligan, Dunn and Brennan. I stared back at them, refusing to lower my head or my gaze. They eventually turned away and continued to chatter amongst themselves with sly and menacing smiles on their faces.

Judge McGuire entered the courtroom and called the first day of my trial to order.

"Mr. Homans, would you like to be heard?"

As I looked around the austere room, I felt like a solitary warrior in the middle of the Roman Colosseum. My enemies were formidable and would use any tactic to win. Flanagan, the prosecutor, and his group of Boston Irish Catholic men were there to protect their way of life, their point of view and their control of the city. McGuire seemed weak and cut from the same cloth as the rest of them. So far, his rulings had been mostly in Flanagan's favor. Could we count on him to be fair and impartial? I said "no." Bill, ever the optimist, held out hope.

We were about to select the jury, the people's representatives in this place of combat. It was our last chance for fairness, balance and justice.

But some anonymous information had been sent to us about how juries were selected in this part of Massachusetts and we had to bring it out into the open.

"Yes, your honor, and I would like to call Mr. James Gibbons to the stand."

James Gibbons was the assistant clerk of the Superior Court for Criminal Business in Suffolk County. It was his job to put together the pool of jurors for both the grand juries and the traverse juries for trials in Suffolk County—grand juries handed down indictments and traverse juries handed down verdicts.

James Gibbons was sworn in.

"Mr. Gibbons, did you bring with you the list of the names of the grand jurors sitting in Suffolk County who indicted Dr. Edelin?"

Gibbons produced the list of the 18 people who had indicted me. Bill studied the list for a moment, then, looking back at Gibbons, asked him how many residents of Suffolk County made up the pool from which my traverse jury would be selected.

"We summoned 150 people from Suffolk County to appear on the special panel for this case, and 131 of them came from the city of Boston," Gibbons responded, as he handed Bill the list of their names as well.

Bill examined this new list and then, addressing McGuire, said, "May it please the Court, 14 members of the grand jury were men and only four were women."

Was this disparity just a matter of chance? Bill handed the list to McGuire. After studying the list of potential traverse jury members, Bill continued, "The list of 131 traverse jurors from the city of Boston contains the names of 99 males and 32 females." He handed that list to McGuire, too. In both cases, there were three times as many men as women.

"What is your point, Mr. Homans?" McGuire asked.

Bill was not finished presenting his evidence. "If I may continue, your honor, I would like to call William Leo Barry to the stand." With that, James Gibbons was excused.

William Barry was the supervisor of the elections for the city of Boston. It was his job to prepare the list of Boston residents who were summoned to serve on both grand and traverse juries.

"Would you describe to us how the list was prepared for grand jury duty?"

He described a system whereby 20,000 summonses were sent throughout the city of Boston. Those who received one were required to come, in person, to City Hall to fill out a questionnaire and appear before an election commissioner who had the power to either accept or reject the person for service on the grand jury. Ultimately, the names of individuals selected by the election commissioners were fed into a computer.

Barry continued. "The current practice is for two male names to be entered into the computer for every female name entered. After the final list is generated, the registrars are told to pick names from each ward in the city on that basis."

"On the two-to-one basis?" Bill asked.

"That's right."

For emphasis Bill repeated, "Two males for every female, is that correct?"

"Yes, that's correct."

"And was that same procedure used to select the special panel which has been summoned for this case, that is, two men selected for every one woman?"

"Yes. The same procedure was used."

Bill made our point. The jury selection process intentionally discriminated against women. As he turned away from the witness stand, he said, "Mr. Flanagan, your witness."

Flanagan now had his chance to cross-examine William Leo Barry, but to me, he only made things worse.

"Isn't the two-to-one ratio of men to women an improvement ovah the previous policy of the election depahtment?"

"Yes. In 1973, it was approximately three to one," Barry responded.

"I have no furthah questions for this witness," Flanagan said. There was nothing else he could say.

"Your honor," Bill said. "I have no further evidence to submit."

"Do you have a motion?" McGuire asked.

Of course we had a motion! Didn't McGuire understand? There was a deliberate scheme used by the election department to discriminate against women in making up juries.

Bill spelled it out. "The US Supreme Court has said that a defendant has a right to be tried by a jury which represents a fair cross section of the community from which he comes and where he is being tried. In this case, the process used by the Boston election department has resulted in a panel with a ratio of men to women of three to one. There have been 99 men and 32 women called as potential jurors. So long as there is an intentional discrimination against a particular class of individuals who will serve on juries, then the right of Dr. Edelin to be tried before a fair and impartial jury, and his right to be tried by a jury selected from a cross section of the community, has been violated.

"Your honor should dismiss the indictment returned by the grand jury because that grand jury was the result of a process which was discriminatory in its selection of men over women. You should also dismiss the panel that has been called to sit in judgment during Dr. Edelin's trial for the same reason."

Flanagan tried to present a rebuttal, but it was weak.

"What Mr. Homans is asking foah is a perfect utopia. He wants to have X numbah of women, and X numbah of men, X numbah of whites, X numbah of blacks, X numbah of Italians, X numbah of Chinese, X numbah of homosexuals, X numbah of everybody. That is impossible. What the defendant has a right to is a fair trial by a jury who was selected in the standahd process of selecting jurahs. The only test heah for both the grand jury and the traverse jury is that they are a fair cross section of our society. Whether they are men or women is not what counts. What counts is that they are a fair cross section. The motions should be dismissed and not allowed."

McGuire looked puzzled. On the one hand was a stronger argument, on the other, his roots.

"Is there anything else?" he managed to ask.

"Yes, your honor," Bill said. He wanted to cover all of our bases. "If you don't dismiss the indictment or this jury pool and you decide to let the jury selection process continue, I would like to be allowed to examine the jurors as part of the selection process. If you won't allow that, I would like you to examine them based upon questions I would like to submit to you."

Our polling had uncovered some serious problems for us regarding the attitudes toward abortion in Suffolk County. In order to lay the groundwork for the questions we would like to have asked of each prospective juror, Bill called Tubby Harrison to testify.

Once he was sworn in, Bill asked, "Mr. Harrison, what was the purpose of the poll you conducted?"

"To determine the attitudes of prospective jurors in Suffolk County toward the subject of abortion in general and at various stages of pregnancy, and the relationship between that and the ability of these prospective jurors to hear the case impartially."

"How did you select the people to participate in your poll?" Bill asked.

"We wanted to interview people who would resemble as closely as possible those on the list from which a jury would be chosen, so we went to officials from each town and asked them how they selected residents to be on the list. In addition to age requirements, they also told us that they tried to get approximately equal numbers of men and women on the list. From what I heard here today, what they told us was not true, especially for Boston."

"What did you do next?"

"We selected 1,000 people to be interviewed from among the four cities and towns that make up Suffolk County and found that 15 percent of prospective jurors say they believe it is *always* wrong for a doctor to perform an abortion. That percentage is significantly higher among certain groups, such as people over the age of 50, people with annual family incomes of less than $5,000, people who did not complete high school and people who identified themselves as Catholic."

Bill stood directly in front of Tubby Harrison. "What did you find out about those who did not feel that abortion was always wrong?"

"Nearly two-thirds of those who believed that abortion was okay in at least some cases said that they think abortion would be wrong beyond the 21st week of pregnancy."

"Were you able to determine if those who had such strong feelings against abortion could sit on a jury and impartially make a judgment about a case such as this one?"

"Ten percent said that they would pre-judge the case if the abortion occurred after the 20th week of pregnancy and a significant percentage of those said they would find Dr. Edelin guilty even if the judge instructed them that abortions performed before the end of the sixth month are legal. These feelings are even stronger among Catholics, people over 50 and those with incomes under $5,000."

Bill grasped the rail in front of the witness stand. "Mr. Harrison, do you believe that your poll results are accurate?"

"Yes. These results accurately reflect the opinion of people from Suffolk County who would be eligible to serve as jurors in this case."

No more questions from Bill.

In his cross-examination of Tubby Harrison, Flanagan tried to discredit his polling methods and the results he presented, but Tubby's confidence in his poll could not be shaken. He stood behind its results and what it told us about the jury pool in Suffolk County.

Still looking puzzled and bewildered, McGuire called for a recess until the next day.

That was it. The first day of my trial was over. We spent nearly the entire day presenting evidence of the discrimination against women in the selection of juries in Boston. It was a metaphor for what this case was about—how women, especially poor women, were treated in Boston and its institutions. We were arguing against powerful forces, all well represented in Room 906 of the Suffolk County Courthouse. And my freedom and career were being offered as a sacrifice in their efforts to resist change.

Bill was beginning to lose hope that McGuire would dismiss the indictment. As we walked back in the January cold to his office and the warmth of the pub in its basement, Bill, in a barely audible voice said, "Maybe I'm wrong about McGuire."

Bill, Frank and I headed straight for the pub to talk over cigarettes and martinis while we waited for the transcript of the day's proceedings to be delivered. When it arrived, his secretary brought it straight down to us.

Bill read it first, a cigarette held between his fingers. As he skimmed through it, the cigarette and his shoulders began to droop. Seeing the proceedings in print underscored our challenges. He handed the bound transcript to Frank and excused himself to work the rest of the evening on his arguments to convince McGuire of the biases of the prospective jurors so they could be eliminated and we would have a "fair and impartial" jury.

The next day, Bill submitted a motion that would allow him to directly question the potential jurors to uncover any bias.

"The questioning of prospective jurors will be very important in this case because impaneled jurors may act on personal feelings extraneous to the facts in this case and thereby deny my client due process. The poll results we have submitted to you demonstrate that it is important to determine whether or not there will be jurors with closed minds. In addition to their own biases, they may poison the judgment of the other jurors. The subject of abortion is controversial. It is important that each prospective juror be questioned thoroughly so that it can be determined whether or not jurors are biased or prejudiced because of outside considerations.

"Our poll indicates that 15 percent of the potential jurors have a fixed position on the question of abortion. On a panel of 12 that represents two jurors.

"Our poll also indicates that 57 percent of the potential jurors believe that abortion is wrong when performed after the 20th week of pregnancy. There is nothing in *Roe v. Wade* that condemns it. Further, 62 percent believe it is wrong to do an abortion at the 24th week of pregnancy, even though it is not prohibited by *Roe v. Wade*. Therefore, it is important to question the potential jurors—and these may be the most important questions to ask—about their views on abortion at various stages of pregnancy. We cannot have even one juror infecting the entire panel of 12 who, before hearing the case, has already made up his mind."

Judge McGuire interrupted Bill. "Mr. Homans, I have determined that I will be the one to question the jurors in this case. I would welcome any suggestions from you as to the questions I should ask the potential jurors, however." He scratched his chin, then leaned toward Bill and said, "Suppose there was a potential juror who thought all abortions were wrong, but stated that he was able to follow the judge's instructions in making a decision, rather than following his own views on abortion. Should he be excused for cause?"

"Your honor, if that juror was not excused by you for cause, we would probably exercise a preemptory challenge, if we had any left."

Since McGuire had determined that he, and not Bill or Flanagan, would question the jurors about their feelings on abortion, Bill wanted questions asked about outside influences on the jurors' decisions.

"Your honor, in our poll, we asked potential jurors if their church said abortion was wrong, whether they felt they would have to find the doctor guilty. Forty-four percent of Catholics said they believed that their church requires them to find the defendant guilty and 46 percent of those who read *The Pilot* regularly believe that abortion is wrong under all circumstances. All of the questions we propose are important for the purpose of determining whether or not a juror is so fixed in a given position that he or she cannot be impartial."

Now Flanagan had his turn.

"Your honah, you have broad discretion as to the questions to be asked of potential jurors. But remembah, I have maintained that this pahticulah crime of manslaughtah was not during an abortion. But if you do want to ask questions about a jurah's feelings regahding abortion, you need to also ask questions which will determine if a potential jurah believes that abortion is always right.

"Furthahmore, I don't know why Mr. Homans is highlighting *The Pilot*. We have seen a great numbah of ahticles that are prejudicial against us. Did you read *The New York Times*? Have you seen the prejudicial advahtisement that's been in theah?"

The two ads the Boston University, Harvard and Tufts physicians had placed in *The New York Times* supporting me had clearly gotten under Flanagan's skin. Good.

Flanagan continued, using our own poll against us.

"The poll also indicated that a significant pahcentage of potential jurors felt that doctahs should get special respect and consideration. You need to ask questions about that. Undah our law, everyone should be treated equally. The doctah should have no special treatment."

McGuire had no expression on his face. It was impossible to know if he would ask our questions. We had to go to our back-up plan.

Bill asked McGuire for additional preemptory challenges, stating that this jury pool was going to be so biased against us that we were going to need plenty to ensure we had as fair a jury as possible. Bill asked for 16; Flanagan wanted the number kept at the usual eight.

McGuire rapped his gavel on his desk.

"We will take a short recess, after which I will give my decision on the various motions before me."

Bill, Frank and I huddled in the hallway outside of Room 906, tucked away in an area away from the large crowd of reporters and photographers. They gave us our privacy.

We didn't say much, but I remained hopeful that Bill's arguments would give me the chance to have a fair trial. We needed to counter Flanagan's fanaticism and unfair tactics with a jury that could consider the information in an unbiased way and render an objective verdict— this was not going to be an easy case to win. Not in Boston.

The recess ended and we filed back into the courtroom to hear McGuire's decisions. My heart was pounding, but I kept my head high. I would not let Newman Flanagan see any sign of weakness or fear.

White-haired and cold looking, Judge McGuire stared down at us from the bench. There was absolute silence in the courtroom except for the noise of reporters scribbling notes on their pads. "In regard to the defendant's motion to dismiss the indictment and to strike the special jury pool, it is denied." That was expected, but I still felt my heart grow heavy. "On the motion for additional preemptory challenges," McGuire continued, "I will empanel 16 jurors and the Commonwealth and the defendant will each be entitled to eight preemptory challenges." A few whispers began among the reporters. McGuire raised his voice. "In regard to the defendant's motion permitting examination of the jurors by the defendant's counsel or, in the alternative, by the court, I will conduct the questioning of each prospective juror as that juror is called, and will ask certain questions which I consider to be appropriate, not necessarily the questions proposed by the defendant." Someone gasped and the room erupted with voices, all talking at once. McGuire banged his gavel and called for order.

"I will now have the 150 members of this special jury pool brought down to the courtroom."

With these decisions, McGuire had closed the door on fairness.

The members of the special jury pool filled the spectators section of the room. It was a sea of white, with only two or three black or brown faces. Whether McGuire noticed this or not, I couldn't tell.

He began his general instruction by talking about the importance of the jury system and their obligation to serve with open minds, using fairness. He told them that juries were seekers of the truth and in doing so, they must put aside all considerations of race, color and religion.

"Justice is served according to the law. This case concerns an indictment for manslaughter against Kenneth Edelin. It is anticipated that the trial of this case will take four weeks or so, and during that time the 16 jurors initially selected will be sequestered. Quarters will be provided at a hotel within the city. The jurors will take their meals together and remain as a group during the entire proceedings. You will be under the supervision of court officers.

"Now you will be returned to the jury room and called down one at a time to answer a series of questions. These questions must be answered honestly. You are not to discuss the case amongst yourselves, or read about it in the papers, or watch the news on TV."

The group was taken back to their room. We were ready to begin.

Flanagan, in the age-old tradition of the courts of the Commonwealth of Massachusetts, rose and spoke.

"May it please the court, the Commonwealth moves for trial in indictment 81823 chahging the defendant Kenneth Edelin with manslaughtah."

"Kenneth Edelin, please rise," said Judge McGuire.

I stood with Bill and Frank on either side of me and looked directly at him. I stood as tall as I could. I had done nothing wrong. I would not cower before him, Flanagan or anyone.

"Kenneth Edelin, you are now at the bar to be tried. These good men and women whom I shall call are to pass between the Commonwealth and you upon your trial. You have the right to challenge eight of their number without assigning a reason therefore. If you do so, or if you object to others for cause, you must do so as they are called and before they are sworn."

That having been said, the process of selecting the jury began.

In all, 69 people were questioned. Fifty-three of them were challenged by either Flanagan, the judge, or us; we used all of our preemptory challenges.

The court called them a "jury of my peers," but the term was hardly fitting. Thirteen were men, three were women. None had completed college. All were white.

Flanagan used preemptory challenges to reject the two potential black jurors who had passed McGuire's questioning and were declared fit to serve on the jury. Flanagan didn't have to give a reason, but it didn't matter. We knew what it was.

Most of the jurors were chosen partly because they were not well informed and said that they had not thought about issues like abortion. Would they be able to follow the complex legal and medical testimony that would be given during the trial? Eleven of the sixteen chosen were Roman Catholic. Would they be able to put their own feelings and what they had been taught about abortion aside and be objective? I was not optimistic. This was not a jury of my peers.

CHAPTER 22

THE CHOSEN

Michael R. Seifart

Twenty-five years old, Michael Seifart was an equipment installer for the New England Telephone Company. He was stocky, with collar-length, reddish-blonde hair and a bushy, drooping mustache. In his red plaid winter jacket, he almost looked as if he had stepped out of a cowboy movie. He was married, had one daughter and his wife worked at Dunkin' Donuts. He was Roman Catholic, a member of St. Matthew's parish in Boston. When asked about abortion, he said he wasn't sure whether or not abortion should be legal.

Joyce Loveter

Joyce worked as a secretary for the Massachusetts Department of Transportation, and was about to turn 22. She was single, attractive, lived at home with her parents in Revere and had attended Beverly Community College for one year. She loved the outdoors, said that she was not a strict Catholic but was a member of St. Anthony's. She couldn't say whether she was for or against abortion; it depended on the circumstances. When questioned by Judge McGuire, she looked petrified. She answered his questions in a small, timid, almost inaudible voice.

Liberty Ann Conlin
A West Roxbury housewife and mother of four. Her husband worked as a construction foreman. She said she had no opinion on abortion.

William F. Sokolowski
Twenty-six, William worked as a laborer in a meat processing facility in Cambridge, but lived in Dorchester, one of Boston's racially charged neighborhoods. He was large-framed with hair over his ears and a dark mustache. Although he identified himself as Roman Catholic, he did not attend any particular church. Still single, he played softball on a tavern team and said he had no opinion on abortion.

Michael Ciano
Short and slightly built, Michael Ciano had a sparse beard and collar-length hair with bangs that made him look much younger than 32. He worked as a materials handler for the Electronics Corporation of America in Cambridge, was single, Roman Catholic and used to attend St. Joseph's Church in Roxbury before moving to East Boston. When asked about abortion, he said, "I have my opinion and they have theirs." He seemed gregarious during the McGuire's questioning, but for some reason, I felt I could not trust him. Perhaps it was that his tie—satin with roses on it—reminded me far too much of Newman Flanagan.

Frederick J. Spencer
A married, middle-aged man from West Roxbury whose combed-back hairstyle recalled the 1940s. He worked as a field service engineer and wore a conservative blue suit. He said he had no strong feelings about abortion, but felt that too many were done.

Vincent B. Shea
A dark-haired, heavy-set, middle-aged man who peered noncommittally through his glasses. He was 51, but looked younger. The father of four daughters, he lived with his wife in Dorchester and worked as an MBTA mechanic. He identified himself as Roman Catholic, a graduate of Nazareth Grammar School and South Boston High and a member of St. Gregory's parish. He said he felt abortions were not wrong if they were properly performed. McGuire would eventually appoint him to be the jury foreman.

Paul A. Holland

Paul was thickly built, in his 40s and had graying brown hair. He was married with four children and worked as a customer contact clerk for Boston Edison. He identified himself as Roman Catholic and a member of St. Margaret's Parish in Dorchester, but said he had no opinion on abortion.

Herbert A. LaDue

A short, balding man of 49, Herbert had graduated from Jamaica Plain High School and worked as a custodian at the JFK Federal Building. He was married and had a 16-year-old daughter. He, too, identified himself as Roman Catholic and was a member of Our Lady of Lourdes Parish in Jamaica Plain. On abortion, he said, "In some cases…I'm not sure."

Anthony Alessi

Thirty. A young family man, the father of three children. Chubby, he appeared confident. He worked as a foreman for the New England Telephone Company, graduated from Jamaica Plain High and attended Northeastern University three nights a week studying business administration. He said he was a Baptist, but his wife was Roman Catholic. He said he never had strong feelings one way or the other about abortion.

Ralph P. Mischely

Twenty-eight years old and a senior draftsman at a company in Waltham, Ralph was a graduate of Alpina Central Catholic High School in Alpina, Michigan. Like Anthony Alessi, he attended Northeastern University at night, where he studied civil engineering. He was married and the father of two children. He was a member of St. Gregory's parish in Mattapan, and though he said he had never really thought about the subject of abortion before, he added, "I suppose if it would injure the mother's health, I'd rather see the mother survive."

Michael Galante

He was a stocky, balding man of 61 with a graying mustache who worked as a press operator in a metal company. He was married, but had no children. He identified himself as a Roman Catholic and a member of St. Mary's Star of the Sea Parish in East Boston. He thought abortions should only be performed if they were absolutely necessary.

Lillian E. Connors
Lillian was a gray-haired, retired switchboard operator, married, the mother of one, Roman Catholic and a member of St. John the Evangelist Parish in Winthrop. When asked about abortion, she said, "I believe where it's legal, it's all right."

Francis McLaughlin
He described himself as a divorced, middle-aged man from Dorchester. He worked as a bartender at Logan Airport.

John G. Kelly
John worked as a teller at a large bank in Boston. He was single, Roman Catholic and a member of Our Lady of Presentation Parish in Brighton. He said about abortion: "I'm against it, but if a woman wants one, that's her choice."

Paul Kolesinski
Thirty-four, Paul had slick hair, was a graduate of Boston Trade High and worked as a shipbuilder at the Boston Navel Shipyard. He identified himself and his wife as Roman Catholic, belonging to St. Monica's parish, but attended church at St. Augustine's in South Boston, where they lived. When asked if he had heard about this case, he said, "I seen it in the papers." On abortion he said, "I think it's wrong," but after repeated questioning, almost to the point of badgering by McGuire, he said that he thought he would be able to decide the case on the evidence. By the time he was questioned by McGuire, we had no preemptory challenges left.

That was it. This was the jury that would sit in judgment of me; the people designated to hear the evidence and find the truth. Newman Flanagan, the little man in the flowery tie, assisted by his Irish gang of three—Joe Mulligan, Charlie Dunn and Donald Brennan—would try to convince this jury that I was guilty of manslaughter, that I had killed a person they called a baby boy. On my side would be Bill Homans, the Boston Brahmin Libertarian, champion of the underdog, and Frank Susman, the reproductive rights lawyer from St. Louis who came with experience, passion and a check for $10,000.

In the middle of all of this was me, the skinny black kid from the streets of Washington who had fulfilled his dream of becoming a woman's doctor to prevent the terrible tragedies that took my mother from me.

January 10, 1975

At 10:45 a.m., the jurors were brought into the courtroom. For the first time, I saw all 16 together—12 of them would ultimately decide my fate and four would be randomly eliminated alternates. They would all hear the testimony and see all of the evidence, but who would be dismissed at the end of the trial?

Thirteen men, three women, all white, mostly Catholic—with my life in their hands. I looked at each of them in turn, thought about our poll results and shuddered. A fair and impartial jury of my peers?

Judge McGuire appointed juror number eight, Vincent Shea, to be the foreman. Once the jurors were seated in the jury box, the clerk, Paul O'Leary, read the indictment in the archaic language of the courts.

"Members of the jury, hearken to an indictment. The Commonwealth of Massachusetts at the Superior Court begun and holden at the city of Boston and for the county of Suffolk for the transaction of criminal business on the first Monday of April in the year of our lord, 1974, the grand jurors for the Commonwealth of Massachusetts on their oath present that Kenneth Edelin on the third day of October in the year of our lord, 1973, did assault and beat a certain person, to wit a male child described to the said jurors as 'baby boy' and by such assault and beating did kill said person; a true bill.

"To this indictment, the defendant at the bar pleads not guilty before trial and places himself upon the country which country you are.

"You are sworn to try the issues. If he is guilty, you shall say so.

"If he is not guilty you shall say so and no more.

"Members of the jury, hearken to your evidence."

After the public reading of the indictment, it was handed to the foreman, who read it to himself, then handed it to the juror seated next to him. Each juror read the indictment in turn.

Assault and beat a baby boy and killed him...

I watched the expression of the jury members as each silently read the indictment. None of them returned my gaze. No eye contact. No reaction. Nothing.

McGuire explained that at the end of the trial, four of them would be randomly withdrawn and not participate in the deliberations, but all of them must pay attention to the evidence. The only one whose place was certain was the foreman, Vincent Shea.

"Mr. Flanagan, you may begin."

CHAPTER 23

THE OPENING ARGUMENTS

Newman Flanagan rose. As he walked to the jury box, he straightened his bright, flowery tie, buttoned his jacket and glanced at me as if to say the battle had begun. He smiled at the jury and began his opening argument. These were his people.

"Mistah foahman, ladies and gentlemen of the jury, the clerk read to you an indictment chahging this defendant with manslaughtah of a male child, a crime that took place on Octobah 3, 1973."

Flanagan then went on to present the case as he saw it, beginning with Dr. Holtrop meeting Evonne in the clinic and arranging for her to be admitted for an abortion. Flanagan also carefully described how both a third-year medical student and a second-year resident—Enrique Gimenez—judged the patient to be 24 weeks pregnant.

"He heard a fetal hahtbeat," Flanagan said, lowering his head and his gaze and pausing, as if saying a quick prayer. "On the next day, Doctah Holtrop examined the patient and concurred with the findings of the medical student and resident...except he made the judgment that she was only 20 to 21 weeks pregnant."

Pausing in key places for dramatic effect, as if deeply saddened by the loss of a fetus' life—but with no concern for mine—he then went on to describe the attempts at saline abortion. "A process by which they endeavah to kill the fetus while it is a paht of the mothah and in the mothah. But they were unsuccessful.

"The next day they tried again to puhfoahm a saline infusion and, once again, they were unsuccessful and obtained a bloody tap. The defendant in this case, Doctah Kenneth Edelin, performed a hysterotomy on this female patient. At the time of this pahticulah hysterotomy, Doctah Gimenez was in the operating room, but not taking paht in the procejah."

Flanagan looked in my direction. "Doctah Gimenez," he said, "does not do abortions."

Flanagan hated those of us who provided abortions for women. This was the opening salvo of his own personal war of revenge.

"When Doctah Edelin detached the placenta from the uterine wall, the child was no longah dependant upon its mothah. The pregnancy had been terminated."

Flanagan then made the most absurd assertion as he continued to paint a picture of me for the jury. "The defendant stood in the opahrating room with his hand in the mothah and watched the clock for a period of at least three minutes. There was no physical connection between the mothah and child for those three minutes. When Doctah Edelin commenced this pahticulah hysterotomy, the baby was alive. When the placenta was detached, the child was alive. After the three minutes passed—during which time he was looking at the clock—Dr. Edelin removed the male child from the mothah's womb. The baby, the male child, was sent to the morgue. There was a pathology repoaht filed and the size and weight of the fetus and placenta were determined.

"In December 1973, I contacted Doctah George W. Curtis, the medical examinah in Suffolk County, and asked him to go to the morgue at the Pathology Depahtment of City Hospital and remove the deceased male child in this case."

"At the time of his autopsy, Doctah Curtis, the medical examiner, made a detahmination that the baby was a male child, 24 weeks gestational age and weighed 700 grams. From his autopsy, he could not detahmine the cause of death. Howevah, he indicated that given the facts that allegedly took place in this pahticulah operation, the cause of death was anoxia." Pausing again, he pointed at me. "This means Doctah Edelin suffocated the baby." A monster who deliberately strangles babies—this is what Flanagan wanted the jury to think of me.

"At the time that this pahticulah male child was detached from the mothah and therefoah, no longah dependant on the mothah, this baby would have lived. There is nobody on earth who can testify as to how long outside of the mothah the baby would have lived. There is no testimony that can say how long *you* will live."

Flanagan then promised to bring into the courtroom "witnesses who weighed less than, who were smaller than and who were born at a gestation lower than the deceased male child in this case." He looked at the jury, his cherub-like face giving them a practiced, kindhearted look.

"There will be a great deal of testimony about the word 'viability' and what that word actually means. It is a word that dethmines whethah or not the male child in this case could have lived outside the mothah. There will be ample evidence submitted to indicate that he would have but for the act of this defendant.

"Subsequent to the Commonwealth obtaining the recahds of this pahticulah female patient, the operative note came into existence in the recahd. It was dictated on the 16th of Decembah and transcribed on the 17th of Decembah, which is approximately two months after the operation. For the pahticulah deceased male child in this case, there was no birth certificate or death certificate filed.

"There will be a great amount of talk concehning of word 'abortion' in this case. The issue in this pahticulah case is not abortion, but the unlawful homicide—the unlawful killing—of a male child: manslaugh-tah. So the issue heah is not abortion but manslaughtah." Flanagan rested his hands on the rail in front of the jury box, looked at each of the jurors, then quietly said, "Thank you."

It was an awful and ugly distortion of the truth. He would do what-ever it took to convict me. The levels he would stoop to frightened me.

McGuire rapped his gavel, breaking the silence that had fallen over the courtroom. He summoned the two attorneys to his bench and looked at Bill. "Do you want to take a recess before you make your opening statement?"

Bill was ready and his adrenaline was flowing. "I don't need a recess. Let's do it now," he said. "What I would like to do, your honor, following my opening, is to move for a directed verdict based on the Commonwealth's opening statement."

McGuire looked at Bill in disbelief. "You want to make a motion for a directed verdict based on the government's opening arguments?"

"Yes, your honor." Homans responded.

"Well, if that is what you want…You may proceed."

With that, Bill Homans moved back to our table, picked up his yellow legal pad full of notes and curled up corners, and turned to the jury. He stood up to his full height and began our defense.

"Mr. foreman, ladies and gentleman of the jury, it is important that you consider and determine not what is said to have happened in terms of the words you hear but what *actually* happened.

"Dr. Kenneth Edelin, a well thought of physician, at the time of the operation in question, was Chief Resident in the Department of

Obstetrics and Gynecology at Boston City Hospital. As such, in accordance with the policies of the hospital, he and other members of the staff performed abortions from time to time. You will hear from witnesses that abortion constitutes the destruction or termination of whatever life there is in the fetus.

"A woman of 17 came to the hospital with her mother, seeking an abortion. She consented to have an abortion performed by the process known as saline infusion. After two unsuccessful attempts, the decision was made to try one final saline infusion. If that was unsuccessful, an operation known as a hysterotomy—which would result in the removal of the fetus from the body of the mother by surgery—would be performed.

"The process of hysterotomy is a recognized form of abortion done in a significant percentage of abortion cases, given certain circumstances. The manner in which Dr. Edelin performed the hysterotomy for the purpose of the abortion was in accordance with generally accepted medical standards throughout the country, including the detachment of the placenta and the removal thereafter of what is known as the products of conception—the placenta, the umbilical cord, the remains of the amniotic sac and the fetus itself.

"Various persons made observations as to the size of the fetus before the abortion. The most experienced physician who examined her estimated her to be 20 to 21 weeks pregnant, much less than the figures given to you by the district attorney.

"This fetus never drew a single breath outside the body of its mother.

"You will hear testimony as to the meaning of words. Words are very important in this trial. You have already heard certain words used by Mr. Flanagan.

"Although the indictment refers to the killing of a 'baby boy,' no 'baby boy' ever existed and certainly no 'baby boy' was ever killed. Mr. Flanagan read to you part of the autopsy report, which said that this was a well-developed, well-nourished black male fetus. We have no disagreement with the words of the autopsy. You'll note that the medical examiner never uses the words 'male *child*' in any place. Throughout the report, the medical examiner refers to a fetus.

"We will also ask you to pay particular attention to the meaning of other words, such as 'anoxia' and 'asphyxia.' We will offer evidence as to the meaning of such words rather than saying 'suffocate,' as the district attorney has done.

"The evidence will show that the existence of this fetus was terminated by anoxia and not by suffocation. We ask you to consider not the words that Mr. Flanagan used, but to consider what actually happened.

"Once you have heard what actually happened, we will ask you to consider whether Dr. Edelin committed manslaughter or performed a proper, correct, lawful abortion following universally excepted medical standards. We ask you to listen to all of the evidence. Thank you."

Bill Homans slowly returned to our table and took his seat next to me. I grabbed his hand and squeezed it.

McGuire then told the jury that there was a matter which needed to be discussed, but since the jury was not permitted to hear it, the court officers led them out of the courtroom.

McGuire nodded at Bill Homans. "I will hear your motion for a directed verdict of not guilty."

From the beginning, the case that Newman Flanagan had brought against me made no legal sense. *Roe v. Wade*, the Supreme Court decision that wiped out all anti-abortion laws throughout the United States, was handed down in January of 1973. The abortion I had performed, and was now being prosecuted for, occurred in October of that same year, nearly 10 months after the ruling. There were no restrictive abortion laws in place in Massachusetts at the time. We knew this. The district attorney knew this. The heart of this trial was really Newman Flanagan's personal views against abortion. Bill Homans had tried several times before to get Judge McGuire to throw the case out, but he had refused to do so. Bill wanted to try again to convince the judge that this was not a case of manslaughter, but one of politics and personal vendetta. To Flanagan, I was every doctor who ever performed an abortion. I was *Roe v. Wade*.

"The defendant respectfully moves that you direct the jury to return a verdict of not guilty. The Commonwealth's opening, accepting all of the facts as presented, does not prove a crime under the laws of this Commonwealth nor under the laws of the United States.

"According to Mr. Flanagan's own opening statement, the death of the fetus, or as Mr. Flanagan chooses to call it 'the male child,' took place nowhere else except within the womb of the patient.

"Even if we accept all of his so-called facts as true, we say that no crime was committed. There is no question that under the language of *Roe* that an abortion is the destruction of fetal prenatal life. The Supreme Court is unquestionably referring to the termination of pregnancy as a result of the termination of the prenatal or potential life of the fetus. In addition, the court said that after viability, the state has an interest in a potential human life which it may protect or promote by the passage of legislation governing the procedure *if it chooses*. On October 3, 1973, there was no legislation in this state governing the abortion procedure and governing the manner in which an abortion procedure should be performed. If we accept Mr. Flanagan's argument, then *Roe* means nothing because an abortion done by D&C, by saline infusion, or by any other means would be illegal.

"Finally, your honor, Mr. Flanagan does not apparently intend to introduce or have evidence that this fetus died anywhere except in the patient's uterus. Under the common law *where* the death occurs *does* make a difference. The common law before *Roe* was that there is no crime if the fetus dies while in the womb of the mother. From the earliest times of common law up to the time of the decision of the Supreme Court in *Roe*, every court which has had to deal with the subject in every state in this country has said that death within the body of the mother is not homicide.

"While Dr. Edelin might like to demonstrate that what he did was in accordance with accepted medical practice, under the facts stated by Mr. Flanagan and under the common law as it existed prior to *Roe* and subsequent to *Roe*—at least in Massachusetts—through October 3, 1973, there is no criminal liability."

Raising his voice slightly and looking McGuire in the eyes, Bill concluded, "This case should terminate now without going through a long, expensive and wasteful trial. We therefore ask you to direct the jury to return a verdict of not guilty."

Newman Flanagan reached deep inside and responded with right to life indignity.

"I think we have been down this *road of life* a couple of times in this case already. We have heahd these ahguments befoah. The Commonwealth's opening is just a brief synopsis of the case. The Commonwealth doesn't even have to make an opening in the case. We made an allegation and during the trial we will introduce each and every essential element to prove the crime which the defendant is chahged. I did not tell the court and the jury all the evidence that I will introduce in this pahticulah case. I made an opening and in my opening I indicated that there was human life in the male child aftah it was detached from the mothah and that the male child would have lived except for the crime which Doctah Edelin committed, whethah it was voluntary or involuntary, whethah it was deliberate or there were extenuating circumstances, whethah it was by willful and wanton conduct. Mr. Homans' motion should be denied and I respectfully ask the court to do so."

"Mr. Homans, do you wish to rebut?" Judge McGuire asked coldly.

"No. I've said everything that needs to be said," Bill responded.

"Fine, then. We will take a recess until 2:00 p.m."

Judge McGuire rapped his gavel. I stood up and went to the back of the courtroom where my family and friends were seated. My sister and Ramona were hopeful that McGuire would rule in our favor. To us, it was clear that my actions were protected by *Roe* and the case should be thrown out.

Bill and Frank came over to me a few minutes later. I bade my family a quick farewell, then my lawyers and I left the courthouse and took the 10-minute walk, through the bitter Boston cold, back to Bill's office. Judi, Bill's secretary, had sandwiches waiting. We sat around the large table in his conference room eating and discussing the morning's proceedings.

We were back in the courtroom just before 2:00. After the jury was brought in and seated in the jury box, McGuire motioned for Bill, Frank and Newman's gang to approach the bench. In a quiet voice so that the jury could not hear, McGuire said, "The defendant's motion for directed verdict on Mr. Flanagan's opening is denied. Mr. Flanagan, proceed with your case."

CHAPTER 24

FLANAGAN'S CASE

"The Commonwealth calls Doctah Mildred Jeffahson."

Up until now, Newman Flanagan's weapons had been words from his own mouth. He was about to introduce his artillery: other "right to lifers"—professionals, experts and physicians who could speak for themselves and weave in their own stories; people who could tell their own lies and inflict their own wounds on me.

And Mildred Jefferson was to fire Flanagan's first shot! The very same strange and unusual woman I had debated shortly after the *Roe v. Wade* ruling. The one who believed abortion was wrong no matter the circumstance. I had hoped to never see her again.

She was a woman of hardened steel—unbending, unyielding and ungiving. With her on the stand, Flanagan hoped to accomplish two things. First, he wanted her to impress the jury with her knowledge and her point of view. Second, because she was black, he would be able to inoculate himself against the charge of racism which was always swirling around my indictment and my case. The racial controversy over busing had moved from the streets of Boston and its own courtroom into mine.

Flanagan let his pal Joe Mulligan question Mildred Jefferson.

"Tell us your name, please."

"I am Dr. Mildred F. Jefferson," she replied, enunciating every syllable through her pursed lips. She sat with her back rigid and her black hair pulled back into a bun so tight that it made her eyes slant. Her hands were cupped primly in her lap.

"And you are a medical doctor?"

"Yes, I am a general surgeon."

"Doctor, would you tell us where you were educated, please?"

She recounted her education, beginning with Texas Christian

College and ending with her medical degree from Harvard Medical School. While her surgical practice was limited and her experience in obstetrics and gynecology practically non-existent, she was a founding member of every right to life organization in Massachusetts.

"I helped found all such organizations represented in Massachusetts, beginning with the educational organization known as the Value of Life Committee and the political organization known as Massachusetts Citizens for Life. Both of these organizations are dedicated to defend the sanctity of life as the basis of a democratic society."

Bill jumped to his feet and objected to Jefferson's discourse on democracy. McGuire ruled against him and let Jefferson's statement stand. Bill stood unbelievingly for a while and then slowly sat back down in his chair.

"Dr. Jefferson, I'm going to ask some questions that will define some terms—mainly medical terms—for the jury. Would you tell us…?"

I grabbed Bill's arm. He stood and objected to what we anticipated to be a series of medical definitions Mildred Jefferson would give as an expert in the areas of fetal development, obstetrics and gynecology. She was not an expert.

McGuire gave Bill permission to question Mildred Jefferson to determine if she was a qualified expert.

Bill moved his hulking frame from behind our table and approached the witness stand, towering over Mildred Jefferson where she sat ramrod straight—cold and ready.

Bill was a polite, but imposing figure in the courtroom. He had a habit of stalking in front of a witness during his cross-examination, lowering his massive head and asking questions in a voice that reflected his upper-class origins. His gentleness was sometimes deceiving, because in his quiet, controlled way he had a reputation for being relentless in his questioning. He was thorough, methodical, determined and brilliant in his cross-examinations.

"Dr. Jefferson, when did you get your medical degree from Harvard?"

"In 1951. Then I did my surgical residency at City Hospital from 1952 until the end of 1955."

Bill began to pace in front of Dr. Jefferson. "When was the last time you had dealings with obstetrical patients?"

"Not since I was a fourth-year medical student at Harvard in 1950."

Bill pressed on. "You are not certified in obstetrics and gynecology?"
"No."

"Have you ever performed an abortion, Dr. Jefferson?"

Her eyes flashed. "No," she said, her voice gaining a slight edge.

"So, you are not qualified as an obstetrician or a gynecologist and you have never performed an abortion."

"That is correct," she said.

"You testified that your experience insofar as far as the question of abortion is concerned has been only political, isn't that right?"

"No, that is not—"

Bill cut her off. "You said that you were a founding member of the Value of Life Committee, which is an educational organization. You also testified that you were a founding member of the Massachusetts Citizens for Life. Is that correct?"

"Yes."

"Neither of these organizations are medical organizations, are they? Aren't they political organizations dedicated to assisting the passage or the defeat of legislation?"

"Yes."

"When was the last time you delivered a baby, Dr. Jefferson?"

"1951."

"Twenty-three years ago! When was the last time you treated a pregnant woman?"

"About three years ago."

"And how many pregnant women did you treat three years ago?"

"One."

"Dr. Jefferson, are you a trained embryologist or perinatologist?"

"No."

Turning to Judge McGuire, Bill said matter-of-factly and with disdain, "In the field of reproduction, obstetrics, embryology and matters of this nature, this witness, by her own admission, is not qualified to testify as a medical expert."

"Your honor," Joe Mulligan pleaded, "I merely intend to have her testify about those things that any medical doctor could testify to—a general definition of terms and basic anatomy."

We waited for what seemed like forever to hear Judge McGuire's ruling. Neither Bill nor Joe Mulligan moved a muscle. Mildred Jefferson stared straight ahead into the crowd, looking icy cold and unapproachable. She was not just any medical doctor. She was a leader in the right to life movement and would certainly inject its philosophy into her testimony. As the lead-off witness, she was going to continue painting the picture that Flanagan wanted his jury to see: Dr. Edelin, the monster baby killer.

McGuire leaned forward and looked at each attorney.

"I will declare her to be qualified to testify as an expert."

"I object!" Bill exploded as he turned and came back to our table.

For the next two hours, Joe Mulligan questioned Mildred Jefferson about the meaning of words—fertilization, eggs, Fallopian tubes, ovary, sperm—which she referred to as the male seed—zygote and embryo. She declared that pregnancy begins with fertilization and that the earliest form of the embryo is the young of humankind. She pronounced that at six to eight weeks, the "newly developing young one of the human family begins to look more like the rest of us."

Bill Homans objected to her use of non-medical terms, but McGuire again overruled his objection and allowed her to continue to use subtly persuasive, non-medical language that "humanized" the embryo and fetus.

Over and over again, Jefferson used the word "baby" and over and over again Bill objected. McGuire told her to stop using the word "baby," but she continued anyway. Each time Bill would object, and each time McGuire would admonish Jefferson and instruct the jury to disregard the word "baby." But it was too late. Being told to disregard a word does not stop a jury from hearing it.

Between his numerous objections, Bill scribbled away furiously on his yellow legal pad, flipping pages and jotting down notes.

"Doctor, what is an abortion?"

"I object, your honor. She is not an expert," Bill said.

"Objection denied."

She said that abortion was the termination of a pregnancy before 20 weeks.

She described spontaneous, therapeutic and induced abortions. Bill objected again that she was not an expert on abortion, obstetrics or gynecology, but McGuire let her continue. And continue she did, using right to life rhetoric to describe D&C, suction curettage, saline infusion and hysterotomy.

"Objection!"

"Denied."

"Objection!"

"Denied."

When she finally finished giving her definitions, Mulligan declared, "I have no further questions at this time, your honor."

Bill Homans slowly rose from his seat and again approached the witness stand, holding his yellow legal pad with its curled up corners.

"Dr. Jefferson, didn't you sign an amicus brief which disputed the position of the United States Supreme Court on the subject of abortion?"

Newman Flanagan jumped up and blurted out, "I object."

Judge McGuire looked at Bill. "Aren't you getting into a matter of law rather than her credentials as an expert witness?"

"I intend to show bias on the part of this witness."

McGuire pressed on. "But up to the present time she has been engaged in defining terms. You claim it is biased?"

"Very. Here is a copy of the of the amicus brief she signed that was filed in opposition to *Roe v. Wade*."

"Does the brief have different definitions than the one she gave here? Is that what you're getting at?"

"The brief has a great deal of difference in it between the Supreme Court holding and her definitions. She says that an abortion is a procedure done before viability. That is not what the Supreme Court says, your honor."

"You may proceed."

Finally, a ruling in our favor!

Bill approached Mildred Jefferson. She looked up at him with that stony stare. "Dr. Jefferson, do you recognize the legality of abortion?"

"I don't understand the question."

"Do you approve of abortion?"

"I do not understand the question," she repeated. I didn't think it was possible, but her back stiffened even more.

"Do you approve of the procedure of dilatation and curettage to accomplish the termination of pregnancy?"

"It…would depend on the medical judgment of the physician," she sputtered.

"Have you taken a political stance against the process of terminating pregnancies by such procedures as dilatation and curettage and saline infusion?"

"My political campaign is to restore the rights of personhood to the unborn."

To make the fetus a person. That has always been part of their strategy. Intimidating doctors was another part. Bill stopped pacing in front of the witness stand and turned to face her.

"Did you testify at a hearing on September 18th before the Boston City Council committee on public health?"

"No. I introduced two speakers at the hearing."

Bill didn't move. He just stared at her. She then added in a somewhat quieter voice, "Perhaps I answered one or two questions."

"Didn't you give a long statement concerning your views on abortion?"

"I gave a long statement at the hearing as part of the introduction of two speakers."

"Didn't you tell the Boston City Council that you disagreed with the Supreme Court in their *Roe* decision?"

"Yes."

"Do you disagree *today* with the *Roe* decision?"

"I object!" Mulligan shouted, leaping to his feet.

We had her! She had just admitted that she told the Boston City Council that she was opposed to legal abortion, and now she was being forced to admit to this jury that she was a biased witness.

Both Bill and Mulligan were standing, facing the judge. The rapid-fire cross-examination of their first witness had raised the tension in the courtroom. Jefferson's next answer would emphasize our point that she was a biased witness against abortion and against me. Her testimony was tainted. Again, silence fell over the courtroom as everyone waited for McGuire's ruling.

He rapped his gavel.

"We will resume this questioning on Monday morning. The court is adjourned."

Like a punctured balloon, the tension and Jefferson escaped from the courtroom. The weekend would intervene, the jury would forget, and Mildred Jefferson would have the chance to regain her composure and prepare herself for the rest of Bill's cross-examination.

Our routine at the end of each day's session became almost a ritual. We would make our way back in the cold January wind to the pub in the basement of the Old City Hall. Bill, Frank and I would gather around a corner table, talk about the day's events in court, chain smoke cigarettes and sip on martinis while we waited for the official typed transcript to arrive. Our discussions were often animated, sometimes heated, sometimes philosophical, but always about how we were going to discredit Newman Flanagan's theories.

With Mildred Jefferson as their lead-off witness, it was clear that this trial was hardly about me. It was an attempt by those who were opposed to abortion to intimidate all doctors willing to perform them.

After the transcript arrived, we quickly reviewed it, and after a few comments, decided that we had had enough for the evening. By this time, Judi Bernstein, Bill's assistant, and Daphne, Bill's girlfriend, had joined us in the bar. We smoked another half-pack of cigarettes and drank several more martinis, trying to talk about anything but the trial. Tipsy, but not sloppy, Judi suggested that we all come to her apartment for dinner. It was the first time all day that I had an appetite.

January 11, 1975

When the trial began, I stopped going to BCH, the Crit and the neighborhood health centers. There were some pregnant women in my private practice that I continued to see on Saturday mornings in my office, but otherwise, I took the time to concentrate on my trial.

Seeing patients became a refuge. They were the link to what I loved and provided me with a sanctuary from the ugliness of the trial. They reminded me that my judgment was sound and that no matter what Newman Flanagan, Mildred Jefferson or any of the self-righteous pro-lifers said about me, my intentions had always been to help women.

After seeing patients, I went directly to Bill's office. Papers were strewn everywhere—across his desk, in messy stacks bound with rubber bands, piled on the floor and pinned to the wall—and open books lay on every available surface. Saturdays were Bill's busiest office day, beginning, after my arrival, with a visit from Bill's estranged wife, Libby, sometimes accompanied by their two daughters. She came by every Saturday to pick up her alimony check, because if she didn't, chances were she wouldn't get it at all. Bill's personal life was a mess. He was caught between his wife, his girlfriend, his daughters and his clients.

From day one, I noticed that whenever Libby came to the office, the tension mounted. That Saturday, she had brought the girls with her. I watched their relationship with their father. As the children of separated parents they, like my children, faced the pain of split loyalties and fractured, tense visits. Partly for their sake, but mostly his own, Bill made sure that Libby and his girlfriend, Daphne, were never in the office at the same time. When Libby left, he announced that he was going for a walk, then popped down to the pub for a quick drink.

By now I had known Bill long enough to know that he tried to escape from the conflicts in his life by drinking. Bill could and did drink a lot.

Judi always worked on Saturdays, but since Bill had started on my case, others began to gather in his office—his partners, physician friends of mine, law professors from Harvard, legal assistants who worked for Bill, and one or two law students who were there to be a part of this case and to do whatever legal chores they could in order to stay involved. The dynamics on Saturday afternoons were free-flowing and free-styling. We talked philosophy, biology, law, medicine and politics. People from all over the country were still offering their help in any way possible. The country's leading civil liberty lawyers and law professors wrote to Bill, offering their theories and help in the case. Some of the most prominent professors in obstetrics and gynecology were in touch with me, lending their ideas and offering to testify as expert witnesses on my behalf. We received mail and articles from ethicists, philosophers, preachers and scientists. Ideas and theories came from everywhere, as did thoughts, opinions, suggestions, insights and information about potential witnesses. The office became a growing repository for everything about abortion.

Late in the afternoon, after everyone else had gone, Bill, Frank, Jeanne, the law students and I would dissect Newman Flanagan's case, his questions and tactics trying to figure out how he was going to prove his theory of the case and how we would defend against it before we went on the attack.

January 13, 1975

We were back in court and Bill, with that engaging, disarming smile on his face, approached the witness stand and resumed his cross-examination of Mildred Jefferson.

"Good morning, Dr. Jefferson," he said. She stared back at him with those steely eyes and did not respond. "On Friday," Bill continued, "you defined abortion as the ending of a pregnancy before viability, or the 20th week. Is that correct?"

"Yes."

"Where did you get that definition?"

"The definition I gave you is a composite that appears in several medical textbooks and in published papers."

She had done her homework over the weekend.

"But you have defined abortion in other ways, haven't you?"

"That is correct."

"Do you recall stating that 'abortion is the name given to the process by which pregnancy is interrupted for the purpose of preventing the birth of the living child'?"

"I use that definition from time to time."

"That is not the same definition used by the Supreme Court in *Roe v. Wade*, is it?"

With that Mulligan jumped to his feet. "I object!"

"Sustained."

Bill retreated and tried a new approach. "As I understand it, Dr. Jefferson, the definition that you gave on Friday is not your definition but the definition of others and not based on your experience. Is that correct?"

"Yes."

With that response, Bill approached the bench. "Your honor, I move that the definition of abortion that Dr. Jefferson gave on Friday be stricken."

As expected, Joe Mulligan objected.

McGuire turned to the jury. "Ladies and gentleman of the jury, we're attempting here to define certain words, to acquaint you with the generally accepted meaning of those words. Dr. Jefferson's testimony is limited to her understanding of those words because of her expertise as a physician. You are to determine what weight to give her testimony. In fact, it is your responsibility to weigh the testimony of all the witnesses. Mr. Homans, you may continue."

Was that it? Was that all he was going to say to the jury about Mildred Jefferson and her testimony? Was he actually going to let her give non-medical definitions and let the jury sort them out? In spite of McGuire's weak instructions to the jury, Bill pressed on, unshaken.

"Dr. Jefferson, it is my understanding that today, when asked to define abortion, you said it is the process by which pregnancy is interrupted for the purpose of preventing the birth of a living child. Is that correct?"

"Yes."

"So the definition you gave us on Friday is not based upon your experience as a physician, is it?"

"No, it is not based upon my experience as a physician."

For all her righteous zeal, Mildred Jefferson was not an expert in the medical practice of obstetrics, gynecology or abortion. Her only exposure to these topics was what she had read in books. She had never heard the pleadings of desperate women wanting to terminate their pregnancies. She had not heard their stories. She was not an expert, but the judge was letting her testify as one. Her definitions were not medical, but political.

"On Friday, Dr. Jefferson, you defined hysterotomy as being one of the forms of an abortion. Is that correct?"

"Yes."

"Dr. Jefferson, isn't the purpose of abortion to terminate prenatal existence?"

"I cannot answer that question."

Judge McGuire looked at her with a quizzical expression on his face. "You can't answer it?"

"I cannot answer that question without knowing the individual and the decision that they made. No outsider can interpret what someone has in mind."

"Who are you referring to?" Homans asked.

"The woman and her doctor."

Seizing the moment, Bill repeated, "So this is a decision arrived at between a woman and her doctor. Is that what you're telling us?" This was the essence of the *Roe*. We had her again!

This time Flanagan jumped in.

"I object!" he shouted.

Again, McGuire stopped us in our tracks and sided with Flanagan. "Objection sustained."

Bill advanced from another direction.

"Dr. Jefferson, on Friday you described hysterotomy as being a form of abortion."

"That is correct."

"The process of hysterotomy for the purpose of abortion involves the separation of the placenta from the uterine wall, does it not?"

"The operation for removing what is growing within the uterus does involve separation of the placenta and the delivery of the unborn offspring within it."

There was silence. The rapid fire of questions and answers stopped. Her last words hung in the air. *Delivery. Unborn offspring.* Bill let them linger for just a moment, then pounced.

"You used the word 'unborn.' During the time that the fetus is within the uterus of the woman, it is unborn, is it not?"

"Until it is delivered it may be considered unborn," she replied.

Again, Flanagan jumped to his feet. "I object!"

Why did he object to that? I thought. Then it dawned on me. *Unborn.* Newman Flanagan and those who were advising him were attempting to craft a new definition of birth. He had to convince the jury that whatever I did occurred *after* the fetus was born, even though it was still inside the womb. Their own witness had just testified that while within the womb, the fetus was "unborn."

Surprisingly, McGuire overruled the objection. "I will let Mr. Homans continue."

Bill nodded, then turned back to Mildred Jefferson. "Based upon your studies, while the fetus is still inside the body of the patient, it is unborn, is it not?"

Flanagan's objection must have caused Mildred Jefferson to realize that she was undermining their new definition of birth. She changed her testimony.

"My understanding, based on my own knowledge of physiology, is that once the placenta is completely separated and the offspring is no longer attached to the mother, even if it has not been removed from the uterus, it has been born."

Bill pressed on. "So that is your own conclusion, not based upon any of the textbooks with which you are familiar and in which you have studied. Is that correct?"

"Yes, that is my conclusion because at that point it must go on its own systems."

"May I ask whether or not the statement you have just made is based upon any of the textbooks or studies you have read?"

"The opinion I gave you is based on my own observations."

Bill pressed on. "The definition of being born is not one that you have read in any textbooks, is it?"

A beat. "That is not correct," she said.

"Would you tell us the name of one textbook or any recognized authority that supports the definition of birth that you just gave?"

"The *Handbook of Pediatrics* defines both 'stillborn infant' and 'live birth.'"

Returning to our table, Bill picked up a copy of the handbook that she just referred to, opened it and tried to hand it to her. She looked down at the book and back up at him with that cold stare. She did not touch the book. Bill began to rapidly page through it.

"Is there any definition of 'being born' that describes it with the fetus still inside the uterus, with the placenta detached, whether or not the uterus was open?"

"No. Not in that wording."

"I have no further questions, your honor."

With that, Bill finished his cross examination of Dr. Mildred Jefferson, confident that he had shown her bias against abortion, her lack of experience with obstetrics, gynecology and abortion, and the absurdity of her attempt to change the definition of birth. She and her definitions had been discredited. The knot in my stomach loosened.

In his Boston brogue, Newman Flanagan said, "Your honah, the Commonwealth calls Doctah Hugh Robert Holtrop."

Holtrop? Why was Flanagan calling him? He would have been one of our witnesses.

Hugh Holtrop didn't look at me as he approached the stand. He was a fuddish looking man, square with a big belly, a face with jowls, and sandy-colored hair that fell over his forehead. He was one of the "visits" in the Department of Obstetrics and Gynecology at BCH and had worked with poor women all of his professional life, first in West Virginia and now in Boston. Though not a very good surgeon, he was committed to the poor, supported abortion and was the one who got me involved with the pregnant teens' program at the Crit. He was the part-time director of the outpatient department. He liked my plan for continuity of care in the clinic and had helped me implement it. It was there in the clinic that he had introduced me to Evonne Gilbert.

He took the Fifth during his grand jury appearance, claiming he did so on the advice of his lawyer. He had left me hanging out there by myself and now he was being called as one of Flanagan's witnesses.

Paul O'Leary, the clerk, swore him in and Flanagan began with the usual "credential assurance"—questions about his training and his affiliation with BCH. He then showed Holtrop Evonne's medical record.

"Do you recognize this recahd?" he asked.

"Yes I do," Holtrop said.

"Tell us about the meeting you had with the patient."

Holtrop described how he had met Evonne and her mother at the clinic when they came in asking for an abortion.

"Did you make a detahmination of whethah or not she was with child?" Flanagan asked.

With child. The horrible little man with the flowery tie would do anything to slip in his wording.

"She was pregnant," Holtrop said, thankfully not falling into Flanagan's trap.

"How fah along was she?"

"According to her last period, she was 17 weeks pregnant. On the basis of my physical, she was about 20 weeks."

"Did you see the patient once she was admitted to the hospital?"

"Yes I did. I watched Dr. Edelin attempt the amniocentesis and observed that this procedure was impossible. He kept getting bloody taps."

"How many times did you observe him attempt this procejah?"

"At least three times, and possibly four."

With that, Flanagan ended his questioning of Hugh Holtrop. Bill and I exchanged a look. I did not understand why Flanagan had called Holtrop. He had said nothing against me. But now it was Bill's turn to cross-examine him.

Bill asked Holtrop more specific questions about his training and experience in obstetrics and gynecology, hoping that the jury would see the differences in the expertise of Holtrop and Jefferson. Predictably, Flanagan objected. Surprisingly, Judge McGuire let Bill continue.

"After you finished your residency, where have you practiced?"

"I had a busy practice in West Virginia for six and a half years. I have been living in the Boston area since 1970 and have been employed for part of that time as the director of the outpatient services in obstetrics and gynecology at City Hospital. I have also been a lecturer and a research associate at the Harvard School of Public Health, Department of Population Studies."

Bill handed Holtrop Evonne's medical record and pointed to a handwritten note. "Would you please read that for us?"

"The history and physical exam noted, except the fundus is consistent with 20 to 21 weeks, measuring 22 centimeters above the symphysis," Holtrop read.

"Who wrote that note?"

"I did."

Bill pointed out to the jury that the other estimations of how far along Evonne was were made by a third-year medical student, with little or no experience, and Enrique Gimenez, who, at the time, was a only first-year resident.

"Is it fair to say," Bill asked, "that your experience in examining pregnant women was considerably greater than their experience?"

Flanagan again jumped to his feet. "Objection!"

Unbelievably, McGuire sustained his objection. Bill paused only a moment to flip up a corner of his yellow legal pad. He switched gears.

"Dr. Holtrop, in the course of your direct examination you referred to what you termed 'bloody taps.' What does that mean when one obtains blood?"

"Attempting the saline infusion would be very dangerous."

"What causes bloody taps?"

"Usually putting the needle into one of the blood vessels of the placenta."

"Could this damage the placenta and the fetus?"

"I object!" Flanagan interjected. "This is pure speculation."

"All right. All right," Judge McGuire said. His voice had a slight edge to it. It was mid-afternoon already. No one had eaten and everybody was tired. "Mr. foreman, ladies and gentleman of the jury, we have a problem here concerning evidence. I'm going to hear it in the absence of the jury."

I could not believe how McGuire catered to Flanagan! I believed that the repeated bloody taps had damaged the fetus by causing hemorrhage inside the uterus. It was dead at the time of the hysterotomy. Holtrop thought the same thing, but Flanagan did not want the jury to know this.

So in another display of his endless Flanagan appeasement, McGuire had ruled that he would hear this part of Holtrop's testimony and decide afterwards if the jury could do so.

After the jury had been taken out of the courtroom, Bill continued his questioning of Holtrop *voir dire*.

"Isn't it true that a bloody tap may occur either from insertion of the needle into a blood vessel of the placenta or into the fetus itself?"

"Yes. If multiple needle punctures were made in the placenta or the fetus, it could die inside of the uterus."

"Your honor," Bill said, "I have no further questions. One of the things the Commonwealth has to prove is that the fetus was alive at the time of the conduct of the defendant. If it turns out that the fetus was not alive at the time of the hysterotomy then there is no object for the alleged manslaughter to have been committed. These bloody taps took place many hours before the hysterotomy was performed, and whatever the condition of the fetus was between that time and the time of the alleged conduct of defendant, we suggest is part of the Commonwealth's burden of proof. The jury should hear this line of questioning and the witness' answers."

Newman Flanagan objected.

McGuire turned to Holtrop. "Do you have an opinion, based on reasonable medical certainty, as to whether or not the bloody taps caused any fetal damage?"

"No, sir. I cannot be certain about that."

"That terminates the *voir dire*," McGuire said. "Bring in the jury. I will see counsel at the bench."

Newman Flanagan and Bill approached the judge. McGuire leaned forward, frowning, as if trying his best to look intimidating to both men. He looked from Bill, to Flanagan, and back to Bill. "In view of the doctor's answer to my question as to whether or not he is certain that there was fetal damage, I am not going to allow any questions delving into *possibilities* of damage caused by the bloody taps."

Holtrop was excused and the jury was back in the box.

The next witness Flanagan called was Alan Silberman, the third-year medical student who had taken the history and performed the physical examination on Evonne when she was admitted to the hospital.

Silberman testified that he did not remember the patient, but recognized the notes he had written on her medical record. He had only three days of experience when he performed the examination on Evonne Gilbert and was therefore not confident about his estimation of how far pregnant she was. His testimony didn't seem to help Flanagan at all. Questioning was brief, and Alan Silberman was excused.

Flanagan is going to have to do better than this, I thought. *This can't be all he's got.* He had to have something up his sleeve. When was he going to show us his big guns?

"The Commonwealth would like to call Dr. James Penza."

Jim Penza had been a mentor and friend since I'd arrived at BCH. He was closer to my age than the other attending physicians and was the most skillful surgeon of them all. He was a graduate of Harvard Medical School and after a year of internship, he spent a tour of duty as a general medical officer in Vietnam. Upon his discharge from the service, he completed his training in obstetrics and gynecology at University Hospital and BCH. He was now board certified. In addition to being one of our few full-time staff members, he was the associate director of the department. He had a very busy private practice. When David Charles fled to Canada to avoid the ridiculous grave robbing charges, Jim Penza and Joel Rankin were appointed acting co-directors of the obstetrics and gynecology department at City Hospital. Jim Penza was a good doctor. His patients loved him and the residents had the utmost respect for him.

Flanagan questioned Jim Penza about the residency structure in the department, as well as the names and positions of the attending physicians. Then Flanagan handed him Evonne's medical record.

"Docktah Penza, look at this recahd and tell us if Docktah Edelin did an operation on this patient."

"Yes, he did."

"Is one of yoah duties to assign residents to perfoahm operations?"

"Sometimes."

"Did you see this pahticulah patient at any time during her stay at the City Hospital?" he asked, tapping his finger on the medical record.

"There is a note by Dr. Edelin on October 2nd in which he claims that I was consulted and that I would attempt an amniocentesis in the operating room on this patient. There is no note that I was in the operating room, but Dr. Edelin has since told me that I was present."

"Do you remembah being there?"

"No."

"Do you recall whethah you were present for the amniocentesis or the hysterotomy?"

"I do not recall being present. However, in the last several months, I have had a conversation with Dr. Edelin which reminded me that when I was in the operating room, I was told that this was Dr. Holtrop's patient. I do remember saying, 'If this is Holtrop's patient, he should be here taking care of her.'"

"How many residents perfoahmed saline abortions at City Hospital in Septembah and Octobah of 1973?"

"To the best of my knowledge, at that time, Dr. Edelin and one other resident were the only ones performing saline abortions."

"How many perfoahmed hysterotomies?"

"Only Dr. Edelin and one other resident."

"Doctah Penza, did you perfoahm hysterotomies or saline abortions at the hospital at this pahticulah time?"

"Yes."

"Would you describe the proceduah for perfoahming a hysterotomy?"

Jim Penza described the operation exactly the way I had done it and exactly as it is described in textbooks. "An incision is made into the uterus to remove the products of conception."

"How are they removed?"

"The uterine cavity is entered and the entire amniotic sac, including the placenta, is dissected free from the uterine wall and the products of conception are removed."

"How long aftah the detachment of the placenta are the products of conception removed?"

"It depends. There is sometimes difficulty dissecting everything cleanly off."

"That period of time can be anywhere from what to what?"

"Several seconds to several minutes."

"What happens aftah the products of conception are removed?" Flanagan asked, straightening that horrible tie of his.

"The sac and the products of conception are removed and placed in a surgical basin, which is then removed from the table and the operation continues."

"Is there any effort made to determine, prioh to the commencement of the hysterotomy, whethah or not the fetus is alive?"

"No."

"What about a fetal hahtbeat? Does anybody check for fetal hahtbeat?"

"There's a protocol for the performance of abortions at City Hospital. Nowhere in that protocol does it mention that fetal heartbeats should be obtained before the abortion is performed."

Flanagan rested his hands on the bar in front of the witness stand and leaned over Jim Penza, his eyes full of religion-fueled accusations. "Is there any reason why you do not take a fetal hahtbeat?"

Jim Penza stared back at Flanagan, unblinking, unflinching. "There really is no reason to check for a fetal heartbeat."

"I have no furthah questions."

Gesturing to Evonne's medical record, which Jim Penza was still holding, Bill began his cross-examination.

"Dr. Penza, please examine the medical record and tell us if the record indicates the location of the placenta in this particular patient."

"The placenta was anterior."

Bill began his usual stalking, back and forth, in front of the witness. "Could you tell us, based upon your medical experience and training, whether or not the effort which you have just described to remove the amniotic sac intact is always successful in the course of a hysterotomy?"

"No, it is not."

"Is this one of the reasons why it could take more time to remove the fetus?"

"Yes."

"You referred to the surgeon having his fingers inside of the uterus for the purpose of removing the placenta. Can you tell us whether not it is possible for an observer to see what is occurring inside the uterus with respect to the surgeon's fingers?"

"It would be impossible for an observer to tell what is going."

Jim Penza was a great witness for us. Why did Flanagan call him?

"I have no further questions, your honor."

January 16, 1975

Newman Flanagan called Helen Horner to the stand as his first witness on the eighth day of the trial. Helen had been an operating room technician for nearly 15 years. Nine of them were at BCH. She had beautiful black skin, full lips and a melting smile. She was more than a little overweight and hands down had the best personality of anyone who worked in the operating room. She was the kind of tech that every surgeon wanted to have standing next to him. She could anticipate the instruments that a surgeon would need so well that she sometimes handed over an instrument that he didn't ask for, but needed.

Flanagan cleared his throat and began.

"Did you evah work as an operating room technician with Doctah Edelin when he perfoahmed abortions?"

"Yes."

"How many times?"

"Many times."

"How many hysterotomies have you scrubbed on?"

"Quite a few."

"Were you working in the operating room on Octobah 3, 1973?"

"Yes."

"Were Doctahs Edelin, Penza and Gimenez working on that day?" Flanagan smiled down at Helen. She did not smile back.

"Yes."

"Were you the operating room technician on a hysterotomy on that pahticulah day?"

Helen straightened in her chair, looked Flanagan directly in the eye and stuck out her chin. "No."

The color drained from Flanagan's chipmunk cheeks. He opened his mouth, then shut it again. He looked down at his notes, back up at Helen, then down at his notes again. He opened and closed his mouth several times, but no words came out. I bit my lip, but I could feel the corners of my mouth twitching.

Helen had testified during the grand jury hearing that she had scrubbed on the hysterotomy with me. She was now giving a different answer that Flanagan had failed to discover prior to the beginning of the trial. I knew that she was not in the operating room on this case. Flanagan didn't. We were one step ahead of him.

He handed her Evonne Gilbert's record.

"Do you know this patient?" he asked, his voice sharp. The color was returning to his face: an angry red that was creeping up into his hairline.

"Not really," she replied, rolling her eyes.

"What do you mean by that?" he snapped, gripping the rail with both hands and leaning over her.

She did not cower or lean away. She sucked her teeth. "I was in another operating room at the time. I don't know this patient."

Flanagan eased away, but kept his grip on the rail. The red in his face was deepening to a purplish color. I would have laughed if the situation were not so serious.

"Ms. Horner, do you recall testifying in connection with that pahticulah hospital record in front of the grand jury in February and again in April of 1974, that you were the scrub technician on that pahticulah patient?"

Bill jumped up and said, "I object!"

McGuire looked at Bill with that quizzical expression of his. "What is your objection?"

"Mr. Flanagan is trying to impeach his own witness."

McGuire ruled Bill out of order.

"Do you recall your testimony in front of the grand jury concehning this pahticulah patient?" a very frustrated Flanagan repeated.

"Yes, I do. I said it was *possible* that I could have scrubbed on the patient."

"Were you the circulating nurse on that pahticulah day? Did you perfoahm a sponge count?"

"Not on this particular case." She turned her head away.

"Ms. Horner, you now say that it was a mistake. You were not on this pahticulah case?"

"That's right."

Newman Flanagan became increasingly frustrated with his obvious screw up. He began to badger her with nonsense questions about minutiae. In his anger, he challenged her use of words. With her Roxbury attitude, she challenged his interpretations of what she had said.

Flanagan said "bucket," Helen said "basin."

Flanagan said "hysterotomy" and Helen said "hysterectomy." She said she was the scrub tech on a hysterectomy that day and not a hysterotomy.

Flanagan then questioned her about the usual protocol in the performance of the hysterotomy. She never flinched. She never stammered. She didn't help him in the least bit.

Finally, in complete frustration and humiliation, he ended his questioning of Helen Horner.

Now it was Bill Homans' turn. He produced several hospital

documents that clearly indicated there was another scrub tech in the operating room when I performed the hysterotomy on Evonne Gilbert. He then produced the pre-operative sheet for Helen to examine.

"Does this sheet contain the patient's name?"

"Yes it does." The bite was gone from Helen's voice.

"Is there any indication on the operative sheet as to who the surgeon was for this case?"

"Yes. Dr. Edelin was the surgeon."

"Does this sheet indicate that the operation listed was a saline/hysterotomy?"

"Yes."

"What does the sheet indicate as to who the scrub tech was on the case?"

"It indicates that Irene Bloom was the scrub tech," Helen said, glancing over in Flanagan's direction.

"Are there other nurses' names on this sheet?"

"Yes. Ellyn Curtis and Eileen Corbett."

Still furious at his failure to prepare himself for his own witness, Flanagan was on his feet again.

"I can't go along with this one, your honah. This looks like...it just doesn't look cricket to me." He could not express himself without sounding like a child having a tantrum. He strung together several incomprehensible, unrelated sentences. "I don't think the records have been kept in the usual course of business. This entry is made aftah these pahticulah entries are all made. I just object to it in general, your honah."

Calmly, Bill turned to Judge McGuire. "We have the custodian of the hospital records here. This OR record was summoned from the hospital and was brought in by the head nurse of the hospital this morning. It has been kept secure since the grand jury hearing. It has been identified as the pre-operative sheet showing the names of the patients and who were present in the operating room."

"I would like to cross-examine her, your honah," Flanagan said.

"She's here," Bill responded coolly.

Flanagan opened and closed his mouth again, then sat down, looking very disgruntled.

With that, Helen was excused and the head nurse of the hospital was called and sworn in. She was able to confirm the accuracy of the records and the fact that the record clearly indicated that Helen Horner had not scrubbed on the case.

Newman Flanagan exploded. He questioned the head nurse about pencil entries, blue ink entries, black ink entries, hash marks through people's names and attempted to create an air of confusion and uncertainty. As the head nurse tried to answer his questions in a logical and calm manner, Flanagan became more and more hostile and hysterical. Finally, Bill rose and objected to his line of questioning.

"What is your objection, Mr. Homans?"

"The district attorney has obviously been trying to imply that there is some conspiracy on the part of every nurse, physician and hospital official to 'cover' for Dr. Edelin. I would invite Your Honor's attention to the fact that what has happened here is a result of the district attorney's own error, as indicated by the mistake he made during the grand jury hearing, which resulted in Ms. Horner giving a wrong answer. Mr. Flanagan misread the book in which the sponge count is kept and thought that Ms. Horner was the person who performed it in this case. When she tried to correct him during the grand jury hearing, he forced her to change her testimony by showing her the hospital record of the patient in this case. She was not involved in this hysterotomy at all. The district attorney is now trying to make it look as if Ms. Horner was deliberately perjuring herself."

Judge McGuire looked at Newman Flanagan and asked, "Is there a question of good or bad faith on the part of this witness?"

"Why didn't she tell me? I know...I can't for the life of me...I am almost sure that there was...I don't know...The first time this came to my attention was just befoah she took the stand...that's the first time she evah told me. Why didn't she tell me?" Flanagan sputtered.

Bill looked directly at Flanagan and shot back, "You haven't interviewed her since her grand jury testimony. She made a mistake then. The whole purpose of your line of questioning about these records is to make it sound as if people on our side were gimmicking up the records, and I am very concerned about this. In addition, you have left the jury with the impression that Ms. Horner for some reason—not necessarily a good or lawful reason—has deliberately changed her testimony."

Bill produced the transcript of the grand jury hearing and pointed out several other places in the testimony of several witnesses that Helen Horner was not the scrub tech on Evonne Gilbert's abortion. Flanagan should have known that, but he had already made up his mind as to what happened on October 3, 1973 and he was not going to let the facts get in his way. There had been ample opportunity for him to have corrected his mistake, but his obsession blinded him. He was trying to impugn the integrity of the head nurse of the hospital and to leave the impression in the jurors' minds that the hospital staff was willing to lie for me.

McGuire finally ruled that Flanagan had to change his line of questioning. He could ask the witness where the records had been kept and under whose control, but he could not impugn the truthfulness of them.

After a few more questions for the head nurse and a few more questions for Helen Horner, the two witnesses were excused.

But Flanagan was single-minded. It didn't matter who the scrub tech was. He had his strategy and was not about to change it. He was ready to call his star witness, the person whose testimony he was sure would give him my conviction.

CHAPTER 25

ENRIQUE GIMENEZ-JIMENO

———

"The Commonwealth calls Doctah Enrique Gimenez-Jimeno."

Tall and haughty, Enrique Gimenez walked up to the stand with his nose stuck in the air. He sat down slowly, as if he was being placed on his throne. He glanced over at me and lifted his chin, looking down his nose at me.

After Dr. Charles left for Canada, Dr. Penza and Dr. Rankin, who were running the department, tried to fire Gimenez for his continued irresponsible behavior. Gimenez hired a lawyer and threatened to sue Penza, Rankin and the hospital. He claimed his dismissal was in retaliation for his testimony before the grand jury in February, even though the grand jury hearings were secret and no one except Gimenez, Flanagan and Mulligan knew what his testimony had been.

Was Gimenez the "inside" person that Mildred Jefferson had referred to when she testified before the City Council back in 1973? The evidence said that he was. Dr. Jefferson had said that the resident who had been secretly working with the right to life groups was afraid to come forward until he could secure another residency slot. It was too much of a coincidence that Enrique was publicly testifying against me now that he had been allowed to resign at the end of his second year, having found a third-year position at Cambridge Hospital.

Flanagan began his examination of Gimenez with the usual questions about his education, both in Mexico and in the United States.

"You completed two yeahs of residency in Mexico and have been in training in this country for fouah yeahs. Is that correct?"

"Yes. Two years in Mexico, four years here."

Newman Flanagan then produced Evonne's medical record and asked Gimenez to look it over.

"Can you tell us if you examined this patient and, if so, what your examination revealed?"

"I examined her on September 30, 1973, when she was admitted to the hospital for a saline abortion. My physical examination revealed that she was 24 weeks pregnant. I also heard a fetal heartbeat."

"Did you ask her when her last period was?"

"Yes. She said it was around the last week of May 1973. According to the last menstrual period, she would have been 18 weeks pregnant. Women"—he said the word with cold disdain —"sometimes give unreliable dates. I depended on my physical examination rather than what she told me."

"When was the next time you saw her?"

"In the operating room on October 3, 1973."

"Which operating room?"

"It was operating room number one."

No, it wasn't, I said to myself.

"Who was there when you came in?"

"Dr. Edelin was the surgeon. There was a scrub nurse, a circulating nurse and a surgical assistant. When I came into the operating room, Dr. Edelin was going through the abdomen in order to get into the abdominal cavity. I positioned myself across the table from Dr. Edelin, next to his assistant."

"How fah away were you from Doctah Edelin?"

"The width of the table. No more than two feet."

"What did he do?"

"He opened the abdominal cavity and exposed the lower portion of the uterus. He then made a low transverse incision into the uterus. As soon as he went into the uterine cavity, he put his left hand inside."

I looked down at my hand, recalling the size of the incision. Impossible! I glanced at Bill. He was writing furiously on his yellow legal pad.

"His entiah hand?" Flanagan asked.

He can't be serious, I thought. *Impossible! Impossible!*

"Yes."

No, I wanted to shout. *Impossible!*

"After that, he made a sweeping motion with his hand with a great deal of force in order to detach the placenta," said Enrique.

"How long did that take?"

"About a minute."

"What did he do next?"

"He left his hand in the uterus and looked at the clock on the wall in the operating room for about three minutes."

I wanted to leap to my feet and call him a vindictive, lazy, incompetent liar. I didn't think even he would stoop this low. This was how Flanagan and Enrique were going to get their revenge. Lies!

"During these three minutes, what did Doctah Edelin do?"

"Nothing. All he did was look at the clock."

Tick tock, tick tock. With that image now embedded in the jury's minds, McGuire banged his gavel.

"I'll have to ask you to stop for now. Court is adjourned. We will see you back here at 10:00 tomorrow morning."

Flanagan's best weapons were lies. My disbelief fed my anger. Bill gave me a look, but I was unable to speak.

The walk back to the Old City Hall was silent. I was lost in my thoughts, trying to find the words for what I was thinking. Only vulgarity came to mind. We settled around our usual corner table in the pub to wait for the transcript. The waitress did not even have to take an order—she just brought over a round of martinis. I gulped down my first, then slammed my fist on the table. Even Bill and Frank jumped.

"That lying bastard! He's making it all up! That son of a bitch…He doesn't even know which operating room we were in!"

Judi, who had joined the table just in time for my little outburst, pushed her martini over in front of me. She gently rubbed the back of my neck to calm me down.

"Don't worry, Ken. We'll get our turn," said Bill.

But I wasn't done yet. Shouting above the noisy pub, I pointed out each and every one of the lies in Gimenez's testimony, hands flailing about, talking through gritted teeth. I didn't even notice that I had stood up. Bill took notes on his yellow pad.

"How do you fight lies, Bill? How do you expose the bullshit when Flanagan and his jury already *want* to believe I'm guilty?"

After my second martini, I left. I couldn't sit around the pub anymore, waiting to read a transcript that would only further enrage me. I was tired, angry and just wanted to go home. Almost immediately, I fell asleep on the couch.

The next morning in court, Flanagan continued his questioning of Gimenez.

"Doctah, when we recessed yestahday, you described how the

defendant opened up the uterus of the patient and insehted his hand into it. Then you said he moved his hand in a circulah motion. What would be the effect of that motion on the baby?"

Baby?!

Bill was on his feet.

"I object to Mr. Flanagan's word. In addition, this witness testified before the grand jury that he has never performed a hysterotomy for the purpose of abortion, and that aside from this case, he has only observed one other abortion by hysterotomy. Therefore, he can't say what the effect of this motion was. Plus there is no evidence that this fetus was alive at the time of the operation."

"Haven't we had testimony that there was a fetal heartbeat?" McGuire inquired.

"Yes," Bill said. "But that was 72 hours prior to this procedure and before the repeated bloody taps."

"But," said McGuire, "there is no testimony that there was any change in the vital signs from that time up to the time of the hysterotomy."

Flanagan chimed in. "I think that the evidence is cleah that there was no change in the life of this pahticulah fetus from the time the fetal heartbeat was heard three days befoah."

"I'm going let him continue this line of questioning," McGuire ruled. I stared at all three of them—Flanagan, McGuire and Enrique.

"Doctah, what effect would this action have?"

"Give birth to a baby," Enrique said.

Bill jumped to his feet again and, in a frustrated tone, implored, "May it please the court, I move that answer be stricken as prejudicial and not in accordance with the facts." McGuire gave an annoyed sigh, as if he were appeasing a child. "I will strike the word 'baby.'" He then looked at Enrique. "'Give birth.' Is that what you said?"

"Yes," Enrique said.

Bill objected again. "I ask that the phrase 'give birth' be stricken, your honor."

"No. I'll allow that to stand."

This was absurd! That was not birth!

Flanagan continued, "Doctah, why do you use the phrase 'give birth'?"

"Because at that time, the baby is not dependent on the mother anymore and that is considered birth. It is on its own systems."

Just like Mildred Jefferson's revised definition. I was beginning to have my own conspiracy theories. On top of that, Enrique had used the word "baby" again.

"It's on its own systems," Flanagan repeated.

"And," Enrique added, "it is no longer dependant upon the mother because its circulation has been cut off."

"How was it cut off, Doctah?"

"By the detachment of the placenta. That is the only attachment to the mother."

"How was the placenta detached?"

"By the motion I described."

"What would you call what is inside the mothah?"

"It is a baby boy or a baby girl."

Bill slapped his hand down on the table in front of us. "I object, your honor, and ask that the answer be stricken!"

"I will allow it to stand." McGuire again sided with Flanagan.

I couldn't believe what I was hearing.

Flanagan walked over to the jurors' box. Enrique's eyes followed him. "Would you repeat that?" Flanagan said, smiling smugly.

"It is a baby boy or a baby girl," Gimenez said, looking straight at the jury.

"Do you have an opinion as to what will happen if the baby boy or baby girl remains in the mothah with no dependence upon her for three minutes or more?" Flanagan asked.

This wasn't happening. This just wasn't happening. Baby boy. Baby girl. Hand in uterus for three minutes. Looking at clocks. It was a nightmare.

Again, Bill rose to object.

Again, McGuire overruled. "Answer the question," he said to Enrique.

I knew Enrique's choice of words before they escaped his lips. He was predictable.

"The baby will die," he said.

"Do you have an opinion as to what caused the baby's death?" Flanagan asked.

Baby again. Flanagan had found a way to keep this image in the jury's heads.

"Lack of oxygen," Enrique answered. "Anoxia."

Flanagan pressed on. "Now, in this pahticulah case aftah he detached the placenta, you observed the defendant watching the clock on the wall, is that correct?"

No, it's not!

"Yes sir," said Enrique.

"Where was his hand while he watched the clock on a wall?"

"Inside of the uterus."

"Could you see his hand?"

"No. It was inside of the uterus."

"And how long a period of time did he watch the clock?"

"For at least three minutes."

"What did the defendant do next?"

"He delivered the baby and the placenta outside of the uterus."

Delivered. Baby.

"Do you have an opinion," Flanagan said, straightening that tie of his, "as to whethah or not the baby was alive at that time?"

Baby.

"I saw the baby and the placenta. The baby had no signs of life, such as breathing or movement."

Baby. Baby. This was their strategy, to humanize the fetus. McGuire refused to make them stop.

"Aftah you observed what took place, what did you do?"

"I didn't do anything. I left the room."

"Are you an abortionist?"

"I object, your honor!" Bill shouted.

McGuire finally ruled in our favor. "Strike that question."

Flanagan rephrased it. "Do you perfoahm abortions, Docktah?"

"No."

"That's all, Doctah. Thank you." With his chest and his chipmunk cheeks puffed, Flanagan returned to his table, grinning.

Now it was our turn. It is said that the only way to fight a lie is with the truth. We had to hope that the jury would see the truth.

A large blackboard was wheeled into the courtroom. Bill turned to McGuire.

"Your honor, I would like to have the witness go to the blackboard and draw for us the layout of the operating room area he is describing."

McGuire agreed. As Gimenez drew, Bill pointed to various parts of the floor plan as they appeared on the blackboard.

"So this is the scrub room. Now, which is the first operating room?

As I recall your testimony yesterday, you said the hysterotomy was done in the first operating room."

Enrique hesitated. "That's the best I can recall. It could have been the other one. I don't know."

Bill feigned surprise. "Didn't you say, with certainty, that it was the first operating room where the hysterotomy took place? Let me refresh your memory from yesterday's transcript." Bill made no eye contact with me as he walked over and picked it up from our table. He walked back over to the blackboard and began to read, "Mr. Flanagan asked you, 'Do you know which of these two operating rooms it was?' and you responded, 'It was operating room number one.'"

Defiantly, Enrique said, "Yes. It was the first one."

I fought the urge to explode.

"So is this operating room number one?" Bill asked, pointing to the drawing on the blackboard. "Can we call this number one where the operation took place?"

"It could have been," Enrique said.

"It could've been?" Bill repeated, stepping back.

"Yes. That's what I said." There was an arrogant edge to Enrique's voice.

Bill didn't falter. "You aren't sure?"

"It's either this one or that," he said, pointing to both operating rooms on his sketch. "I don't know. To the best of my recollection, it was number one."

"Well, let me come back to that a little later," Bill said. He paused for a moment, then changed directions.

"By the way, did you perform an operation that day, Dr. Gimenez?"

"I can't remember."

"You don't remember whether you had another operation?"

"No, but we always had operations so it is possible."

"But you do remember that you took pains to go see Dr. Edelin's operation."

"Yes."

"And you do remember enough to have described the operation to us in some detail."

"Yes."

"But you are unsure as to which operating room it was in. Is that what you're telling us now, Dr. Gimenez?"

"That's correct."

"You don't know whether it was operating room number one or two, do you?"

Flanagan stood up. "Your honah, please, I think he has answered that."

Bill persisted. "You are not sure whether it was the first or second operating room. Is that correct?"

"Yes," Enrique said, anger apparent in his sharp tone. "That is correct."

"Now, Dr. Gimenez, could you show us where the operating table was during this operation that you have described for us?"

Enrique held the chalk up to the board for a moment, but didn't draw. He moved his wrist a few times, then, turned to Bill. "The operating room was the same as any other operating room in BCH, so the table could have been here," he pointed to one spot, "or here." He pointed to another.

"Was there an anesthesiologist present?" Bill asked.

"There is always in anesthesiologist present," Enrique answered. He was shorter than Bill, but somehow managed to look down his nose at him.

"And where was he seated?"

"The anesthesiologist is always next to the patient's head."

"Then obviously the legs of the patient or the body of the patient extend down in this direction. Is that right?" Bill pointed.

Flanagan rose and asked, "Is that in both operating rooms? Are you talking about both rooms?"

Bill looked at Flanagan, "I am asking about the first one—the one he described to us yesterday." Turning back to Enrique, Bill continued, "Referring to OR number one, would you tell us where Dr. Edelin was standing?"

Flanagan again jumped to his feet. "Your honah, I think the testimony is faihly clear today that he testifies he doesn't know whethah it was the first or the second operating room."

Bill stood his ground. "He swore under oath yesterday, your honor, that it was OR number one."

Judge McGuire became Solomon. "I'm going to let him describe both rooms."

"Dr. Gimenez, assuming, for the moment, that this procedure was in the first operating room as you testified yesterday, kindly tell us where Dr. Edelin was standing when you say he performed this procedure."

"On the left-hand side of the patient."

"Would you indicate that on the blackboard?"

Enrique put an "E" on the board next to the operating table he had sketched.

"Now can you show us, Dr. Gimenez, where Dr. Edelin's assistant was standing?"

"In front of him, on the other side." He marked the blackboard with an "A."

"Do you know whether that assistant was a student or physician and whether it was male or female?"

"I can't recall," he said, lowering the chalk and looking at Bill, his eyes flashing. "How do I know?"

Bill remained calm. "Where did you stand?"

Enrique put a "G" right behind the assistant.

"Was there a scrub nurse and a circulating nurse present?"

"There always is."

"Who were they?"

"I don't remember."

"Can you describe what you saw?"

"I saw the baby and the placenta. The baby had no signs of life such as breathing or movement."

There it was again for the jury to hear. *Baby.* But whatever they thought it was—baby or fetus—Enrique had just testified that it was stillborn.

"Dr. Gimenez, let's assume that the operation took place in the second operating room, which, as you say today, it might have been. Please indicate where Dr. Edelin, his assistant and you were standing in relationship to the operating table."

Gimenez marked the blackboard with the letters again.

"Do you remember yesterday, Dr. Gimenez, that when you were asked the question, 'Do know which of the two operating rooms it was?' you responded, 'In the first one?'"

"Yes."

"Yesterday there was no question in your mind, was there Dr. Gimenez?"

"No."

"But there is some question today?"

"Yes. I was thinking about it last night and I want to be sure when I say something."

"You decided that you've got to be sure when you say something, is that correct?" Bill asked. I knew where he was going with this—he was dangling the noose.

"That's correct."

"You decided that yesterday?"

"No. Always." He raised his voice.

"Let me show you the operating room schedule, Dr. Gimenez, and ask you to look at it. Does it refresh your recollection as to which operating room you were in?"

Gimenez studied the schedule, and with a smile responded. "Yes. It was operating room number one. The first one."

"The operation done by Dr. Edelin was in operating room number one?" Bill asked.

"Yes. The first one."

"You are sure of that now, is that correct?"

"Yes."

Sensing the noose, Flanagan stood up and warned Enrique—he objected. "I move that ansah be stricken. The question was, does it refresh his memory on that pahticulah date."

Bill shot back. "And then he said, 'It does, number one.'"

Judge McGuire intervened. "Wait. Give me that paper." He looked it over, then addressed Enrique. "Does looking at the paper refresh your recollection as to which operating room it was? Just say yes or no."

Enrique, taking Flanagan's cue, backtracked a bit. "It doesn't refresh my recollection," he said. Then he added, "It says that it was number one so I'm happy about that."

McGuire immediately countered, "Strike that. I told you to answer yes or no and nothing else. Does this refresh your recollection, yes or no?"

Gimenez started to answer, "I feel..."

Flanagan jumped up, "Your honah, please..."

McGuire banged his gavel. "This court is in recess."

Just when we were getting ahead, McGuire once again stopped our counterattack, giving Flanagan and his star witness time to regroup during the recess.

Bill and I knew which operating room it was, but Gimenez was not sure. His memory of details was very selective in favor of Flanagan. How convenient.

After the 20-minute recess, Enrique Gimenez went back on the witness stand.

"Do you know which operating room you were in, Dr. Gimenez?"

"I am not sure."

McGuire interceded to help him. "Keeping in mind that your testimony yesterday was that you were in the first operating room, do you now want to change the statement you made yesterday, Dr. Gimenez?"

"Yes. I am not sure which it was."

Unfazed, Bill continued with his questions. "In any event, Dr. Gimenez, the operating table was in the same place no matter which room it was in. Is that correct?"

"Yes."

"No matter which operating room it was you stated that Dr. Edelin was standing on the patient's left, his assistant was across the table from him and you were standing behind the assistant. Is that correct?"

"Yes."

"Now, Dr. Gimenez, in your testimony, you referred to a clock in whichever operating room you were in. Would you kindly go to the blackboard and indicate the position of the clock?"

Gimenez didn't budge. "I don't know. I don't remember."

"You are unable to tell us where the clock was that Dr. Edelin was allegedly watching?"

"Not the exact place on the wall. I couldn't tell you because I'm not sure. I know there was a clock there."

"Let's refer to the drawing you made of operating room one. Can you tell us which wall the clocks were on?"

"It could have been on any of the walls."

Bill approached the sketch and pointed. "Was it on the wall opposite from the anesthesia equipment, the wall adjacent to the anesthesia equipment, the wall on the side where you say Dr. Edelin was standing, or on the wall near where you say you and the assistant were standing?"

"I don't know."

Bill then produced a photograph of one of the operating rooms and continued. "Let me show you this photograph, Dr. Gimenez. Is this a fair representation of operating room number one?"

"I can't be sure," he said.

"Do you recognize the door, for example, Dr. Gimenez?"

Determined not to get trapped again, he replied, "It looks like any other operating room."

"Let me show you this photograph," Bill said, producing a second photograph. "Do you recognize the clocks in this operating room, Dr. Gimenez?"

"I see two clocks here. Is this where the clock was?"

"I'm asking you, Dr. Gimenez," Bill said with a smile. Enrique did not smile back.

"I don't know. I can't tell you for sure."

"You don't recognize this as operating room number one?"

"Not with what I see here."

"Can you tell us anything that distinguishes operating room one from operating room two, Dr. Gimenez? Were the operating room tables the same? Were the lights the same? Were the doors in the same position?"

"I'm not sure," he said

Bill pressed on. "Did operating room one have two clocks like in this photograph, Dr. Gimenez?"

"I know there was a clock in each operating room."

"Do you remember whether there were one or two clocks?"

"I remember there was one in the operating room. I don't remember that there were two."

"Is your statement today that there was only one clock in each operating room?"

"No!" he shouted. "My statement is that I don't remember. I am not sure. I remember there was one clock. *That's* my statement! I don't know if there were two."

Ever calm, Bill said, "Let me show you a photograph of operating room two. Are you able to recognize this as operating room two?" He handed Enrique a second photo. "Look at the anesthesia machine. Look at the doors. Look at the position of the lights. Look at the operating table. Can you identify this as operating room number two?"

"It could be any operating room from any hospital," Enrique hissed.

Bill cut in a new direction. "Dr. Gimenez, you say you were on the gynecology service at City Hospital for 12 months. How many operations were you involved in during the time you spent on the gynecology service at City Hospital? Several? More than three?" There was a quiet chuckle from the back of the room. Bill ignored it. "More than 10? More than 20? Fifty? A hundred? More than—"

"It's possible," Enrique interrupted, "that it could have been a hundred. I. Don't. Know. I couldn't tell you for sure."

"And during all those operations, did you ever look at the clocks in either of these operating rooms?"

"Yes."

"But you can't tell us today where the clocks were located, is that correct?"

"I can't tell for sure."

Bill paused and flipped the pages in his yellow legal pad.

"Dr. Gimenez, you went into some detail about the position of Dr. Edelin's hand and that he permitted his hand to remain in the uterus of this patient, isn't that correct?"

"Yes."

"You described the period of time during which his hand was inside uterus as being at least three minutes, is that correct?"

"Yes."

"Did you time that on one of the clocks, Dr. Gimenez?" I wanted to smile.

"Excuse me?"

"Did you time the period of three minutes on one of the clocks on one of the walls in the operating rooms?"

"Yes. I was looking along with everybody else in the room at the clock."

"You were looking at the clock. Can you tell us which direction Dr. Edelin was looking in when he was looking at the clock?"

"I recall he was looking at the clock."

"Was he looking straight ahead at the clock?"

"I'm not sure."

"Was he looking to his right?"

"I'm not sure."

"Was he looking to his left, Dr. Gimenez?"

"I'm not sure." Enrique carefully pronounced every syllable as his entire body tensed up. Bill was getting under his skin.

"Was he turned around, looking behind him like this?" Bill asked, twisting his body around.

"I'm. Not. Sure," Enrique said through gritted teeth.

"Would you have remembered if Dr. Edelin had turned around looking behind him like this while he had his hand in the uterus for three minutes as you have described?"

"It is my recollection that he looked at the clock and he was still."

"But you don't recall how he looked at the clock, is that correct Dr. Gimenez?"

"No, I don't recall."

"Didn't you say that everyone in the room was looking at the clock?"

"Yes."

"Dr. Gimenez, was there anyone who was not looking at the clock? How about the operating room technician? The anesthesiologist? The circulating nurse? The scrub nurse? Dr. Edelin's assistant? How about you, Dr. Gimenez? Was there anyone among all those people in the operating room who was *not* looking at the clock?"

"I remember the whole group was looking at the clock."

"Your best recollection is that you all were looking at the clock."

"Yes."

"But you can't tell us which position Dr. Edelin was in when he was looking at the clocks, is that correct?"

"I am not sure."

His voice dripping with sarcasm, Bill said, "You vividly recall Dr. Edelin standing with his hand motionless in the uterus for at least three minutes, but you can't tell us anything else about the direction he was facing when he looked at the clock."

"That's correct." I was not amazed at Enrique's ability to lie without flinching. I knew he was a gifted liar—it was what made working with him so difficult. But now his lies were all swirling around me and I felt powerless to stop them. No one knew the real essence of our relationship. No one could see a reason for him to lie.

Bill Homans, however, was unraveling his house of fabrication one lie at a time, and Flanagan's fingerprints were all over the wrappings. This was not a trial for Flanagan, this was a crusade. Enrique Gimenez had a grudge against me and was all too willing to help Flanagan win.

Bill asked McGuire's permission to have Dr. Gimenez go back to the blackboard.

"Would you draw for the jury the exact shape and size of a 24-week pregnant uterus?"

Gimenez lifted the chalk to start his drawing, made a couple of attempts, then stopped.

"Does anyone have a measuring tape?" he asked.

"Yes, sir. In fact, I do have one with me." Bill reached into his coat pocket with a slight smile on his face and withdrew a tape measurer. He handed it to Enrique.

Enrique began to draw the inverted pear-shaped outline of the uterus, measured, made some adjustments, then stepped back from the board. Bill asked him to indicate the area on the uterus where I made the incision. He pointed to the narrowest part of the chalk sketch.

"Can you tell us how wide this area is where the incision was made?" Bill asked. "It is roughly eight to ten centimeters."

Bill took a step closer to Enrique so that they were standing nearly toe to toe in front of the blackboard.

"But you told us Dr. Edelin made an incision 10 centimeters in length, is that correct, Dr. Gimenez?"

"That's right."

"From one edge of the uterus to the other?"

"That's right."

"But aren't there some very large arteries in this area? Wouldn't cutting an incision that long cut into these large arteries? And wouldn't that cause a lot of bleeding? Didn't you previously testify that there was *not* a lot of bleeding during this operation?"

"That's correct."

A 10-centimeter incision would have been a surgical catastrophe. There was no way one that length could have been safely made in the lower portion of an 18- to 24- week pregnant uterus without causing severe bleeding and putting Evonne's life at risk. The incision I made was just big enough for me to get two fingers inside. His whole description was a lie.

"Isn't it true, Dr. Gimenez, that the description of the operation that you have given here is different from the testimony in front of the grand jury? Didn't you say in front of the grand jury that you could not remember what kind of incision Dr. Edelin made at the beginning of this operation?"

"That's true."

"Isn't it true, Dr. Gimenez, that during your grand jury testimony, when Mr. Flanagan asked the question, 'And what did Dr. Edelin do after he removed the placenta?' you answered, 'He removed the placenta and I think he looked at the clock.' Do you recall giving that answer?"

"Yes."

"Do you remember Mr. Flanagan pushing you and saying 'Not what you think? Do you recall whether he looked at the clock?' and you responded, 'Yes'?"

"I was not certain at that time and didn't say 'yes,' but then he pushed a little and I said the truth. I said 'yes.'"

"Who was the first person to bring up the issue of the clocks in the grand jury, Dr. Gimenez?"

"Mr. Flanagan."

Moving on to unravel another thread in the fabric of lies, Bill turned to the newfound definition of birth—upon which Flanagan was basing his entire case.

"Dr. Gimenez, in your earlier testimony you referred to what you termed 'birth' as a result of the separation of the placenta."

"That's right."

"When did you arrive at that that definition of birth?"

"I always believed that birth occurs when the baby is not dependent on the mother after the separation of the placenta."

Again, he sounded like Jefferson.

"Is there any source or textbook that will give us this same definition of birth?"

"Yes. There is a textbook entitled *Clinical Obstetrics and Gynecology.* It is authored by Dr. Stanley Asencio. It was published in September 1974—not too long ago."

Enrique had done his homework…but so had we. Bill picked up a copy of the book which, conveniently, we had on our table. "Is this the book you are referring to?"

"Yes. That is the book."

"Would you point out to me where there is a definition of 'birth' as including a process where the fetus is not removed or not separated from the body of the mother?"

"I cannot answer your question! It is misleading. You are defining birth in your question for me."

Bill rephrased it. "Would you show us where in this book there appears a definition of birth where the fetus has not been removed or expelled from the uterus of the mother?"

"I have to read it, Mr. Homans, and then I'll explain it."

"Before you explain," Bill said, "could you tell us whether such a definition appears in this book?"

McGuire interrupted. "Let him read it to himself." Bill stepped back.

After a few minutes of reading, Enrique looked at Bill, but avoided his eyes.

Bill approached him again. "Does the word 'birth' appear anywhere in the portion you have just read?"

Flanagan objected, but McGuire overruled.

"Would you tell us, Dr. Gimenez, whether the text you have in front of you contains a definition of birth?"

"As I said before, this is the source of the definition of birth."

Avoiding the question again. I hoped the jury could see that.

"It doesn't have a definition of birth, is that correct?" Bill asked.

"It doesn't say, 'This is the definition, this is birth.'"

"It doesn't use the word 'birth,' does it?"

Enrique hesitated. "No," he said.

"Doesn't this book describe an operation in which an abnormal fetus was removed from the uterus of the mother, still attached to the placenta, had a surgical procedure performed on it to correct the abnormality, then was placed back into the uterus which was filled with water and the incision closed?"

"Yes," Enrique said weakly.

"And after the fetus was placed back into the uterus and the incision sutured, the fetus remained alive for 45 hours thereafter. That was the operation described in this article, was it not?"

"Yes."

"This article does not involve a definition of birth as you describe it, does it?"

"This text describes the delivery of a baby outside of the mother—not birth, just the delivery!" Gimenez shot back.

"Dr. Gimenez, you're saying that when it was removed from the uterus of the mother and placed on the mother's abdomen, it was not born?"

"That's correct. It was not born."

Scratching his head, Bill asked, "Let me see if I understand you. You were telling us that this fetus, although removed from its mother's womb for the purposes of an operation, was not born because the placenta was still attached, and that therefore, the opposite must be true: if a fetus remains inside of the uterus but with the placenta detached, it becomes 'born.' Is that what you are telling us?"

Fetus outside, placenta attached: not born. Fetus inside, placenta detached: born.

Flanagan objected to Bill's question. McGuire sustained it.

Bill tried again, his voice becoming deeper and more forceful. "Is there anywhere in this book that describes being born as including the process where the fetus remains inside the uterus of its mother with the placenta having been detached?"

"No. It doesn't."

The definition of birth that Gimenez was using was ridiculous, but we had no way of knowing what kind of an impact this would have on the "jury of my peers." Did any of this matter? This was a homicide trial, not a scientific medical meeting. But what the jury believed about accepted medical practice was important. Words were important. Imagery was important.

Bill moved on to the next lie.

"Dr. Gimenez, you stated that you measured the height of this patient's uterus to be four finger breadths above the umbilicus, is that true?"

"Yes, that's what it was."

"From that measurement you judged that she was at least 24 weeks pregnant."

"Yes."

"Isn't it true that the height of woman's pregnant uterus can vary, depending upon her size, her weight, and whether or not she had a full bladder at the time the measurement was made?"

His definition of birth already exposed for the distortion that it was, he slumped in his chair a little and could not hold Bill's gaze.

"Yes. All of those things can affect the height of the uterus and the estimation of the length of a pregnancy in a particular woman."

"One final question, Dr. Gimenez. Isn't it true that you have pronounced views against abortion?"

"I object," Flanagan blurted out.

"What is your objection?" McGuire asked.

"I think we're going too fah afield heah on this pahticulah mattah," Flanagan said, conveniently forgetting his own questions regarding Enrique's views on abortion. "We have maintained all the time that this is not an abortion case, therefoah, his views about abortion are not material to this case."

Bill shot back. "And we, on the other hand, have maintained at all times that what Dr. Edelin did here *was* an abortion and carried out in accordance with not only medical, but legal standards as well. The witness' views on abortion are important concerning his credibility because he may be biased, just as Dr. Jefferson was biased."

"Then I would ask for a *voir dire*, your honah," Flanagan insisted. He didn't want Gimenez's views on abortion revealed in front of the jury.

McGuire agreed and had the jury taken out of the courtroom again.

Bill continued his questioning. "You feel strongly about the question of abortion, don't you, Dr. Gimenez?"

Enrique sat back in his chair and said, "I don't perform abortions, but if a patient wants an abortion, I refer her to a doctor who will. I think that a woman has the right, but I don't perform them. That's all."

It was not the answer anyone in the courtroom expected to hear. It cemented what I had known from the beginning. For Flanagan, this trial was about manslaughter. For me, it was about abortion. For Enrique Gimenez, it was payback.

"I have no further questions for this witness, your honor."

With that, Bill returned to our table and sat down next to me. Enrique was excused. After two days of testimony against me, his chance for revenge was over.

CHAPTER 26

FLANAGAN'S EXPERTS:
A NEIGHBOR, A DEMON AND A COUPLE OF RODENTS

———

"The Commonwealth would like to call Doctah Fred Mecklenburg."

Fred Mecklenburg was an obstetrician and gynecologist from Minneapolis, Minnesota. He was a member of Minnesota Citizens Concerned for Life, a statewide right to life organization. His wife, Marjorie, was president of that organization. She had been a long-time activist in the right to life movement and a founding member of the National Right to Life Committee. A Republican, she testified before the Republican Platform Committee to have a right to life plank inserted into the party's platform.

Was the entire right to life movement at Flanagan's disposal?

Mecklenburg was a bigger threat than Jefferson. He was a board-certified OB/GYN and had been brought here to criticize and discredit my competency as a physician. And criticize me he did. He stated that his review of Evonne Gilbert's medical record indicated that I should never have performed a hysterotomy. He testified that I put Evonne in danger by operating on her and that she must have lost a lot of blood during the surgery, a conclusion contrary to the testimony of even their star eyewitness, Enrique Gimenez. Mecklenburg used the word "baby" 18 times in his testimony and McGuire allowed his anti-choice, right to life rhetoric to stand throughout his testimony. He had credentials as both an obstetrician and a fanatic.

While he painted a picture of me as an incompetent doctor, he attacked my character and colored my soul with evil. The operation on Evonne, he said, was not like any other he had seen or performed.

He agreed, however, that the purpose of abortion was to terminate a pregnancy and the life of the fetus.

The advantage I had over Mecklenburg and all of Flanagan's experts was that I knew Evonne and they did not. I had looked into her eyes every day for nearly a week. I listened to her words. I studied her face. I learned about her life, her mother, her father and the dreams all three had for her future. I had agreed to help her by terminating her pregnancy. Mecklenburg made his judgment based on a medical record. I had a patient and he had a chart. He was dealing with pieces of paper, and I was dealing with pieces of a young woman's life. He sided with fetal rights and I, with the rights of this young woman—as guaranteed by the Supreme Court.

It was as simple and as complicated as that.

January 21, 1975

In the middle of Mecklenburg's testimony, the Supreme Court handed down a ruling in a jury selection discrimination case from Louisiana that could have had a direct impact on me. Billy Taylor, a black man in Louisiana, had been convicted of a crime by a jury selected from a panel on which there were no women, because Louisiana had a statute that declared that women could not be selected for jury service. The Supreme Court ruled that a jury must be selected from a representative cross-section of the community, guaranteed by the Sixth Amendment of the Constitution. Taylor's conviction was reversed and a new trial was ordered.

This was very much like my case! Armed with this new ruling, we again went to McGuire and moved to have the charges against me dismissed because of the gender bias against women in the Suffolk County jury pool. McGuire said that he would give both sides time to prepare their briefs on this motion and would schedule oral arguments at a later time. For now, he allowed Mecklenburg to continue his testimony.

Flanagan introduced the results of the medical examiner's autopsy of the fetus, which Mecklenburg described in detail. During Bill's cross-examination, Mecklenburg agreed that all of the organs described were too immature to sustain life.

The medical examiner found red blood cells inside the immature lungs of the fetus, indicating that there was blood in the amniotic fluid that had been inhaled into the tiny, immature air sacs. How did the blood get into the amniotic fluid? It got there because of the multiple bloody taps that resulted in the puncture of blood vessels. The medical examiners report confirmed the fear I had that there was hidden bleeding inside of Evonne. This complication and her insistence that the pregnancy be terminated meant that I had to proceed with the only option left—a hysterotomy. The report proved that my decision to proceed was not bad medicine. It was the best thing for Evonne. Even Mecklenburg had to admit that one of the indications for hysterotomy as a means for abortion was a failed saline infusion.

Finally, after being on the witness stand for nearly two days, Mecklenburg's testimony was over. He had served Flanagan's purpose. Not only had he managed to insert his views against abortion into the testimony, he had humanized the fetus by the repeated use of the words "baby" and "child." Though he had failed to portray me as an incompetent physician, he tried to make me look cruel and heartless.

———————

"The Commonwealth would like to call Doctah Denis Cavanagh."

Denis Cavanagh was Flanagan's academic heavyweight warrior. Enrique Gimenez was only an OB/GYN-in-training. Mecklenburg's credentials in the right to life movement were solid, but his academic credentials were meager. Cavanagh had both.

He had been chairman and professor of obstetrics and gynecology at St. Louis University in Missouri for eight years. He was an Irishman, born in Scotland and had all of the academic credentials and awards. He belonged to all the important academic professional organizations in both the United States and England. He had published over a hundred scientific articles in the medical literature and written two books.

He seemed eager to testify against me.

He, too, had examined Evonne's medical record and had estimated that she was between 24 and 28 weeks pregnant, challenging Holtrop's estimation that Evonne was, at most, 21 weeks.

During his testimony, Denis the Demon, as I nicknamed him, defined abortion as "the termination of pregnancy prior to 20 weeks," which was the definition used in most textbooks when referring to miscarriages. In defining birth, Denis the Demon said it was "a process of expulsion or extraction of the unborn child" that, in this case, began "at the time the incision was made in the uterus."

He continued. "The separation of the placenta would be a further stage in the birth process. A fetus *is* an unborn child. From the time of conception until the baby is delivered."

Child. Baby. Denis the Demon even used Flanagan's word: "suffocation." He said that my attempts to do a hysterotomy at this stage of gestation made a relatively easy operation difficult. It would be impossible, he claimed, for me to extract the placenta, the sac and the fetus intact. He also thought the patient had excessive blood loss and was going into shock.

Several times during his testimony, I wanted to leap to my feet and shout at him. Did he know Evonne? Did he care about her situation? Did he examine her? No! He was working from a hospital record!

Flanagan finished his direct examination of Denis the Demon, satisfied that he had discredited me as a doctor and my technique for performing the abortion. Then, Bill rose to conduct the cross-examination.

In the eight months that I had known him, Bill had been a good student of obstetrics, gynecology and abortion. He also fully understood the power of words to the right to life movement. Most lawyers that I had consulted before I hired Bill had seen my indictment and trial as part of the larger assault on abortion. A few had seen it purely as a criminal indictment of manslaughter against me. Only Bill Homans understood that this trial was about both and more. Although Brahmin Bill Homans had many personal flaws and weaknesses, he was brilliant in the courtroom. He relished the opportunity to cross-examine Denis Cavanagh.

He approached Denis the Demon in his slow and deliberate way, straightening his suit jacket over his large frame. His salt-and-pepper hair was neatly parted with a thick lock falling over his forehead. He was a giant of a lawyer, intimidating to opponents, protective of his clients. His weapon, the yellow legal pad with the curled corners, was in his hand at the ready.

He started out by acknowledging the fact that Denis the Demon had authored more than a hundred scientific articles in medical literature.

"Have you written any non-medical articles, Dr. Cavanagh?"

"Yes sir," Cavanagh said.

"Tell us about them. Did you ever write an article on the subject of abortion?"

"Yes. I don't recall the exact title of it, but it was an article that I wrote for the lay public."

"In that article, you took a position against abortion, didn't you?" Bill knew the answer.

"Yes I did."

"Haven't your thoughts and views on abortion been entered into the *Congressional Record*?"

"Yes. My views on abortion were placed in the *Congressional Record* by a member of Congress."

"Hasn't that member of Congress proposed a constitutional amendment to overturn *Roe v. Wade*?"

"Yes, sir, he has."

Through Bill's questioning, Cavanagh also admitted that since the ruling in *Roe v. Wade*, he had tried to get himself appointed "guardian *ad litem*" for all of the fetuses in Missouri in an attempt to prevent women from having legal abortions. In the struggle for women's right to control their own childbearing, Denis the Demon thought he knew what was best for the women of Missouri and the rest of the country.

Bill stood against the rail of the witness stand and leaned in close to Cavanagh.

"Do you know what today's date is, Dr. Cavanagh?"

"January 22, 1975."

The second anniversary of *Roe v. Wade*!

"Did your name appear this morning in a newspaper advertisement in the *St. Louis Democrat*?" Bill asked.

"I agreed to sign an ad sponsored by Missouri Doctors for Life that would appear today."

"Your name appears under a full page ad which reads, 'Abortion Degrades Women, Our Profession and the Country.'" We had a copy of the newspaper ad. Bill showed it to Denis the Demon.

"That is the statement I agreed to support."

Having exposed Denis the Demon's anti-choice views for the jury, Bill moved on. He questioned Cavanagh about his experience in performing abortions.

Denis the Demon was not one of those who objected to all abortions. He believed that abortions could be performed to protect women's lives, but said he only performed abortions for "medically" indicated reasons. He disagreed with the reasons Evonne wanted an abortion and why I was willing to perform it. He disagreed with us philosophically, piously, personally, professionally and paternalistically.

He believed he knew best what women and doctors should do, and he wanted his views written back into law.

"How many abortions have you engaged in directed toward terminating a pregnancy and terminating the prenatal existence of the fetus?"

Flanagan jumped to his feet. "I object to the question, your honah. There is no definition of abortion that includes the destruction of the life of the fetus."

Judge McGuire looked down from his bench at both of them.

"There seems to be some difficulty in defining terms here. We will continue to hear Dr. Cavanagh's testimony in the absence of the jury."

McGuire had the jury led out once again and we entered into another *voir dire*. My heart sank. So far, the jury had heard none of the testimony McGuire heard first.

"I will allow you to inquire of the doctor as to his understanding of the legal definition of abortion in *Roe v. Wade*. I will also allow you to explore any difference in that definition and the definition he gave."

Flanagan objected. "You're asking a non-legal witness to give an opinion as to what the legal definition is, your honah." To my surprise, McGuire overruled him.

Bill continued his questioning.

"Dr. Cavanagh, do you limit your definition of abortion to prior to 20 weeks of pregnancy?"

"Yes I do."

"You would not apply term 'abortion' to an elective termination of pregnancy after 20 weeks, is that correct?"

"That's what I'm saying, Mr. Homans."

"Have you ever used the word abortion as an operative procedure regardless of whether or not the procedure was done before or after 20 weeks?"

"If I did, it was inaccurate to do so," Cavanagh said. His voice suggested uncertainty. I sat up straighter in my seat.

"Didn't you write an article entitled 'Legalized Abortion: The Conscience Clause and Coercion,' which appeared in 1971 in a publication called *Hospital Progress*?"

Bill handed him the article. In it, Cavanagh had riled against abortion at any time during pregnancy, unless it was needed to save the life of the woman. He wrote that it did not matter when in a pregnancy it occurred, an abortion was an abortion.

"You are correct, Mr. Homans. You've refreshed my memory on that."

McGuire had heard enough. He ordered the jury to be brought back into the courtroom to hear Cavanagh's testimony under cross-examination by Bill. A rare ruling in our favor!

During the rest of his testimony in front of the jury, Cavanagh repeated his definition of abortion as the termination of pregnancy prior to the 20th week, but, he insisted, after the 20th week, termination of pregnancy was not an abortion, contrary to what he had written in the article.

"Dr. Cavanagh, does your definition ever include termination of the prenatal life of the fetus?"

"No, it never does."

What a contradiction!

In a victory of sorts, Bill got Denis the Demon to agree that according to the description of the fetus given by Gimenez, it was stillborn.

On the issue of the bloody taps, Cavanagh conceded our position when he said, "I think every time you get one, there is a bit more danger to the fetus. Nobody would want to infuse saline if they were getting repeated bloody taps."

After a few more questions, Dr. Denis Cavanagh was excused from the witness stand. The bias of his testimony had been firmly established and his attempt to portray me as incompetent and reckless had failed. If he had been able to inflict any damage, it appeared to be minimal.

January 23, 1975

The 13th day of my trial brought us to a crossroad. After the jury had been seated, Flanagan and Bill approached the judge's bench. Speaking in a low voice so that the jury would not hear, Flanagan said he wanted to introduce two photographs of the fetus that had been taken by Dr. George Curtis, the medical examiner. McGuire ordered the jury to be taken out of the courtroom, yet again, so that he could hear arguments from Flanagan and Bill as to the admissibility of the two photographs.

Flanagan began his argument.

"Your honah, I have two photographs of the deceased taken on

February 7, 1974 that the Commonwealth proposes to introduce. I hope to introduce evidence that this photograph is a fair representation of the deceased in this case as he appeahed on Octobah 3, 1973. The jury has heard us talking about a 24-week-old fetus and they heard Mr. Homans say in his opening that there will be no evidence that a baby was born. I think the photograph will give the jury evidence that there *was* a baby boy. Secondly, it would provide the visual image in connection to the testimony that will be given by the medical examinah, Doctah George Curtis."

Bill shot back. "These photographs should not be admitted. They were taken on February 7, 1974, four months after the abortion. The changes that have occurred over these four months are as a result of fixing of the fetus in formaldehyde as well as the general passage of time. These changes have been so significant that they give a distorted view of what the fetus looked like at the time of the abortion. The reason I said there was never a baby born, your honor, is because the fetus was never born and therefore could not be a baby or a person *within the meaning of the law.* We have argued that a subject of manslaughter must be a human being or person. To show that there is a human being or a person in existence, the Commonwealth does not need these photographs.

"Finally, these photographs are inflammatory. None of us—not me, not Mr. Flanagan, not you and certainly not the jury—is used to seeing photographs of this nature. Mr. Flanagan's purpose for introducing them is not as evidence but as a means to inflame the emotions of the jury. The issue before the court and the jury is whether this fetus—or, as Mr. Flanagan calls it, a 'baby'—was born or ever became a 'baby boy.' This case involves the issue of whether an abortion was done. There is nothing in the photographs to indicate that an abortion was done or, as the Commonwealth states, was not done properly. The impact on the jury would be so inflammatory as to overcome their probative value. Therefore, I oppose the introduction of these photographs."

McGuire didn't make a decision right away. He said he would later and told Flanagan to call his next witness.

"The Commonwealth calls Doctah George Curtis."

————

Flanagan had received information late in 1973 from a right to life group working inside the BCH mortuary that there was a second-trimester fetus in the morgue which had resulted from an abortion. In February of 1974, Flanagan asked Dr. Curtis, the medical examiner of Suffolk County, to take jurisdiction over it.

This was the kind of abortion that Flanagan and the national right to life organizations were looking for. Flanagan's advisors had told him that an abortion by hysterotomy would likely produce a live fetus— then the facts could be twisted, making that fetus the subject of homicide. Although they found similar cases in other cities around the country, it was only in Boston where they were able to get an indictment.

As Dr. George Curtis, the slight, white-haired, bespeckled coroner, took the stand, McGuire tried to halt the battle of words before it began.

"Before Dr. Curtis testifies, let's get an agreement on what word or words you want him to use in his description."

"How about 'the fetus' or 'the subject'?" Bill suggested.

"How about 'the deceased'?" Joe Mulligan said.

"The autopsy report," Frank Susman said, "uses 'fetus.'"

"If you're going to be that way, how about 'baby boy'?" Flanagan fired back.

Finally, McGuire rapped his gavel. "I instruct Dr. Curtis to use the word 'subject.'"

The testimony of Dr. George Curtis began.

"Doctah Curtis," Flanagan said, "please tell us what you found in the City Hospital Morgue when I asked you to take jurisdiction ovah the subject."

"I found the subject fixed in a 10 percent formalin solution. That is a solution used to preserve tissue."

Throughout his questioning, George Curtis described his findings from when he performed the autopsy on the fetus. The fetus had extremely immature organs which would not have been able to sustain life. The lungs, Curtis said, were firm and contained little, if any, air. They were solid in consistency. When looked at under a microscope, he saw that the immature air sacs were collapsed for the most part, with some of them partially collapsed and a few expanded. Then he said, "Most of them were empty, but a few contained red blood cells. That indicates that there was blood present in the amniotic fluid. When I placed the lungs in a container of water, they sank to the bottom. If the lungs had been expanded with air, they would have floated."

"As a result of your examination, did you form an opinion as to whethah the subject had any respiratory activity?" Flanagan asked.

"It did have respiratory activity."

"What was your opinion as to the gestational age of this subject?"

"Twenty-three or twenty-four weeks."

"Doctah Curtis, do you have an opinion as to the cause of death of this pahticulah fetus?"

"Death was due to anoxia."

"I have no furthah questions for this witness." Flanagan returned to his table.

To make matters worse, Bill was not feeling well. The intensity of the trial, his preparation and our daily meetings were taking their toll, while the tensions of his personal life ate away at him. He tried to ease the pain with alcohol, but that only made things worse. The lines in his face had become deeper, his eyes redder and sadder, and his posture was even more stooped. He asked McGuire's permission to cross-examine Dr. Curtis from his seat. It was granted and he began.

"Dr. Curtis, when you describe the organs as being 'fetal organs,' that means that they are not fully developed organs, is that correct?"

"That is correct."

"Would you agree that the lungs were not fully developed?"

"No, they were not fully developed."

"Are you aware of the phenomenon known as fetal respiration?"

With that, Flanagan jumped to his feet. "I object to the word 'phenomenon.' I think life itself is a *phenomenon*."

"I will withdraw the word 'phenomenon,'" Bill said. He paused and looked up at McGuire. "I'm trying to think of a better word, your honor."

Sneering, Flanagan said, "Why don't you call it a miracle?"

"I object and ask that Mr. Flanagan's speech be stricken," Bill said.

"Strike the miracle," McGuire ruled. There was a chuckle in the back of the courtroom. "Continue, Dr. Curtis."

"Fetal respiration involves the inspiration and exhalation of amniotic fluid into the lungs of a fetus while it is inside of the uterus."

"Isn't it true that as a result of this activity, some of the lung sacs may become distended?"

"That is correct," Dr. Curtis responded.

"In order for the lungs to be fully expanded with air, there must be several breaths taken outside of the uterus, is that correct?"

"That is correct."

Bill struggled to his feet and slowly walked over to the witness stand. "Let me show you the pictures you took of the lungs. Is there anywhere in the pictures that show that the air sacs are fully expanded with air, Dr. Curtis?"

"Not in this photograph."

"Isn't it true that the distention you observed in some of the lung sacs was as a result of the inspiration of amniotic fluid rather than air?"

"Yes, that is correct."

"When you felt the lung tissue, it had a solid consistency, didn't it?"

"Yes, it did."

"And when you placed the lung tissue into water it sank to the bottom of the container didn't it?"

"Yes, it did."

"And what does that indicate to you, Dr. Curtis?"

"That they were not fully expanded with air."

"You also described blood in the alveoli, didn't you, Dr. Curtis?"

"Yes, I saw blood in some of the alveoli."

"And how would that blood get into the alveoli?"

"There must have been blood in the amniotic fluid."

"Do you have an opinion as to how this blood may have gotten into the amniotic fluid?"

"My opinion is that the blood would come from the passing of the needle through the placenta and its blood vessels during the multiple attempts at amniocentesis."

Every day of the trial, watching Bill in action reaffirmed that I had made the right decision in hiring him. Sick, even having difficulty standing, he was still sharp. He took this opportunity to begin to set up the case to be presented by our expert witness.

"Dr. Curtis, as a result of a court order, did you send microscopic slides of the fetal lungs to California?"

"I did. I sent the slides to Dr. Kurt Benirschke."

"Who is Dr. Kurt Benirschke?"

"He is a specialist in fetal and neonatal pathology."

"Dr. Curtis, I would like to turn your attention to the weight of the fetus. In the pathology report filled out shortly after the operation in October 1973, the pathologist recorded a fetal weight of 600 grams, didn't he?"

"Yes, sir."

"Do you have an opinion of the gestational age of a fetus that weighs 600 grams?"

"That would be approximately 21 or 22 weeks."

"When you weighed the fetus some four months later, you got a weight of 700 grams, didn't you?"

"Yes, I did."

"Do you have an opinion as to which of these two weights should be the most accurate?"

"Yes. The weight taken just after the removal from the uterus should be the most accurate weight. The difference in these two weights could be that the scales were not the same, that one of scales was inaccurate. If they were both calibrated correctly, then the weight taken immediately after the fetus was delivered surgically would be the most accurate."

"Just two more questions, Dr. Curtis. You are not a member of Doctors for Life, or any other right to life organization, are you?"

"No, I am not."

"You call them as you see them, don't you, Dr. Curtis?"

"That is cor—"

"Wait a minute! I object." Flanagan was on his feet. "I hope every witness 'calls them as they see them.' I ask that the statement be stricken."

"It is stricken," McGuire said.

Bill came back to our table and eased himself into his chair. He flipped through the pages of his yellow legal pad, leaned back in the hard oak chair and said, "I have nothing further for this witness."

Flanagan stood up. "Your honah, I would now like to introduce the photographs of the fetus as evidence and have them viewed by the jury."

I held my breath, dreading McGuire's ruling.

"I have decided that I will let the jury see only one of the photographs," McGuire said. He motioned to the court clerk, Paul O'Leary, who handed McGuire an envelope containing the two photographs. McGuire picked one out, placed it in a folder and instructed the clerk to give it to the foreman, Vincent Shea.

"Examine this photograph, and when you are through, pass it along to the juror next to you."

For the next 10 minutes, we watched the faces of the jurors as they looked at the photograph. McGuire's "compromise" was really a victory for Flanagan. All it would take was one photo to humanize the fetus. If it looked like a baby, then the jury would think of it as a baby. We watched their faces as the folder containing the photograph was passed from juror to juror. No expressions changed, but we could not read their minds. When the last juror finished looking at the photograph, the clerk retrieved it and kept it at his desk.

"Your honah, the Commonwealth would like to call Doctah Norman L. Vernig."

———

Norman Vernig, from St. Paul, Minnesota, was a neonatologist—a specialist who takes care of babies during the first month of their lives, usually in the Intensive Care Unit. A little man with mouse-like features, he was an assistant professor of pediatrics at the University of Minnesota Medical School. Flanagan had sent him copies of the fetal autopsy report and Evonne's medical record.

After reviewing the autopsy report, Vernig said, "I would place the baby's gestational age at 24 weeks."

Baby. Throughout his testimony, Vernig the Vermin, as I nicknamed him, repeatedly used the word, searing it into the jury's minds if it wasn't there already.

It was Friday afternoon, the end of a long week. McGuire halted questioning for the day and told us he wanted to hear our argument to dismiss the case based on the Supreme Court's ruling in *Taylor v. Louisiana* on Monday. After that, the examination of Vernig the Vermin would resume.

Court was adjourned for the weekend, but there would be no time off for me.

After I saw my remaining prenatal patients on Saturday morning, Frank Susman and I flew to Washington where I gave a speech to a large gathering of pro-choice activists who had come to the nation's capital to strategize on ways to keep *Roe v. Wade* intact and protected against the onslaught of anti-choice efforts to overturn it. My trial was central to the right to life efforts to intimidate doctors and others who provided abortions. The hotel ballroom where I spoke was full, and at the conclusion of my speech, I received a standing ovation and thousands of dollars in donations to help with my legal fees. One of the television reporters there said the pro-choice movement had found a new hero. I was flattered, but it was not how I saw myself. I was a defendant on trial for manslaughter.

Frank and I returned to Boston on Sunday and went straight to Bill's office, where they worked on our motion to dismiss the charges against me. This time, we had the Supreme Court on our side. McGuire would be forced to rule in our favor.

January 27, 1975

After we had all gathered in Room 906, the jury was brought in. McGuire spoke to them from his perch.

"A discussion concerning a decision in another court will be discussed by counsel with me this morning. I brought you down so that you would know that you've got about an hour to wait, so you may be excused and go back to the jury room." With that, they were escorted out of the courtroom.

The decision by the Supreme Court in *Taylor v. Louisiana* was taylor-made for us. We had already argued that the systematic exclusion of women from the jury pool in Suffolk County was illegal. The Supreme Court had just ruled the same thing. Therefore, the jury sitting in judgment of me was illegal, as was the grand jury that had handed down the indictment.

This time, Frank was going to argue the motion for us. He had become a good, trusted adviser and friend. He had a unique midwestern view of life and freedom. The argument he made was simple. The Sixth Amendment of the Constitution says that the accused has the right to a speedy and public trial by an impartial jury in the state and district where the alleged crime was committed. In case after case after case brought in the 20th century involving the composition of juries, the United States Supreme Court had been consistent in its rulings: "A state cannot, consistent with due process, subject a defendant to indictment or trial by a jury that has been selected in an arbitrary and discriminatory manner. This is in violation of the Constitution and laws of The United States of America."

Up until now, much of the legal attention on jury composition focused on discrimination against blacks. In the *Taylor* decision, the United States Supreme Court said that women should have the same status to be on juries that had been gained by blacks. My trial was a carbon copy of the case in Louisiana.

By the census, women constituted 53 percent of the population in Suffolk County, but only 25 percent of the jury pool. There were only three women out of 16 jurors on my jury—18 percent!

The Supreme Court said that "the purpose of the jury is to guard against the exercise of arbitrary power, to make available the common sense and judgment of the community as a hedge against the overzealous or mistaken prosecution. This cannot be achieved if the jury pool is made up of only special segments of the population or if large distinctive groups are excluded from the pool." The jury system was supposed to protect others and me from the Newman Flanagans in our country.

"The system in Suffolk County was one in which the grand jury and the jury sitting here excluded a fair cross-section of the community," Frank argued. "The system excluded a recognizable class, a class defined as being at least 50 percent of the population, but a class that came to represent only 25 percent of the total jury pool. The system can't discriminate on the basis of race *or* gender.

"We believe that these proceedings must be terminated immediately and the indictment dismissed as required by the rights, privileges and benefits guaranteed Dr. Edelin by the United States Constitution."

In his rebuttal, Flanagan brought in another lawyer who was more of an expert on the US Constitution than the gang sitting at his table.

The expert was weak, because their position was weak. He began by pointing out that prior to 1950, no women sat on juries in Suffolk County. Since that time, he claimed, there had been a steady increase.

This was supposed to justify discrimination? Improvement?

Then, in possibly the most ridiculous argument I've ever heard, he said that discrimination against blacks could not be compared with discrimination against women. He went on to say that the kind of discrimination found in the Suffolk County jury pool was not the same as that in the *Taylor* case.

Ironically enough, his concluding sentence was, in fact, the very essence of our defense: "We are living in shifting times when ideas are changing regarding the respective roles of the sexes."

After listening to both arguments, McGuire declared, "We'll continue with the trial pending my decision on the motion to dismiss the case."

What was there to decide? How could we make it any clearer that this trial was unconstitutional in so many ways?

The jury was brought back in and Vernig the Vermin retook the stand. Flanagan continued his direct examination.

"You've examined the recohd of this patient. If the placenta was immediately detached once the uterus was opened, would the 'subject'"—Flanagan paused briefly, almost mocking the word—"be alive?"

"Yes, the baby would be alive."

Baby. He did it again.

"If the 'subject'"—pause—"was removed immediately from the womb, would it still be alive?"

"Yes, it would."

"I have no furthah questions," Flanagan said.

I looked over at Bill. Vernig's answer was a slight change in direction for Flanagan. Up until now, he had argued that even if the fetus died inside of the womb, I was still guilty of manslaughter because it had been "born" once the placenta was separated. Now Flanagan was going down another path—trying to say that the fetus was alive when it was removed from the uterus, and allowed to die outside of the womb. He was now giving the jury a second choice for conviction. Either this or that—pick one!

Bill, feeling better and stronger than he had the week before, rose and walked around the wooden table. With his well-worn yellow legal pad in hand, he approached the witness.

"Do you have an opinion as to what percentage of babies weighing 700 grams, at 24 weeks gestational age, would survive?"

"There are no exact figures that I can find."

"So there are no exact figures." Then, in an off-handed way, Bill asked, "By the way, how many ounces is 700 grams?"

"It would be roughly 23 or 24 ounces."

The bait taken, Bill sprung the trap on Vernig the Vermin.

"Dr. Vernig, do you recall speaking in St. Cloud, Minnesota, on April 15th of last year at a dinner honoring a Congressman Zworch?"

He hesitated, obviously surprised. "I…recall speaking at a dinner in St. Cloud, but I'm not sure when it was."

"Do you recall saying, quote, 'Realistically, a baby born less than 28 ounces will have about a 99 percent chance of dying'?"

Flanagan jumped to his feet. "I object, Your Honah. We're talking about now, not then."

McGuire overruled his objection.

"Let me repeat the question. Do you recall saying, quote, 'Realistically, a baby born less than 28 ounces will have about 99 percent chance of dying, and if that baby survives, there certainly is a significant chance for permanent neurological defect,' unquote?"

"First of all," Vernig responded nervously, "as far as I know, there was no actual record made of my talk at that time."

Then, in a dramatic move that Frank had suggested, I reached into my briefcase and grabbed a tape cassette. I placed it on the table in clear view of Vernig the Vermin and quietly drummed my fingers on it. When his gaze met mine, he quickly looked away.

A network of pro-choice supporters had developed around the country and were helping us. They sent us information about each of Flanagan's out-of-town experts, so we could know their bias and anti-choice connections. The Vermin's speech *had* been recorded and we not only had a copy, but also a typed transcript.

"I didn't say exactly that," Vernig squeaked, his eyes constantly darting back to the tape.

Bill handed him a typed copy of his speech. "Dr. Vernig, examine this transcript and especially these two pages that I'm pointing to."

His mouse-like face whitened. I imagined whiskers twitching and had to bite my lip to keep from snickering.

"Does that refresh your recollection as to what you said that night, Dr. Vernig?" Bill asked politely.

"Yes, it does."

"Didn't you say that a baby born less than 28 ounces will have about a 99 percent chance of dying and if it does survive, it certainly has a significant chance of permanent neurological defect?"

"Yes, I did," he said quietly.

Not satisfied with the first mousetrap, Bill sprang another.

"Dr. Vernig, you defined neonatology, which is your specialty, as the practice of pediatrics that cares for babies during the first 28 days of life, is that correct?"

"That is correct," he answered. He was still visibly shaken by the revelation that we had his speech.

"Can you tell us if any baby you have ever cared for that weighed less than 800 grams survived through the 28th day?"

"No sir, I cannot."

"Based upon your examination of the autopsy report, are you able to tell us with medical certainty that this fetus was 24 weeks?"

"It was"—his eyes darted back to the tape—"*approximately* 24 weeks."

"I have no further questions for this witness."

With that, Vernig the Vermin was excused from the witness stand. The mouse had been captured and destroyed.

He walked over to Flanagan and said something to him in a low voice. Flanagan stood up and addressed Judge McGuire. "Your honah, Doctah Vernig still has several hours befoah his flight back to Minnesota. He would like to stay in the courtroom, if that is possible."

The wrinkles in McGuire's forehead deepened. He looked confused.

"Mr. Homans, do you object to that?"

It was Bill's turn to look confused. "I have no objection to the prior witness being here," he said.

"Very well. He may resume the stand."

"No," Bill said. "He's all through."

"He's just waiting for an hour," Flanagan piped up.

Bill nodded. "I just said no objection as far as—"

"All right," McGuire said impatiently. "He's excused then."

"No, no," said Flanagan. "He's in the courtroom, your honah. He would like to stay."

As if a light bulb had clicked on over his head, McGuire finally understood. "Oh. Okay. He can stay."

The intensity of the first three long weeks of the trial was taking its toll on everyone. I hoped it had not befuddled Judge McGuire's mind too much. Already his rulings had not been favorable for us and I needed him to have a clear head when he made the decision on our new motion to dismiss the charges.

After the confusion with Vernig the Vermin was settled, Flanagan said, "I would like call Doctah William O'Connell to the stand."

———

O'Connell was sworn in.

"Please state your name."

"Dr. William T. O'Connell."

"Where do you live, Doctah O'Connell?"

"In West Roxbury, next door to you."

Laughter came from the spectators behind me. I could not believe what I was hearing. Was he joking? Had Flanagan really called his next-door neighbor as a witness? First Denis the Demon, then Vernig the Vermin and now, Newman's Neighbor?

Newman's Neighbor gave a brief description of his education, background and experience as an obstetrician and gynecologist. His practice was limited mainly to the Catholic hospitals in Boston, and he taught at several Catholic colleges in the area. Flanagan asked if he had examined Evonne's medical record. He had.

"And did you come to a conclusion as to how far pregnant she was?"

"Twenty-four weeks." Newman's Neighbor went on to say that the technique I used in performing the hysterotomy was dangerous and that I put Evonne at risk. He also said that once the uterus was cut into, the process of birth had begun. Flanagan then pursued his new line of questioning, broadening the jury's options for conviction.

"At the time the placenta was detached, do you think the 'subject' was alive?"

"Yes."

"If it was removed immediately from the uterus, would this 'subject' have continued to live?"

"Yes, it would have continued to live."

"I object," Bill interrupted. "There is no evidence that the fetus was alive when it was removed from the uterus of the woman. Mr. Flanagan's own witnesses said that the fetus was not alive when it was removed. The testimony of Drs. Gimenez and Jefferson said this was a stillbirth. The testimony of the medical examiner is, at best, equivocal."

McGuire overruled Bill.

Newman's Neighbor repeated himself, saying that, in his opinion, the fetus would still be alive after it had been removed from the uterus, and not only that, it would continue to live. He did, however, admit that the survival of a fetus so small is rare.

Flanagan nodded to Bill and said, "Your witness."

Bill approached the witness stand and faced the gray-haired, rosy-cheeked, pale-skinned neighbor of Newman Flanagan. They immediately began a banter regarding the definitions of birth and stillbirth, but Bill knew how to direct the questions where he wanted them to go.

"Birth is not complete if the fetus is still within the uterus, is it, Dr. O'Connell?"

"No, it is not."

"The purpose of abortion, as you understand it, is not to deliver a liveborn fetus, is it?"

"My understanding of abortion is that it does not contemplate the delivery of a liveborn fetus." At least Newman's Neighbor agreed with our understanding of the outcome of an abortion.

Bill then went on to show O'Connell's bias.

"Dr. O'Connell, are you a member of an organization called the Value of Life Committee?"

"Yes I am."

"Are you presently, or have you been, the treasurer of that organization?"

"I am still the treasurer."

"Isn't the president of that organization Dr. Mildred Jefferson?"

"She was president up until three or four months ago. Dr. Joseph Stanton is now the president."

The same Joseph Stanton who, along with Mildred Jefferson, gave testimony in front of the Boston City Council and began the process that resulted in my indictment.

"Doesn't the Value of Life Committee oppose abortion?" Bill asked.

"Yes we do."

"Weren't you a member of a group that submitted an amicus brief against *Roe v. Wade* to the US Supreme Court?"

"Yes I was."

"Have you ever performed abortions by hysterotomy, Dr. O'Connell?"

"No I haven't."

"Have you ever been present at a hysterotomy done for abortion?"

"No."

"So how can you say that Dr. Edelin's technique was poor medical practice?"

"I object, your honah!" Flanagan shouted. Maddeningly, McGuire upheld Flanagan's objection and refused to make Newman's Neighbor justify his criticism of my surgical technique. Bill went in a different direction.

"Did you sign a letter to the president of the United States requesting a constitutional amendment to overturn the Supreme Court decision in *Roe v. Wade*?"

"Yes," he said defiantly.

In disgust, Bill turned and walked away. "I have no further questions for this witness."

Flanagan approached McGuire.

"Your honah, I would like to bring in, for the jury, babies who have been born weighing less than 700 grams and lived."

What?! I almost leapt to my feet, but Bill beat me to it, objecting to this ridiculous request. McGuire had the jury taken out of the courtroom so he could hear our arguments against this dramatic request.

Bill began by citing *Roe v. Wade*. Because of *Roe*, and because Massachusetts had not enacted any laws to restrict that decision, viability was not an issue in this case. "Secondly," Bill went on, "testimony of Mr. Flanagan's own witness, Dr. Vernig, stated that the universal opinion is that a 700 gram fetus has little or no chance of survival. Mr. Flanagan is attempting to raise possibilities rather than probabilities. Finally, your honor, this kind of testimony is being offered to inflame the jury. The babies that he is proposing to bring in will not be able to testify about their gestational age. They can't testify as to their birth weight. They can't testify how the physician examined their mother's abdomen to determine their gestational age just before delivery. The babies can't do any of these things. For all of these reasons, your honor, I suggest that the evidence is not admissible."

McGuire leaned forward and rested his arms on his bench. "This is evidence of similar, but unrelated events. I will sustain the objection and not allow it."

I exhaled. With all of McGuire's absurd rulings, I did not put it past him to allow this sideshow. Visibly annoyed, Flanagan called his next expert witness.

"I would like to call Joseph Kennedy to the stand."

Dr. Joe Kennedy was a neonatologist and the director of the Newborn Nursery at St. Margaret's Hospital. He was an associate professor of pediatrics at Tufts University Medical School and had all the right credentials. He was also one of the "visits" at BCH.

Flanagan asked him if he, after reviewing the autopsy report of the fetus, had come to a conclusion as to its gestational age. He said that he surmised that it was "about" 24 weeks. He also testified that the fetus died secondary to asphyxia.

"Doctah, what is the purpose of the intensive care nursery at City Hospital?"

"To care for sick, small and premature infants."

"Does this include 'subjects' 24 weeks of age?" Flanagan asked. I bristled. I hated his snide tone.

"Yes, it does."

"Do you believe that this 'subject' was alive at the commencement of the hysterotomy?"

"Yes, it was."

"Do you have an opinion as to whethah the 'subject' was alive once the placenta was separated?"

"Yes. It was."

"Finally, do you have an opinion whether the subject would still be alive if it was immediately removed from the uterus?"

"Yes. It would be."

There was no three-minute wait, but we hadn't had our chance to state that yet. In anticipation of our defense, Flanagan was shoring up his second theory of the case for the jury to consider. When I claimed that I had, indeed, immediately removed the fetus from the uterus, then according to Flanagan's latest expert witnesses, the fetus must have been alive. By not ordering the fetus to be taken to the intensive care nursery, I was guilty of manslaughter. Or, at least, that was one of the choices he was giving the jury.

"Doctah Kennedy, what is the generally accepted definition of the term 'viability'?"

"A viable infant is one that is at the stage of development when he has a chance to live."

"Do you believe that this pahticulah 'subject' was viable?"

"I believe that the subject was viable and that he had a chance for life."

"What condition would the 'subject' be in?"

"The subject would have been in the state of very severe anoxia and asphyxia. I can't predict what would happen other than that the subject would be severely ill as a result of anoxia and asphyxia."

"Your witness, Mr. Homans." With a dramatic gesture and a grin at his Irish gang, Flanagan sat back down at his table.

Bill rose, picking up his beat-up yellow pad and several notes I had written to him during Kennedy's testimony. He approached the witness stand. I was not feeling very confident. All of these technical terms had to be confusing to the jury. They were not doctors—anoxia, hypoxia, asphyxia, alveoli, gestational age, viability, fetus, amniotic fluid and on and on and on. I recalled the frustration of my first year of medical school. All the new words were difficult to understand and remember back then. How could I expect members of a jury—some of whom had barely completed high school—to understand these words and the implications behind them? Were they confused? Were they tuning out? Were they bored?

Bill picked up where Flanagan left off.

"So it is your opinion that the subject was suffering from anoxia or asphyxia, is that correct, Dr. Kennedy?"

"That is correct."

"But you are unable to tell us whether or not the subject in question was alive or dead as a result of the anoxia or asphyxia."

"That is correct."

"Dr. Kennedy, you said that viability is the condition of an infant when it's at a stage of development where it has a chance to live outside of the womb."

"I would change my definition slightly to say that it has a chance to live and survive for a prolonged period of time."

"For a prolonged period of time," Bill repeated with his eyebrows raised. "So we can modify your definition that viability is a condition of an infant when it is at a stage of development where it has a *chance* to live for a 'prolonged period of time.'"

"Yes."

"Are you aware of any fetus of 24 weeks surviving for a 'prolonged period of time' at City Hospital in the newborn nursery?"

"No."

"Are you aware of any babies of 24 weeks' gestation surviving for a 'prolonged period of time' at St. Margaret's Hospital?"

"No, I am not."

In all of his years of practice, and from his experiences at both BCH and St. Margaret's Hospitals, he had never seen a 24-week fetus or baby survive.

"Coming back to the issue of viability, Dr. Kennedy, you said there was a 'chance' of survival for a prolonged period of time. When you use the word 'chance,' you mean less than a probability, don't you?"

"Yes."

"A chance," Bill repeated. "And that chance would be very small, wouldn't it?"

"Yes, that chance would be very small."

"I have no further questions for this witness."

Red-faced and clearly annoyed, Flanagan bellowed, "The Commonwealth calls John F. Ward to the stand."

Dr. John Ward was an assistant clinical professor of pathology at the University of Pittsburgh Medical School. Like Vernig the Vermin, he was a little man, with very pale skin, thick glasses and the features of a rodent. Flanagan used him as a consultant throughout his investigation of his case against me. He even went to Pittsburgh to bring Ward a special set of microscopic slides. I nicknamed this latest witness Ward the Weasel.

"Doctah Ward, would this 'subject' gain or lose weight after being in formaldehyde for four months?"

"It would lose weight."

Absurd! Ward the Weasel was saying that at the time of the abortion, the fetus weighed even more than 700 grams! From this ridiculous assertion, he went on to the next.

"Doctah, did you fohm an opinion as to the age of this fetus?"

"On the basis of my calculations, the fetus was approximately six and a half months gestation—26 weeks."

Ward the Weasel had taken the measurements to their most extreme possibility. Bill objected to his testimony and wanted to challenge his credentials. He was not an expert in the field of estimating fetal gestational age and the tables he used to come to his conclusions were outdated and incorrect. Ward the Weasel and Flanagan, driven by fanaticism, were saying the most outlandish things and posing them as scientific facts.

"Your honor, this witness is not qualified to testify on these matters," Bill said.

"Would you like to cross-examine him on his qualifications?" McGuire asked.

"Yes, I would."

"Very well. We will excuse the jury."

After the jury had left the courtroom, yet again, Bill approached the witness. Ward the Weasel sat meekly in the stand.

"Have you ever conducted any experiments for the purpose of determining loss or gain of weight as a result of fixation in formaldehyde?"

"No."

"Have you ever observed a study being performed for that purpose?"

"No."

"What publications have you used to support your contention that tissue loses weight as a result of formaldehyde fixation?" Bill asked.

Pointing to a book on Flanagan's table, he said, "I used that green-covered textbook on the table over there. I think the author's name is Cheswick."

Flanagan looked at the cover of the book in front of him and corrected his expert.

"Uh…the authah is Ludwig, your honah."

The Weasel didn't even know the name of the author of the book he was referencing!

Bill then asked him if he was familiar with specific articles that appeared in the scientific literature concerning whether tissues gain or lose weight as a result of formaldehyde fixation. The Weasel did not know any of the articles.

We had done our research and everything we found concluded that a fetus would gain weight when fixed in formaldehyde. This explained why the fetus weighed 600 grams at first and 700 grams four months later after being fixed in formaldehyde. Ward relied on an out-of-date textbook, had done no research himself and was unfamiliar with the current information related to formaldehyde fixation. This was Flanagan's expert?

Bill then approached McGuire. "I object to the witness' qualifications on this issue."

McGuire looked down and without hesitation said, "He's qualified and I will allow him to testify."

I was stunned. How could McGuire allow Ward the Weasel to testify as an expert? Was McGuire also confused by the medical words and facts?

The jury was brought back into the courtroom and Flanagan continued his direct examination.

"From your examinations of the slides I brought you in Pittsburgh, do you have an opinion as to whethah this pahticulah 'subject' breathed outside of the uterus?"

"Yes. The subject did breathe outside of the uterus."

No! I wanted to shout. *It did not!*

"On what do you base your opinion?"

"I base my opinion solely on the microscopic appearance of the lung tissue."

"Based upon your examination of the lungs, was this 'subject' a stillbohn?"

"No, it was not."

"The report by the medical examinah indicates that there were few red blood cells in the alveoli. How do you explain that?"

"Red blood cells that we see in the lungs at an autopsy come from the blood vessels in the lungs. Generally they leak out of the tiny blood vessels."

"Do you have an opinion as to what caused the death of this 'subject'?"

"I believe that this baby died from hypoxia, or lack of oxygen due to the separation of the placenta."

Baby!

"I have no furthah questions."

Bill was on his feet and approaching Ward the Weasel even before Flanagan reached his chair.

"Did you use charts and tables to determine the gestational age of this fetus?"

"Yes, I did."

"When you referred to these charts, you used estimates that would produce the greatest gestational age, didn't you?"

"I object, your honah!" Flanagan yelled.

Bill tried another approach. "The tables you referred to give a range of gestational ages for a particular weight, don't they?"

"Yes. One fetus at 24 weeks could weigh 600 grams, another could weigh 700 grams."

"Couldn't a fetus that weighed 700 grams be at a gestational age *less* than 24 weeks?"

"Yes, it is possible."

Leaving the Weasel's ability to stretch the truth for a moment, Bill moved in to challenge his competence as a pathologist.

"Dr. Ward, let us turn our attention to the issue of fetal respiratory movements. Wouldn't you agree that there is respiratory activity in the fetus involving the inhalation of amniotic fluid into its lungs?"

"In certain circumstances, but not all the time."

"And you reached this conclusion based upon your reading, didn't you?"

"Yes."

"One of the authorities you rely on is a Professor Dawes, isn't it?"

"Yes."

The Weasel was using old and outdated articles published by Dawes that said intrauterine fetal respiratory movements were very rare and occurred only very occasionally. What he did not know was that Professor Dawes had recently changed his mind based on his own experiments and now agreed that respiratory movements occur regularly *in utero*. But was all of this too much for the jury to understand? Did they even care? Would it make a difference?

"Are you aware that Dawes has now come to the conclusion that respiratory movements occur in the fetus most of the time while it is inside the uterus?"

"No, I am not."

Bill produced the most recent article by Professor Dawes and asked the Weasel to read it. After a few minutes of rustling pages, Bill asked, "Do you have an opinion, Dr. Ward, as to whether respiratory movements take place in utero or not?"

"Relying on what I have read, I conclude that this is a distinct possibility."

"Relying on what you have read *when,* Dr. Ward?"

"Just now."

"Do you now agree that respiratory activity takes place in utero during a substantial portion of pregnancy?"

"I'm having difficulty answering this question. It appears that Professor Dawes has changed his mind."

The Weasel had not done his homework to prepare for this trial. He was incompetent. Bill paused to let the Weasel's answer sink in. Moving in closer, Bill continued.

"Let's get back to the issue of fetal weight and the affect formaldehyde has on it. You testified that the fetus fixed in formaldehyde would lose weight, is that correct?"

"Yes, that is correct."

"You relied on the Ludwig textbook for that information, is that correct?"

"That is correct."

Bill picked up the copy of Ludwig's book sitting on Flanagan's table. Handing it to Dr. Ward, he asked, "Can you show me anywhere in this text where Ludwig describes the effect of formaldehyde on the weight of a fetus?"

Ward flipped through the pages of the book until he found the section he was looking for. Reading it to himself for a moment, he looked up at Bill. His eyes darted quickly over to Flanagan, then back to Bill.

"There is no place in this text where he describes the effect on the fetus. Only on individual organs," he replied.

Bill then produced enlarged photographs of the microscopic slides of the fetal lungs which had been taken by the medical examiner.

"Dr. Ward, examine these photographs for a moment."

The Weasel took the photographs and looked at them. His shoulders slumped and there was a fine tremor to his hands.

Giving him time, Bill asked, "Do you see alveoli, blood vessels and bronchioles in these pictures?"

"Yes, I do."

"Can you point out the blood vessels?"

"Blood vessels?" he asked nervously. "I would have trouble identifying those for sure in the photographs. I have to confess that I don't have the best eyesight in the world. I couldn't be sure about the blood vessels."

"I don't have the best eyesight in the world!" Bill let the words sink in for the jury. After a moment, he launched another attack on the Weasel's credibility.

"Do you see any fully distended alveoli in this photograph, Dr. Ward?"

"Fully expanded alveoli?" he repeated. "I don't see any that I can identify offhand. I'm not sure whether these are blood vessels or alveoli."

Bill took the photographs and stared at Ward the Weasel for a long while.

"Your present practice," Bill said calmly, "is in Pittsburgh, isn't it, Dr. Ward?"

"Yes, sir, it is."

"Are you a member of the advisory board of People Concerned for the Unborn Child?"

"Yes, sir, I am."

"Is that organization associated with the National Right to Life movement?"

"Yes it is."

"Are you in opposition to abortion as permitted by the Supreme Court decision in *Roe v. Wade*?"

The Weasel squared his shoulders. "Yes, sir, I am."

"I have no further questions for this witness, your honor."

Bill returned to our table. He was calm, but I was furious. This incompetent, right to life "expert" witness that Flanagan had found in a small hospital it Pittsburgh, like all the rest, was willing to distort the truth to promote his anti-abortion philosophy. Their beliefs were not the law! How many people were willing to convict an innocent man of manslaughter to further their own ends? It made me sick!

Ward's scientific knowledge was outdated, his eyesight was poor and his motivation was to destroy the truth and me. The Weasel was Flanagan's last hope as an expert witness.

Flanagan rose from his seat. "Your honah, the Commonwealth rests its case against Kenneth Edelin."

After 17 days and 16 witnesses, Flanagan was finished. It was our turn.

CHAPTER 27

OUR TURN

Newman Flanagan knew his jury. He gave them two options for conviction. He slipped in words and phrases to convince them that it wasn't a fetus, it wasn't an abortion; it was a baby, and it was manslaughter. Flanagan's expert witnesses were willing to stretch the truth, lie outright, make unsubstantiated charges against me and question my skill and judgment as a physician—and they all had some sort of membership in a national or local right to life organization.

Just as Flanagan rested his case, we received word that the United States Supreme Court had handed down a further decision related to the case of *Taylor v. Louisiana*. We had argued twice before that the jury for this case had systematically excluded women from the jury pool, and was therefore illegal, but while we waited for McGuire's decision, the Supreme Court amended its ruling. They now said that it could not be applied to cases already completed *or* in progress. This took James McGuire off the hot seat and cut the legs out from under us.

But we were not ready to give up on the illegality of Flanagan's charges and his jury. Before the jury was brought into court for the day, Frank Susman rose to argue for dismissal again, in spite of the amended decision of the Supreme Court. This time, Frank based our arguments on the laws of the Commonwealth of Massachusetts, which stated simply that if an injustice is found, it has to be corrected, even retroactively. The Massachusetts Constitution stated that every defendant is entitled to a fair trial. It was a strong argument. Flanagan's argument against our motion was simply restating the lie.

"The Commonwealth is not in violation of this defendant's rights concehning the trial panel that he received in this case. There was no intent to exclude anyone on this pahticulah jury."

For the third time, McGuire dismissed our arguments. He didn't want to determine the outcome of this trial himself. He wanted the jury—this jury— to do it.

We were determined not to let McGuire off the hook. We had yet another motion to make. Based on the weakness of Flanagan's case and his witnesses, we asked McGuire to direct the jury to bring in a verdict of "not guilty"—even before we presented our defense. Based upon English Common Law, the laws of the Commonwealth of Massachusetts and *Roe v. Wade,* I could not be guilty of manslaughter.

Bill rose to make our argument.

"This was an intended abortion performed by Dr. Edelin. The Commonwealth's eyewitness, Dr. Gimenez, said that whatever was removed from the womb of the patient—'subject,' 'fetus,' 'baby' or whatever you will—showed no signs of life. He said that without hesitation. There is no evidence that the fetus was born alive. As long as it remained in the womb and was not expelled or removed, it was not born and therefore not a person and cannot be the subject of homicide. Since there is no proof that this fetus was born alive, there was no human being for Dr. Edelin to kill and therefore this case should not go to the jury.

"The Commonwealth's position is that abortion does not include termination of prenatal life of the fetus. We maintain that the Supreme Court's definition of abortion is a process which results in the termination of fetal life. Dr. Edelin performed an abortion. An abortion was contemplated and an abortion was performed. There is nothing in the manslaughter statute taken in light of *Roe v. Wade* which gave the defendant the slightest warning that his conduct in performing an abortion would make him subject to a criminal charge. As a matter of constitutional law and due process, the defendant shouldn't be here because he wasn't given any warning that his conduct made him guilty of the crime of manslaughter. Shouldn't Dr. Edelin have been warned that performing an abortion following *Roe v. Wade,* even after consulting with at least two other physicians, may subject him to criminal liability for the crime of manslaughter? In *Roe v. Wade,* the court stated that a state could regulate abortions in the third trimester so as to take into account its interest in the potential for life of the fetus. At the time of this abortion, Massachusetts had no restrictive laws as to when abortions could be performed. Even though viability is not an issue here, this fetus was certainly not viable. The testimony of the Commonwealth's own witnesses, Drs. Mecklenburg and Cavanagh, were not able to give us any opinion whatsoever as to the potential for survival for this particular fetus. Dr. Vernig testified that he could not recall any case where a fetus of 800 grams or less survived for more than 28 days. The Commonwealth has offered nothing beyond remote possibilities. This fetus has not been shown to be viable in any way. It was not born alive, and even if it had been, it would not be capable of sustaining life and therefore never became a human being subject to the protection of our laws. This indictment never should have been brought and therefore you should direct the jury to bring a verdict of 'not guilty.'"

Bill's argument for a directed verdict was complete, passionate, detailed and long. When he finally finished, Flanagan slowly rose from his seat, looked over at Bill and said in his usual sarcastic way, "Your honah, befoah I start, I just want to say I won't be as long as Mr. Homans was." He paused. No one laughed. He cleared his throat. "As I stated in my opening, and as I have argued previously in this case, we're not concehned with an abortion. Abortion concehns an unborn child. That's what the Supreme Court has said. But the Supreme Court said something else in *Roe*. They said that the states have the right to intervene if the fetus has reached a stage in the mother where it is viable, though unborn. We are intervening on behalf of the fetus. *Roe v. Wade* concehns only abortion. It does not concehn the homicide statutes of the Commonwealth of Massachusetts, and that is what we are dealing with here. Once the unborn became independent, on its own systems, not a paht of the mothah, and no longah dependant upon her, *Roe* does not apply. *Roe* applies only to the unborn. Nowhere in *Roe* do I see any discussion as to the rights of the independent human being. The action of the defendant in this pahticulah case is that he allowed an independent human being, on its own systems, to remain in that pahticulah environment for at least three minutes. These actions caused the death of a viable, independent human being—either born or in the process of being born—on its own systems. Not an unborn fetus."

McGuire interrupted him. "Can a fetus in the process of being born be the subject of manslaughter?"

Flanagan jumped on McGuire's question. "In this case, death was caused by lack of oxygen—anoxia—because of the acts of Doctah Edelin in connection with this independent human being, on its own systems, in the process of being born. The killing of a viable child shall have the same consequences whethah it is during the birth process or aftah its completion. Nowhere did *Roe* sanction the deliberate killing of a child aftah it has been detached from the mothah." Flanagan's cheeks became redder and redder and his lower lip quivered with passion. "If that were true, then *Roe* would stand for the right of a woman and her docktah to commit infanticide. The question in this case is whethah a viable child, detached from its mothah, has a right to be killed. I have introduced evidence sufficient for a jury to determine that there was a viable child, that it was detached from its mothah, that it was a human being and that the unlawful killing of this human being constitutes manslaughtah. Homicide statutes apply in this pahticulah case." He glared in my direction, then turned back to McGuire.

There was a long silence. McGuire looked down at Bill and Flanagan, his face impassive.

"I will take this matter under advisement," he said. "We'll take a short recess."

No one in the courtroom moved, though voices buzzed around, echoing in every corner. I caught scraps of conversations filled with hope, anger, pessimism and confident self-righteousness. I tried to tune them out. McGuire returned in about 20 minutes.

"The defendant's motion to strike the jury and to dismiss the indictment is denied." I had expected as much. As soon as I learned about the amendment to the Supreme Court's ruling in *Taylor v. Louisiana*, I knew McGuire would not rule in our favor. "The defendant's motion for directed verdict is also denied. Mr. Homans, would you like to proceed with your case?"

Bill, like me, was disappointed, but not surprised. He stared at McGuire for a moment then said, "Yes, your honor." He looked over at me. "Dr. Edelin, would you take the stand?"

CHAPTER 28

My Story

January 30, 1975

As I rose from my hard, wooden chair and made my way around the large table to the witness stand, I knew that I was going to have to be my own best witness. All the others who followed me on the witness stand could confirm and corroborate, but only I could present this case, the facts and the truth to the jury. McGuire was not going to grant us either of our motions to throw the case out, but we had to try. We had spent the day before preparing for my testimony. I was ready. I wanted the jury to hear my side of this case and the events that led to my indictment. I wanted to go first to lay the groundwork for the rest of the testimony the jury would hear. They had to learn the truth. They had to know my thinking to understand why I did what I did.

There were only two people who understood the agony of the decisions that were made—Evonne and me. Bill, Frank and I had argued for weeks about whether we should put Evonne on the stand. Flanagan had his photographs, but we had the young woman who made the decision to have the abortion. Abortion, after all, is about a woman's ability to make decisions for herself.

In the end, I wielded the power I had reserved for myself when I'd hired Bill: final decisions were mine and I did not want her to testify. Her privacy would be invaded, her identity known and her anonymity destroyed.

"Do you swear to tell the truth, the whole truth and nothing but the truth?" Clerk Paul O'Leary asked me as I raised my hand in the air.

"I do."

With that, I took the witness stand. From this angle, the courtroom I was so familiar with looked completely different. To my left sat the 16 people who were judging me. At a table in front of them were Bill Homans and Frank Susman, their faces empty of emotion. Beyond them were the scores of spectators, filling the visitors' section. To my right sat Newman Flanagan and his gang of three, defending their way of life and trying to convince the jury to set a ridiculous precedent. In front of them was Paul O'Leary, the court clerk.

Sitting above it all was Judge James McGuire, keeping the Commonwealth's order and shaping the truth—generally not in my favor.

It was me against them, them against me.

What *was* the truth? What was *my* truth?

I was a light, bright and damn-near-white looking, bushy-headed black man on trial for murder, angry at the injustice of the entire situation and terrified of the lengths my enemies would go to convict me. How do I defend myself? Where do I begin?

My story began deep inside the warm darkness of Ruby Marguerite Goodwin Edelin. She was the reason I existed and the reason I became a doctor—the first in my family. There were white Edelin doctors in Maryland, but they were not *my* family.

I was one of those accidental babies, conceived in unrestrained passion. At that point, my parents already had three children and weren't planning on having more, but I was a welcome and loved addition to the family. I was the baby-dear.

By the time I came along, my two brothers and my sister were in school during the day. Dad was at work. It was me and Momma, just the two of us. She read books to me and taught me how to use the crayons to color in my coloring books. Saturday nights she gave me my bath and covered my skin with Vaseline. When I was sick with fever— which was often—she would rub my back until I fell asleep. I would awake from my nap feeling better, my fever gone. I always felt she had healing hands. I hoped that one day I, too, would have that ability.

From my childhood of brick sidewalks in segregated, wartime, colored Washington, DC, through the blooming of my adolescence in the green, lush and rocky Berkshire Mountains in western Massachusetts, to riding in the subway on the cusp of the liberation decade of the '60s in Greenwich Village and Manhattan, and ending up in the country town of Nashville, Tennessee, attending Meharry

Medical College—the only private black medical school in the country—
the journey I took to have my dream of becoming a doctor come true
was a long and challenging one. Painted on this canvas was a picture of
birth, life and death. The birth of my family emerged from the bodies
of slave women impregnated by their owners. Their lives and mine in
this hostile and schizophrenic country of opportunity and oppression,
hope and hopelessness, freedom and fear was all a part of my journey.

I was six years old when World War II ended in 1945, and the
celebration in Washington went on for days. There were parades and
parties and everybody danced in the streets. I rode my bike from one
end of Maryland Avenue to the other with red, white and blue crepe
paper streamers fluttering behind me, ringing my bicycle bell and blowing
my noisemaker the whole time. It was wonderful not to have to worry
about the searchlights, the sirens, the ration stamps, the smashed tin
cans, the SPAM and the darkness anymore.

The war was over and life was one new fascination after another.
One of my favorite memories was when Dad would say, "Kenneth, I'm
walking to H Street. Come walk with me. Maybe we'll get a root beer
while we're there."

I loved to walk with him. We didn't do it enough. He was always
working. He held my hand tightly in his as we started off on our journey
to H Street.

There were lots of small shops there and Dad made frequent trips
to the hardware store. There was always something broken at our house
that needed fixing. We would walk along and look in the windows of
the other stores until we came to Woolworth's 5- and 10-cent store.
After a Saturday morning of hard play in the middle of August in hot
Washington, there was nothing better for a six-year-old than a cold root
beer and a hot dog!

Woolworth's had two lunch counters. One was tall and too high for
me to see over. On the corner of this counter sat a large, polished,
brown wooden barrel of root beer served in chilled mugs for a nickel.
The hot dogs were 10 cents—I always had mine with mustard and relish.
Dad would lean on the countertop and give the hot dog man our order.
There we stood, drinking cold, sweet root beer and eating the world's
best hot dogs.

The other counter was much longer and much lower. It extended
half the length of the store, and in front were a line of stools which

swiveled on their permanent fixtures in the floor. I never got a good answer when I asked Daddy why we couldn't sit down on the stools to eat our hot dogs and drink our root beer. I didn't understand when he finally said we had to stand at the colored counter. After a while, I stopped asking the question.

Washington, the nation's capital, was fiercely segregated. It had two separate school systems: one black, the other white. Separate, but not equal. In a city with sweltering summers, there were two public swimming pools for colored swimmers, whereas whites had many more.

Water fountains in Union Station were segregated. We had to ride in the back of the bus on a trip through Virginia when I was six. All of the movie theatres were segregated. Whites and coloreds were separate.

But there were many different layers of coloreds in Washington. The elite were light-skinned and college educated—the professors at Howard University, the doctors, dentists, undertakers and some businessmen. Our family never made it there. Our skin was light enough, but Momma and Dad never went to college.

At Lovejoy Elementary School, all of our teachers were Negroes. Teachers and other important colored people were always called by the proper name, "Negro." It was a word that signified respect and a special place; it was a proper noun and as far away from the improper "nigger" as a colored person could get.

At the beginning of each year, our Negro teachers distributed textbooks to us, depicting white *Dick and Jane* in white America with their dog, Spot. They were in the old, worn and outdated textbooks that had been used at the white elementary schools in previous years. Sometimes pages were torn. Sometimes pages were missing. Most of the time, the pages were full of pencil marks and scribbles. We had to record the condition of our books on its inside cover. More than once, I witnessed a teacher's anger explode when one of us found a message that had been written in the margin by the book's previous owner: "niggers!"

It was hard for me to understand why someone I didn't even know could hate me so much.

Momma got sick in the spring of 1949, just before my 10th birthday. Life was never the same after that. She told me that she had to go to the hospital. She didn't tell me why. There were whispers that I was too young. Weeks later when she came home, I went into her bedroom where she was laying down and begged to know why she had been away.

"They had to remove my breast," she said quietly, pulling the strap of her nightgown down. I was petrified. She slipped her arm out of her gown and peeled away the bulky white bandage that covered the left side of her chest, revealing a long, red, serpentine scar. It was raised and angry, extending up toward her left armpit, slithering across her ribs which were covered only by a thin, tight layer of skin. She wanted me to see. She tried to help me understand. I didn't. What is cancer? How do you get it? What does it do? Why couldn't I hug her anymore? I was her baby—her last child, her youngest son. I was used to getting my hugs. When I was little and we were alone together she used to pick me up and give me long wonderful hugs. My brothers and sister were older and had theirs. This was my time and I reveled in her affection. I lived for the closeness. She was my first and longest love. We were inseparable.

I didn't understand. I felt sad for her. I felt sad for me. I cried. She carefully drew me to her lap, comforting me with a gentle backrub. "I'll be all right and you'll be all right, too," she promised. She would have to take some medicine and go to the hospital all that summer, but she promised that she was going to be all right.

Momma decided that I should go to New York to live with my Aunt Martha and her husband for the summer. My mother had three sisters who lived in New York City and they all agreed to help take care of me, but only one had a house big enough for a rambunctious, sometimes angry 10-year-old. I didn't know them very well and didn't want to go.

"Don't send me away, Momma," I begged her. "I don't want to leave you."

She held me as close as she could, rubbing my back until I began to calm down.

It was a miserable summer in New York. I cried, had temper tantrums, lied and swore. I talked back. I spat. I didn't care. I didn't want to be there. My aunts put up with me because they loved their sister, and Ruby didn't want her baby to see her sick. That summer, she underwent treatments with radium and took hormones that caused her to grow thick, coarse hair on her chin. She didn't want me to see her vomiting after a treatment. She had allowed me to see her scar, but she would not let me watch her body deteriorate as she was given the poisons meant to kill the cancer left in her body—poisons that almost killed her.

Finally, the days became shorter and cooler as the summer was coming to an end. Aunt Martha and her husband, Uncle Harold, decided that they would drive me back to Washington. They wanted to see Momma, too. The six-hour car trip had to be planned very carefully.

Enough food and sweet tea had to be brought along because there were no restaurants on the road to Washington where Negroes could stop and eat. Most gas stations would not even let us use their bathrooms.

When I got back home in mid-August, my temper was under control. I just wanted to be home with Momma. She seemed to be stronger and happier, and I refused to let her go very far without me. I would tag along wherever she went. I was tied to her apron strings.

When the school year began, Momma was stronger. She came to the first PTA meeting of the year. But happiness and sunshine soon disappeared with the arrival of winter. Momma began to have back pains. I arrived home from school one afternoon in December and found her with her head in Dad's lap, her hands covering her face. She was crying. He stroked her head with one hand as he held the phone to his ear with the other. The test showed that the cancer had spread to her spine.

My mother continued to cry. I cried. Dad showed little emotion, but it was not easy for him. Soon, she needed a cane to walk. In spite of all the treatments, the cancer had continued its relentless and ravenous journey through her body. She began spending most of her time in bed and had to be carried up and down the stairs. When nothing else seemed to be working, she went into a Christian Science nursing home, hoping that their special ways of healing would help. She did not get better.

Shortly after she entered their nursing home, while sitting up in bed crocheting, there was a loud *snap*, like a cold, dry stick breaking in the dead of winter. Her right arm had broken spontaneously, a further sign that the cancer was spreading. There was no turning it back. The surgery, the radium treatments, the hormone pills, the prayer with the Christian Scientists, the Sunday and evening prayers from Calvary Episcopal Church...none of it was stopping the cancer as it marched through her body. She was transferred to a hospital, where her arm was set in a cast, but all that did was permit her to continue her crocheting and wait for the end.

When spring came, she seemed to improve a little. She began to smile again. We all began to smile again. Hope rose in me. I thought the cancer was leaving her body.

My graduation from elementary school was near, and I had been chosen to give the graduation speech. We all worked on writing that speech—Daddy; my brother, Milton; my sister, Norma; my teachers; everybody. It was to be a special day. I practiced over and over again until I knew the words by heart. They gave me lessons on how to use my hands and change the inflections in my voice when I spoke. They taught me about making eye contact with the audience and how to slow down my delivery and to let the natural rhythm of the words dictate the speed. "Carve each word before you let it fall," they said.

"Momma, can you come to graduation?"

"I don't know, Kenneth."

"Momma, please."

"I don't think so, Kenneth."

"Momma, please."

"I'll try, Kenneth."

Dad tried to arrange for Momma to come to graduation. He said he was to going to bring her by ambulance in a special chair so she could watch and listen as her son, her baby, her 11-year-old man delivered the speech as he and his classmates left sixth grade.

On graduation day, I was up early, standing in front of the mirror, practicing my speech one more time, watching my hands and listening to the changes in my voice. I put on my new blue graduation suit, a crisp, white shirt and the bright, iridescent blue clip-on bow tie. I repeated my speech one more time in front of the mirror. By the time I got to the bottom of the stairs, with the excitement filling my chest, my heart and my head, the faces of my father, brother and sister told me something was wrong.

"Momma won't be able to come to graduation," one of them said.

The excitement and joy escaped from my being.

"She's not feeling well and the doctors think its better if she doesn't travel."

I had practiced it for her, so she could see and hear me. In front of all those people, I wanted her to be proud of me and to say, "That's my baby! That's my son!" Now, I didn't even want to go to the graduation.

"After graduation, she wants you to come to the hospital and give your speech to her. Just to her. She wants to hear it."

We left for graduation. When the time came for me to give my speech, I rose from my chair on the stage and walked to the front. My eyes scanned the audience and I found the row where my family sat— my father, brother, sister, grandparents, aunts, uncles and cousins. I looked toward the back of the auditorium, still hoping that Momma would be wheeled through the door, just in time to hear my speech. She never came.

Later, we went to the hospital. My mother's frail body was bolstered by pillows. I stood on a box so she could see and hear me. My eyes fixed on her half-opened lids, my arms and hands moved with the cadence of my speech. It was my graduation gift to her. When I finished, she managed a weakened smile as her body seemed to disappear more and more into the pillows and bed sheets. Everyone else applauded. I went over to her bed and someone lowered one of the side rails so I could give her a kiss.

As I pressed my lips to her cheek, the pungent odor of her cancer entered my nostrils and was permanently imprinted in my brain. I wished I could heal her. I wished I could touch her and make all of her pain go away. I wished I was a doctor.

Someone said, "It's time to go." We all left the hospital except for Dad, who always stayed behind.

Every day after work, Dad would walk from his job at the post office in downtown Washington to George Washington Hospital to be with his Ruby. He sat with her for hours, brushing her hair, holding her hand. Every night was the same, just sitting and stroking her hair. Saying goodbye. He loved his Ruby.

Near the end of her illness, as the cancer consumed her body, he couldn't hold it in any longer. In a secret diary, on April 23, 1951, he wrote a prayer for her. The doctors were failing. The prayers of others were failing. Maybe God would listen to "Ruby's Prayer."

Jesus healed the lepers,
One came back in prayer.
O, my tortured body,
My soul in dark despair.
He commanded the lame to walk,
He made the blind to see.
O, my weakened limbs,
Carry me to Galilee.
What ailment this that holds me
No earthly remedy to cure.
O, God in Thy infinite mercy
Make me whole and pure.

I was not allowed to visit Momma much in the hospital. "Too young," they said. One Saturday evening, as he was about to make his regular evening visit to the hospital, Dad turned to me and said, "Do you want to go see your mother?" I quickly grabbed his hand and we headed out to the streetcar.

By the time we arrived, it was dark outside. Her room was dark as well. Dad took me up to the side of Momma's bed, let go of my hand and said, "I'll be back in a minute."

I looked at Momma's sunken face, outlined by the bones of her cheeks. Her breath was weak. There she was, hopelessly and helplessly lying there. I did not know how close she was to death. What 11-year-old momma's boy could ever imagine that his momma would leave him—would die? I leaned over the rail and touched her face. She opened her eyes and looked at me. She tried to smile.

"Do you want me to rub your back?" I asked.

She looked at me again and whispered, "Yes."

Summoning all of her strength, she grabbed the bed rail and turned on her side. I opened the ties on the back of her hospital gown and rubbed her back, the way she had always done for me when I was little. I could feel the bones lying beneath her frail and wasted body. Some of them were tender, especially in the middle and she would twitch and wince when my hand passed over them. Finally, she rolled onto her back, not having the strength to hold herself any longer.

"Thank you," she whispered, breathing even harder now.

Dad came back in. He went over to the opposite side of the bed, leaned over, kissed her lips and began to stroke her hair. I hoped my back rub would be as magical as hers had been for me. I was willing her to get better.

Back home, I prayed all night for her to get well.

The next day, we all went back to the hospital. As we walked into Momma's room, Grandma let out a cry. Momma was lost in the pillows and sheets, her eyelids nearly closed. Her mouth was open and a grunt accompanied each infrequent breath. I didn't understand. What was happening? They all began to cry. I walked over to the rail of the bed and called her.

"Momma? Momma! Wake up, Momma!"

But she didn't wake up. No movement. No acknowledgment. No recognition. I began to cry. Someone was told to take me home. They did not want me to stay until the end. I had rubbed her back the night before. The last words she ever spoke were to me: "Thank you."

I had rubbed her back, but she didn't get better. I didn't have the magic in my hands, the way she did.

Shortly after I arrived back home, Dad called and said that she was gone. When the end came, her labored breathing stopped. Her eyes opened and she sat up in the bed, looked straight ahead for a brief moment, then fell back down in the bed and was gone. Grandma said that was what happened when Death walked through the door. Momma sat up to greet him, and Death took her away.

Many of the details of her life escape me, but the memory of my mother dying haunts my being. The pain was searing. The scar that remains is tight, ungiving, unforgiving and painful.

They brought Momma home in a casket. For two days and two nights, she lay in our living room, surrounded by flowers and all of her friends and family. I wanted to run and hide, to escape from the presence of death.

"Why did she have to die?" I asked.

"God took her. The good always die young."

Why did He take her? I asked myself. I hated God for taking her.

Later that night, when I went to bed, I pulled the covers over my head but the mixed sweet fragrances of the flowers in the living room reminded me of death. I couldn't sleep. When morning finally came, I waited until the last moment before going downstairs. As the four of her children stood in front of her for the last time, Dad lifted the veil and kissed his Ruby on her lips. I cried through the funeral and at the cemetery as they lowered the casket containing her body into the ground. I didn't care who saw me cry. Momma was gone. I would never see her again. She was in the cold ground. I was alone.

I promised myself I would help women like her one day. I would heal them. I would be a doctor.

CHAPTER 29

IN DEFENSE OF MYSELF

Bill Homans approached me in the witness stand.

"Would you state your full name, please?"

"Kenneth Carlton Edelin."

When prompted, I told the jury my story of becoming a doctor at Meharry Medical College in Nashville, Tennessee. Meharry was the oldest private, all-black medical school in America. It had been educating black doctors for more than a century. Nearly half of all black doctors still living had been trained at Meharry.

I then told them how I had joined the Air Force to help pay for part of medical school and to help support my new wife. I told them how I had to spend an extra year on active duty during the Vietnam War. I described my three years in the Air Force as a doctor, including when I worked as an obstetrician and gynecologist in the Air Force Base Hospital in England, and how I became the chief of the General Practice Clinic there, and the chief triage officer of the Air Transportable Hospital, a unit which could leave on a moment's notice to set up a field hospital anywhere in the world. For extra credentials, Bill asked the right questions, giving me the opportunity to tell the jury that I received two medals—one from the Air Force, one from the Army.

I gave the jury a detailed description of my training in obstetrics and gynecology at BCH. I told them I had delivered hundreds of babies, done both major and minor surgeries and abortions.

I told them I was able to estimate how far pregnant a woman was by knowing the date of her last period and by measuring the height of her uterus. I had done this thousands of times. Ultrasound was in its infancy and the one machine available at BCH was crude and unreliable.

253

Bill asked me to list and describe the various kinds of abortions I had done as a first-year resident. I described abortions by D&C, saline infusion and hysterotomy that I either performed myself or assisted others in.

Bill wanted to know how women were able to get abortions at BCH. I explained that if a woman came to Boston City Hospital before January 22, 1973, requesting an abortion, she could be no more than 20 weeks pregnant, and it had to be shown that continuation of the pregnancy would be detrimental to either her mental or physical health. After that diagnosis had been made, her case was presented to the Abortion and Sterilization Committee at City Hospital. If the committee approved the request, then the patient was scheduled for the procedure and it was carried out. This could take weeks, and meanwhile, the pregnancy continued. He wanted to know how many abortions I had done under those policies. I couldn't give him an exact number, but most of them were D&Cs. There were a few that had progressed beyond 12 weeks, which required either saline infusions or hysterotomies. If women came to BCH requesting abortions, it was the policy of the hospital to provide this service for them. David Charles was a strong proponent of that.

As a first-year resident, I scrubbed with more senior residents who were performing hysterotomies and from them, I learned how to do the operation. The operation was not uncommon and was performed all over the country and the world. Saline infusions and hysterotomies were the only two techniques we had to offer patients who wanted second trimester abortions at BCH.

Bill wanted to know what happened on January 22, 1973. Flanagan objected, saying that I was not a legal expert, but surprisingly, McGuire let me answer.

"My understanding of the Supreme Court ruling of January 22, 1973 was that a woman could have an abortion during the first third of her pregnancy and that request and decision was between herself and her physician."

Flanagan objected again, but McGuire let me continue.

"During the second trimester—up to 26 weeks—a woman could still request an abortion and a physician could still carry it out. The state could, if it wanted to, intervene to direct where the abortion could be performed so as not to put women's health at risk."

Flanagan fumed, chipmunk cheeks purple with frustration. He objected yet again. But I was allowed to continue.

"During the third trimester," I said, "or the last 13 weeks of pregnancy, a woman could still request an abortion and the request could still be carried out by the physician. However, during this time, the state could intervene to prohibit abortion on behalf of the unborn 'child,' unless there was some medical reason which meant that the continuation of the pregnancy would be detrimental to the woman's health or life."

Bill paced in front of me, his yellow legal pad tucked under his arm. "What change in the gynecology service did you notice after January 1973?"

"The requests for abortions increased dramatically."

"By the time you were Chief Resident, how many other residents performed abortions at City Hospital?"

"Most of the residents who performed abortions had finished their training and graduated. As a result, there were only two of us left who were willing to do them. My personal caseload increased tremendously, and included women who were requesting second trimester abortions. With the assistance of the nursing department, we established a Saline Abortion Unit on the GYN service, the only one like it in the city of Boston. A woman could be admitted on any Monday, have the saline infusion, abort and usually be discharged from the hospital on Wednesday or Thursday. There were three beds in the saline abortion unit and we could take care of three to four women each week who wanted second trimester abortions."

Bill asked me to describe the surgical techniques for performing a hysterotomy in detail. I did.

"Dr. Edelin," Bill said, "based upon your experience and training and based upon accepted medical practices, are hysterotomies generally done in the fashion that you've described?"

"Yes, they are."

Bill then asked me to describe a saline infusion. In doing so, I emphasized that the injection of this concentrated salt solution into any place other than the amniotic sac could be fatal to the woman. If the concentrated salt solution got into her bloodstream, she would have convulsions and die. It was very important to be absolutely sure that the needle was in the amniotic sac prior to injecting the concentrated salt solution.

"We know this when clear amniotic fluid comes out of the needle."

As I answered, I began to feel more confident. I knew my specialty.

"As Chief Resident, did you establish procedures to be carried out in the event of a live birth occurring as a result of a hysterotomy or saline infusion?"

"Yes. I established a policy that if there was a live fetus resulting from any abortion, it must be taken immediately to the newborn nursery."

Bill paused a moment to let that answer sink into the jury's minds. He then asked me to recount my care of Evonne Gilbert.

"The first time I saw the patient was in the outpatient department and Dr. Holtrop introduced me to her. She had come to the hospital with her mother, asking for an abortion."

"When was the next time you saw the patient?"

"The morning of October 2nd. She was in a bed in the saline abortion unit…"

I recounted, in detail, how I had examined Evonne's abdomen and estimated that, since her uterus was no more than a fingerbreadth above her umbilicus, she was 20 to 22 weeks pregnant. I told the jury about the numerous attempts I made to insert the needle into the amniotic sac, but with each attempt blood, rather than amniotic fluid, came out of the end.

"What conclusion did you draw from these bloody taps?" Bill asked.

"I didn't know for sure, but I presumed that I was dealing with an anterior placenta and knew that I could not proceed with the injection of the saline because of the dangers it would pose for the patient."

"Following these attempts, when was the next time you had any contact with this patient?"

"It was some time around noon."

"What happened?"

"I tried to do the amniocentesis again, using the same technique I had used in the morning. I got the same results. I tried a different technique by inserting the needle in an area lower down on her abdomen to avoid the placenta. Again, the same results—bloody taps. I explained to the patient the difficulty I was having and the reason why I couldn't proceed with the injection of the saline solution. After that, I consulted with Dr. James Penza because he had more experience in saline infusion than I."

"Who is Dr. Penza?"

"Dr. Penza was the associate director of the Department of Obstetrics and Gynecology."

"What took place as a result of this consultation?"

"Dr. Penza indicated to me that he would attempt to perform the saline infusion the next day in the operating room. If that failed, I would have to do a hysterotomy. I scheduled the patient for the operating room the next morning."

"What operation was intended for the patient?"

"Dr. Penza was going to try the saline infusion and if that failed, I was prepared to perform a hysterotomy," I repeated.

Bill handed me a sheet of paper.

"What are the entries on the operative sheet?"

"There are the names of the anesthesiologist, the nurse anesthetist, the scrub tech and the names of the circulating nurses. In the next column, it indicates that the procedure was scheduled to take place in operating room number two."

Bill stopped his pacing, showed me several other papers and asked me to identify them.

"These are City Hospital authorizations for surgery. One is for a saline infusion, another is for a D&C and the third is for a hysterotomy. They were all signed by the patient's mother."

Bill then asked me to review the patient's chart and explain the discrepancies between the gestational ages as estimated by Dr. Gimenez, the medical student and Dr. Holtrop.

"Dr. Holtrop," I added, "was the more experienced of the examiners and therefore, I believe that his estimation was most accurate. In addition, if the patient had not emptied her bladder before being examined by Dr. Gimenez and the medical student, the uterus could have seemed larger than it actually was."

"Do you recall whether or not there was another patient in the Saline Unit on that day?"

"Yes, there was."

"Did you perform a saline abortion on the other patient?"

"Yes, I did. After the first attempt to do the saline on the 17-year-old patient failed."

"What was the result of the saline on the second patient?"

"I was able to perform the saline infusion without any difficulty."

Bill produced a photograph of the second operating room and

asked me to identify what I saw. I pointed out the anesthesia equipment, cardiac monitor, the door leading to the scrub room and the double doors through which the patient came in on a stretcher.

"Is this a fair representation of the operating room as it looked on October 3, 1973?" Bill asked.

I hesitated for a moment, and then replied, "I don't think so."

"In what respect are they not the same?"

"The clocks…"

Expressionless, Bill resumed stalking back and forth in front of the witness stand, tapping his fingers on the back of his yellow legal pad.

"What is it about the clocks that do not appear to be the same?"

"I think they were both broken and out for repairs. They are present in the photograph, but they were not there on October 3, 1973."

There was a murmur of revelation in the courtroom. Flanagan shifted in his seat and fixed me in his gaze. I did not flinch. I did not blink. The murmurs died down and a still silence fell over the courtroom.

Bill continued. "Otherwise, is it a fair and accurate representation of the condition of the operating room on October 3, 1973?"

"Yes, it is."

"Can you tell us what happened to the patient in the operating room?"

"Dr. Penza attempted to do the saline infusion. The result was the same for him—another bloody tap—so the decision was made to go ahead with the hysterotomy. I left the operating room to explain to the patient's mother what was going on and asked one of the third-year medical students to assist me with the surgery. Once the patient was asleep, I prepped her abdomen with an antiseptic solution and covered her with sterile sheets and towels. I stood on the left side of the patient, with my surgical assistant standing across the table from me. To my left was the scrub nurse, Irene Bloom."

Not Helen Horner. I glanced over at Flanagan. He glared back at me, then began scribbling furiously on his own legal pad.

Bill then asked me to describe the operation, which I did in great detail, pointing out the size of the incision and the reasons for every decision I made.

"Once the fetus was removed, I observed it and in the process of passing it from the operative field to the stainless steel basin the scrub tech was holding, I put my fingers on its chest to feel for a heartbeat."

"You were looking for signs of life?" Bill asked, raising his voice for emphasis.

"Yes," I said. "I was."

"Was there a heartbeat?"

"No, there was not."

"Was there any time, Dr. Edelin, when you looked at the clock in the operating room, holding your fingers or hand in the uterus for a prolonged period of time?"

"Absolutely not."

"I show you this picture and, assuming that you may be mistaken as to whether or not there was a clock there, if you had looked at the clock, where would you have had to face with respect to the patient for a period of three minutes or more?"

"I would have had to turn my entire body around. The area where the clocks are located was directly behind me."

"Did you ever put your hand inside of the uterus?"

"No. The incision was not big enough for me to insert my hand inside the uterus."

Bill then turned to Judge McGuire. "May I ask the witness to come the council table for the purpose of demonstrating for the jury the position of his hands and himself during the operation?"

Flanagan objected. McGuire overruled. I stood next to our table, facing the jury.

"Put your left hand in the position it would have been in when you detached the placenta," Bill instructed.

Facing the jury, I placed my left hand palm down in front of my abdomen just above the table.

"Keeping your hand in place, turn your body around to your left and attempt to look behind you as if you were looking at the place where the clocks were in the operating room."

Flanagan objected.

McGuire asked Bill and Flanagan to approach the bench.

"Mr. Homans, what are you trying to show here?"

"I want to demonstrate to the jury what Dr. Gimenez said the defendant did. I want them to see how long three minutes is and the position Dr. Edelin's body would be in for those three minutes. I want the jury to see for themselves and draw their own conclusions."

Flanagan objected, but McGuire overruled him.

Bill nodded to me. "Dr. Edelin, please resume the position you were in, this time with your left hand in front of you and your body and head turned to your left so that you could see the clocks if they had been on the wall."

I turned my head over my left shoulder and then twisted my body at the waist to the left. It was an awkward, contorted position.

"Now, Dr. Edelin, I want you to hold that position for three minutes." Bill looked down at his watch.

There I stood, my legs leaning against the table, my left hand reaching across the front of my body, with my head and upper torso twisted in the opposite direction to look behind me at a place where the clocks would have been had they been present. This was the position in which Enrique Gimenez claimed I stood for three minutes. The strain of turning around while keeping my hand in that position caused my muscles to tighten, my hand to quiver and my neck to ache before the first minute was up. By the time Bill said that three minutes had gone by, my shoulder was twitching and my left hand was shaking. I had to stretch out my back when I was allowed to turn back to normal.

"You may resume the witness stand," Bill said.

"Dr. Edelin, did you ever remain motionless with your left hand in the womb of the patient for three minutes or any other significant period of time?"

"No I did not."

"What did you do after the fetus was removed?"

"I sutured the incision and dictated the post-operative orders to one of the nurses."

"Did you ever make a handwritten note of the operative report?"

"No, I did not."

Bill turned to McGuire again. "I would like to ask the witness to approach the clerk's desk, your honor."

McGuire agreed. On Paul O'Leary's desk was the photograph of the fetus.

"I show you exhibit nine and ask whether it is a fair representation of the fetus involved in this case at the time of its removal from the body of your patient on October 3, 1973?"

"No."

"Tell us what differences there are between what you see now and what you saw on October 3, 1973."

In the brief moment before I answered, Flanagan, under his breath, but loud enough for me to hear, said in his thick, South Boston brogue, "It was beautiful."

He momentarily stopped me in my tracks. It was a remark intended only for me to hear. I looked at him for a second, then back at the photograph.

"Usually," I said "in a fetus of this size and gestational age, the skin is smooth and almost transparent. In this photograph, there is also a distortion of the face."

Again, under his breath, Flanagan said, "With pain."

I ignored him. I couldn't let him rattle me.

"I ask you, Dr. Edelin, on October 3, 1973, did you do anything that was not in accordance with accepted medical practice?" Bill asked.

"Everything I did was in accordance with good medical practice."

"On October 3, 1973, did you intend to, or in fact, violate the law as you understood it?"

"No, I did not."

"I have no further questions for this witness, your honor."

With that, Bill turned me over to Newman Flanagan for cross-examination.

I had already been on the stand for a day and a half and was emotionally drained, but I was ready for his attack.

His first lunge was an oblique one in an attempt to impugn my credentials.

"Doctah, are you board certified?"

"I took the written part of my board examinations in June of 1974."

"Have you taken your oral examinations?"

"No. That comes two years after the completion of residency."

"So the answeh to my question, 'Are you board certified?' is 'no.'"

There was no sneer on his face, but there was one in his voice.

"No, I am not yet board certified."

Then he moved in for a direct blow.

"Assume that the 'subject' in this case was 24 weeks of age. Priah to Octobah 3rd, 1973, how many hysterotomies had you perfoahmed when the 'subject' was 24 weeks of age?"

Bill was ready. He had faced Flanagan enough times to know his tricks. "I object, your honor. There is a double-barrel nature to the question." It was a warning for me. I had to listen to every question carefully.

McGuire thought for a moment. "Dr. Edelin, you may answer that question."

"I have never performed any."

Now the trick question.

"So, this was your first?"

He was trying to get me on record as saying that Evonne was 24 weeks pregnant.

Bill was waiting. "That's what I object to, your honor."

Flanagan retorted. "I would press it, your honah. This is cross-examination."

"Try rephrasing your question, Mr. Flanagan," McGuire said.

"Assuming this was a 24-week-old 'subject'"—the word dripped out of his mouth as if it had a foul taste—"was it your first?"

Bill, still standing, objected again. "I have no problem if Mr. Flanagan wants to ask him whether he's ever performed an abortion on a woman who was 24 weeks pregnant, but I suggest the way the question is presented is unfair because it has an assumption in it. This was not a 24-week-old fetus."

McGuire looked over at Flanagan. "Try a new approach, Mr. Flanagan."

"How many hysterotomies had you perfoahmed, priah to Octobah 3rd, where the 'subject' weighed approximately 600 grams?"

"None."

I had barely finished answering the question when Flanagan, in rapid-fire staccato style, shot off another one. "Doctah, priah to Octobah 3rd, 1973, how many hysterotomies for the purpose of abortion had you been personally involved in?"

"I would estimate about 12."

"Where did you get your training in perfoahming hysterotomy for abortion?"

"At City Hospital."

"When did you first perfoahm an abortion by hysterotomy?"

"Sometime during my first year at City Hospital—between July of 1971 and June of 1972."

"Have you evah even seen any textbook with pictures of a hysterotomy for abortion where the woman was 20 weeks pregnant?"

"Not that I can recall."

"Didn't you tell us that you learned how to do hysterotomies for abortion from standard textbooks in obstetrics and gynecology?"

"Yes."

"Can you show me anywhere in these books where they discuss an abortion by hysterotomy in excess of 20 weeks?"

With that, he placed three large textbooks up on the witness stand. Ignoring the books, I answered, "No, not that I can recall."

"If I show you these books, would that help to refresh your memory?"

Without sparing the books a glance, I looked directly at Flanagan and repeated, "Not that I can recall."

"Would you look through these books to see if it would help refresh your memory as to whethah or not—"

I cut him off, speaking slowly. "I said, 'No, not that I can recall.'"

"Dr. Edelin, you testified that it was good medical practice to perfoahm a hysterotomy the way you did on a woman who was more than 20 weeks pregnant, didn't you?"

"Yes."

"Didn't you say that the textbooks I have put befoah you were the ones that you used to come to that conclusion?"

"In part, yes."

"How about *Williams Obstetrics*? Did you use it to come to that conclusion?" *Williams Obstetrics* was the Bible of obstetrics. Every obstetrician had read it many times.

"Yes," I said.

"Doctah, would you show us anywhere in these three textbooks where—"

I cut him off again. "I will show you in this one." I selected a book from the pile, then another. "And also in this one."

"Show me," Flanagan challenged, grinning at me.

I opened up the first book to the section that described abortion and tried to hand it to Flanagan. He just stood there, looking at me, letting my outstretched arm stay put.

"Have you found something that describes a hysterotomy for abortion in a woman over 20 weeks pregnant?"

"It doesn't set an upper limit."

"Do any of these books define an abortion?"

"I see one definition in this one," I said, giving the book I was trying to hand to him a little shake.

"Read it," he commanded.

Without looking at it, I said, "The definition of abortion in this textbook is 'the expulsion of the products of conception before 20 weeks of gestation.'"

"How would you define abortion?"

"An abortion is the termination of pregnancy prior to viability."

Flanagan reached in front of me and picked up *Williams Obstetrics*. "Is there a definition of abortion in this book?"

"Yes."

"Don't they define it up to 20 weeks?"

"No."

I had read *Williams Obstetrics* so many times that I knew it almost by heart. Flanagan paused. He cocked his chin up to look down his nose at me.

"Read to us what it says."

I couldn't believe he was letting me read this definition of abortion. He obviously had not read it carefully. I opened the book, found the page and read aloud: "'Abortion is the termination of a pregnancy at any time before the fetus has attained a stage of viability.'"

"Do they have a definition of what viability is?"

"Yes, they have a discussion of it."

"Read that."

"You want me to read the whole thing?"

"Yes."

He asked for it.

"'Attainment of a weight of 1,000 grams is therefore used as a criterion for viability.'"

"Read the whole paragraph, Doctah," he snapped.

I did not cower, I did not slouch, I did not flinch. I read, carving my words before letting them fall: "'Interpretations of the word viability have varied between fetal weights of 400 grams at about 20 weeks of gestation and 1,000 grams at about 28 weeks of gestation. Survival with a weight between 400 grams and 800 grams is very unusual. Attainment of a weight of 1,000 grams is therefore widely used as a criterion of viability. Infants below this weight have little chance of survival, whereas those of 1,000 grams have a substantial chance of survival.'"

The entire courtroom could feel the hatred and tension between Flanagan and me. Our eyes were locked. The room was hushed.

McGuire broke the silence. "We've come to the end of today's session.

We will resume at 10:00 Monday morning. Ladies and gentlemen of the jury, have a good weekend."

He rapped his gavel and adjourned the trial for our two-day break.

I was relieved. Flanagan had come at me with several trick questions that I was not ready for. Bill's objections to some of them gave me a chance to think about how I would answer. I needed to step back, regroup and get myself ready for his attack on Monday morning.

I had developed a regular weekend routine during the trial. As usual, after court on Friday, Bill and I would meet in the pub in the basement of the Old City Hall. A crowd would always gather and join us for drinks and talk. Many were lawyers from Bills office, some were politicians. Friends and supporters would drop by and visit. People knew that if they wanted to get in touch with me after court, the pub was the place to go first.

Bill almost always focused on every hopeful sign that things were going our way. I was much more pessimistic. After looking over the transcript when it arrived until we were totally spent and exhausted, I would drive Bill home to Cambridge and then go back to my new apartment, also in Cambridge, where I had moved after I'd finished my residency at BCH.

On Saturday morning, I went to my office to see prenatal patients. Most were due to deliver in the spring and they had every confidence that I would be around to deliver them. One was a nurse from City Hospital and she, her husband and I had become good friends even before she got pregnant. They were sure that that I was going to deliver their baby, which was due near the middle of that month—February. They wanted me to be its godfather.

After seeing patients in the morning and going through a week's worth of mail, I went to a meeting of the KEDF. The defense fund had become so busy and the contributions and mail so heavy that we made the decision to hire a full-time coordinator, Carol Cohen, the wife of a prominent kidney specialist in Boston. The KEDF was housed in Bert Lee's office.

Saturday night, I usually spent with friends. On this particular Saturday night, Judi came to visit. She brought two friends with her, Connie, a third-year law student at Harvard, and her boyfriend, Terrell. Terrell had recently been released from Norfolk State Prison. Connie had met him while working on the Harvard Prison Project in Norfolk.

She had visited Terrell regularly, and their friendship had grown into love. After he was released, Terrell moved in with Connie in her Harvard Square apartment.

He was shorter than me, with brown skin, and had several scars on his face. When he spoke, his voice was always filled with passion. As the four of us sat around my apartment, drinking wine, I asked Terrell about life in prison. While I tried not to think about going to jail, it was a very real possibility that hung over my head like a guillotine—especially considering the tactics Flanagan was using to win.

Terrell had been following the trial through television reports and in the newspapers. For him it was the white justice system beating up, once again, on a black man. Only in this case, it was not a black man from the streets of Boston, but one from the corridors of a hospital.

He told me exactly what I would be facing if found guilty. There were, apparently, inmates at Norfolk who wanted me to be sent there. They had psychotic scores to settle—just like Flanagan.

Flanagan's trick-filled cross-examination on Friday had unnerved me. I could not let him trick me into making a mistake. I wished this terrible nightmare would go away. I wanted to run and hide. I felt like the lonely, frightened child I used to be after Momma died. Sometimes all I wanted to do was to get in bed and pull the covers up over my head, just as I had done back then. But just like then, there was no place to run now. There was no place to hide. There were no sheets that would make this awful nightmare go away.

The four of us talked about the trial and what I would face on Monday morning.

"Ken, there is nothing he can do to hurt you," Terrell assured me. "You are smarter than he is, but he is sneaky. Remember this: you know yourself. You know this case. And you know medicine better than Flanagan will ever know any of those things. You know about some parts of the law better than he does. He is not as smart as you and he can't get you. Don't be afraid of him. Don't lose your cool. Listen to his questions and think about them before you answer. Prepare yourself tomorrow, then go in there Monday and kick his ass."

CHAPTER 30

Battling Flanagan

The next morning, I went to Bill's office around 10:00 a.m., so I could prepare for the rest of the cross-examination. Bill and Frank critiqued my testimony. Frank told me to be aware of my facial expressions when I spoke. I confessed how close I'd come to falling into Flanagan's trap and testifying that this was a "24-week-old fetus."

"Thank God Bill objected. It gave me some time to think," I said.

"Take your time," said Frank. "Listen to the questions, think about them and then try to answer in a way that will cut off Flanagan's attacks."

It was like chess, except it was not a game. Bill suggested a few approaches that Flanagan might take and gave me some likely questions to answer.

The day went by way too fast. I left Bill's office as the sun was going down and went back to my apartment in Cambridge. I sat in my living room, alone, staring out the window at the neon sign across the river, watching it change from red to white as it spelled out "*Coca-Cola*." I went over the sample questions again and again in my head, trying to think of some of my own. Even my dreams were filled with potential scenarios.

I woke up on the couch before the sun rose. I took care of my body, mind and my spirit, then drove along the frozen, snow-covered Charles River, bracing myself for battle.

Every day during the trial, the spectator gallery was jammed. By 9:00 a.m., the hallway outside the courtroom began to fill, and when, shortly before 10:00, the thick, double doors were unlocked, the crowd broke through in a rush. Some were forced back outside, their penalty for not having been quick enough to claim one of the hundred or so seats available at the trial each day. Most of the spectators were women—young, old, those who'd had abortions and those who would never have them. They came for all different reasons, and many of them wanted to make me a hero of sorts.

"I had an abortion," said one 28-year-old Somerville woman to a reporter outside of the courtroom. "And I simply don't know what I would have done if I couldn't have. It must be awful to bring a child into the world that you can't support financially, emotionally or in any other way. People like myself owe it to Dr. Edelin to be here."

Aside from pro-choice women, there were other supporters who came to the trial. Sitting shoulder to shoulder on folding chairs and benches in the rear of the uncarpeted courtroom were the nurses and technicians from BCH, the medical students I had taught at Boston University, friends and relatives, like my sister, Norma, and my brother, Milton.

Along with all of those who were drawn to the trial because they either supported or denounced abortion, there were those who competed for a seat for a much less emotional reason. They came to witness the courtroom battle between two skilled and seasoned lawyers, Newman Flanagan and William Homans.

Flanagan was not to be underestimated, but, as Terrell had reminded me, I was smarter than him.

"Doctah," Newman Flanagan began, "when we left off on Friday, we were talking about these textbooks. What is the definition of abortion as described in these books?"

"*Williams Obstetrics* defines abortion in several ways. The first is 'the termination of pregnancy before viability has been reached.' In the second definition, it defines it as 'a time before the fetus has attained a weight of 500 grams.' However, in a later chapter concerning therapeutic or induced abortions, it refers to abortion as 'the interruption of pregnancy before viability.' Do you want me to go on to the others?"

"Is your definition of abortion found in these books?"

"Yes. It is found in *Williams*."

"What is your definition of abortion?"

"It is the interruption a pregnancy before viability."

"Is there, anywhere in any of those books, a discussion or description of the termination of the potentiality of life within the uterus?"

"I think that concept is inherent in the word 'viability.' I assume that if I am going to do an abortion on a woman who's carrying a fetus before viability, then the fetus is going to succumb as a result of the abortion."

"Didn't you testify the othah day, in connection with *Roe v. Wade*, that your opinion was that unless there's a law contrary to it, you can perfoahm an abortion up to 40 weeks?"

"That is what my interpretation of *Roe v. Wade* is."

I would not fall into his trap. I would not let him make a fool of me.

"Would you conclude that the termination of the potentiality of life after viability is the law?"

"No."

"Would you say that a 38-week-old fetus was viable?"

"Yes."

"When do you draw the line as to when you can terminate that potentiality of life?"

"I would place viability at somewhere between 24 and 28 weeks, usually clustered around 28 weeks. My actions in the past and my beliefs now are that I have never performed an abortion on a woman who was carrying a fetus that I considered to be viable. In fact, I have refused to do abortions on several women who I thought were carrying viable fetuses."

"I move the answer be stricken!" Flanagan snarled.

"I will allow the answer to stand." McGuire said looking down at Flanagan.

Red-faced, Flanagan continued, "Can you tell me where in these books it indicates that the operation you perfoahmed—with the detachment of the placenta first—is good medical practice on 'subjects' that weigh 600 grams?"

"None of these textbooks discuss 600 grams specifically. They don't discuss 400 or 500 grams either. They describe a technique for performing an operation. I don't think they are limiting the technique to a pregnancy that is only 16 weeks just because the photographs in the books are of 16 weeks."

His advance blocked, Flanagan changed his line of questioning. He asked me a series of inconsequential questions about surgical permits, who signed them and who witnessed them and on what dates were they signed. I listened carefully to every single one, taking my time to answer them, trying to figure out where he was going with this. Was he trying to throw me off? Taking a breather to figure out his next approach?

"Aftah Doctah Holtrop introduced you to the patient in the clinic, where did you next see her?"

Hadn't I answered this question already? "I saw her in the saline abortion unit on the second floor of the GYN service at City Hospital."

"What is a saline abortion?"

I described it again in the same way that I had described it so many times before.

He asked me again how many attempts I made to perform the saline abortion. I described the numerous attempts on two separate occasions—once in the morning and once during my lunch break.

"What happened after the second attempt in the afternoon?"

I relayed the story again. There were no discrepancies for Flanagan to jump on, from my description of how I explained what was going on to the patient and her mother, to asking Dr. Penza for his help and advice, to entering the patient's name and other information on the operative schedule.

"Did you write a note on the patient's chart describing your two failed attempts at saline infusion?"

"Yes, I did."

"Where?" he asked, handing me the chart.

Pointing to a few lines, I said, "Here. That's my note here."

"Would it be good medical practice to perfoahm a hysterotomy on a woman where the fetus is already dead?"

"Yes. It certainly would be."

"Before you did the hysterotomy, did you have an opinion as to whethah or not the 'subject' was alive?"

"I had very serious doubts as to whether it was."

"Isn't it a fact that 'subjects' are always alive before the commencement of the hysterotomy?"

His snide tone suggested that he thought he knew the answer, but Flanagan was not a medical expert. He did not know medicine as well as I did.

"No, that is not always true."

"Did you know if this fetus was alive or dead?"

"No, I did not."

"Couldn't you have found out whethah or not the 'subject' was alive?"

"I could have."

"Why didn't you?"

"Because at this particular stage of this particular abortion, for this particular patient, I didn't think is was necessary or indicated."

"Suppose the fetus was dead. It could have aborted itself, is that right?"

"That's a possibility."

"You just have to wait to see what is going to happen, isn't that right?"

"Sometimes it is detrimental to wait. For this patient, we and she couldn't wait."

Flanagan placed his hands on the bar in front of the witness stand and leaned in. He lowered his voice. "Would it have made any difference to you whethah the fetus was alive or dead?"

"No."

Flanagan stood up, his voice returning to normal. "Assume that the fetus was alive. Would you have a pediatrician in the operating room with you?"

"No."

"Why not?"

"Because," I said firmly, "this was an abortion."

"What does that mean to you?"

"It means that I was performing an abortion before viability. Having a pediatrician there would be contrary to the patient's wishes and contrary to good and ethical medical practice."

Suddenly there was a commotion in the courtroom. An old white man seated in the visitors' section jumped up and took off his heavy overcoat, revealing a sandwich board he was wearing. Glued to it were pictures of babies and fetuses, surrounding big red letters that spelled out "Abortion is Murder."

The court officers rushed over to him to cover his sign and escorted him from the courtroom. McGuire shouted as he rapped his gavel.

"Sheriff, we're going to take a short morning recess. I want quiet in the courtroom when the court is sitting. And I want quiet in the corridor when we are in recess. If anyone can't comply with those orders, you will see that they are removed."

After the recess was over, and once order had been restored, Flanagan asked me questions about saline abortion technique and the configuration of the operating rooms, but his questions seemed to be disconnected.

"Is all of the equipment in the operating room moveable?"

"No. The lights from the ceiling and the outlets for electricity and anesthetic gasses are fixed in one place."

Then, with the sarcasm and sneer I had come to expect from him, Flanagan said, "Well, we know the clocks are portable. You can take them off the wall and repaih them, can't you?"

I ignored his question.

"The clocks are portable, aren't they? They can be carried out."

"And fixed, too," I said, handing some sarcasm back to him.

He asked me to describe other things in the OR. Then he wanted to know how many people were in the operating room, what time I started the hysterotomy, and how I could know who the people were if they were all wearing hospital hats and masks. Was he kidding me? Did he think I didn't know my co-workers?

"When you started this operation, the patient was undah sedation, is that correct?" Flanagan asked.

"She was asleep," I corrected him.

"So she was undah sedation, I would assume."

"She was under anesthesia. That is more than sedation."

Flanagan again asked me to repeat the description of the operation that I had already given Bill. Afterwards, Flanagan paused and glanced at some of his notes. He grinned at his gang, then looked back at me.

"What is the standard procedure concehning written operative notes at City Hospital?"

"The standard procedure is that the surgeon writes a brief description of the operation by hand in the patient's record at the end of the operation."

I had not done so immediately after Evonne's procedure. I was wrong. I focused on keeping my facial expressions smooth, bracing myself for Flanagan's attack. He produced the records of another woman I had operated on that day.

"I want to show you the record of Mary Quinn and ask you if you made a handwritten note here."

Before I could explode in anger, before Bill could leap to his feet and object, Judge McGuire stopped Flanagan in his tracks. "Wait just a minute. What right do you have, Mr. Flanagan, to invade the privacy of someone who is named here?"

Turning red, Flanagan responded, "I'm sorry, your honah," he offered meekly. But it was too late. He had blurted out the name of another patient in open court, in front of the jury, the reporters and everybody else in the courtroom. Question stricken or not, the crowd had still heard the name. Flanagan's carelessness didn't stop him. He pressed his point.

"Aren't handwritten operative notes and the dictation of the operative note supposed to be done right aftah the operation?"

"That is correct."

"So when you dictated the operative note on the 16th of Decembah of 1973, two and a half months afterwards, it was from memory, wasn't it?"

"Yes," I said. "And from reviewing other parts of the patient's record."

"You have testified that you made a low transverse incision in the uterus, but the operative note that you dictated does not indicate what kind of incision you made, does it?"

"The operative note states, 'An entrance was made at the anterior surface of the uterus in its midportion,'" I said.

Flanagan had found a weak point. My failure to dictate the operative note was inexcusable, but dictating medical records was a low priority for me. It was important for a complete and accurate medical record, but in addition to my duties as the Chief Resident, I had been taking care of a large number of patients in obstetrics and gynecology, both in the clinic and once they were admitted to the hospital. As one of only two residents who performed abortions, I was responsible for the patients who were admitted to the second trimester saline abortion unit, and half of all of the first trimester abortions that were done at BCH. Somehow, I did not think that Flanagan or the jury would be understanding or forgiving of my reasoning. Still, I refused to let Flanagan see me cower.

"You are telling us now that you made a low transverse incision into the uterus. You remember that now?"

"Yes, I do."

"Is there any advantage in detaching the placenta first when you entah the uterus of a 24-week pregnant woman?"

"The biggest advantage is that the placenta, the sac and the fetus can be removed all together. This is done to prevent leaving any of the products of conception behind, which could cause complications for the patient later."

"Ah there any risks in doing that?"

"There is a small risk of hemorrhage."

"Do you agree that if the placenta is detached the fetus is in trouble?"

Bill objected to the question, but McGuire allowed it.

"Once the placenta is detached, the oxygen and nutritional supply to the fetus are cut off. Whatever potential for life the fetus may have, it will not have any longer."

"How big was the incision you made into the patient's uterus?"

"It was about six or seven centimeters—less than three inches long."

"You say you then placed two fingers into the uterus. What did you do with your fingers?"

"I swept them from side to side between the sac and the wall of the uterus."

"Could you reach the top of the uterus?"

"I'm not sure. I tried."

"If you had stuck your hand in and went up, you could have reached the top, isn't that right?"

No, Mr. Flanagan. You will not hook me so easily, I thought.

"I couldn't have gotten my hand in an incision that small," I said.

Flanagan frowned. He pointed to the medical record. "Where does it state how small the incision was?"

"It doesn't."

"You are testifying from memory, aren't you?"

"Yes."

"In an abortion, do you consider whethah or not you owe any duty to the fetus?"

"Not at the outset, no."

"So your only duty at the outset is concehning the mothah. Just prior to the commencement of your hysterotomy in this case, you felt you had no duty to the fetus, is that correct?"

"That is correct."

"And you felt that whethah the fetus was alive or not was not important, is that correct?"

"That is correct."

"Your only concehn at that time was for the mothah?"

"Yes."

Flanagan paused to straighten his flowery tie.

"Assume that the fetus was dead just prior to the commencement of your hysterotomy, what would be good medical practice in that case?"

"To proceed with the hysterotomy."

"What do you base that on?"

"On the situation that surrounded this particular case, and my own medical experience."

"Did you feel that you had any duty to that 'subject' prior to the commencement of the operation?"

"If I had delivered a liveborn fetus as a result of an abortion, I would have made sure that it got to the nursery."

"But you don't make any effoht to determine whethah or not the 'subject' is alive or dead befoah the commencement of a hysterotomy, is that a fair statement?"

"Yes."

"Why is that?"

"Because the patient had come into the hospital requesting an abortion."

"So, you had no obligation to the 'subject'?"

"My obligation to the fetus could only commence after it had been extracted from the uterus. As I said before, if I had delivered a liveborn fetus, I would have made sure that it was taken to the nursery. That has always been my philosophy and the policy I established."

"Do you know how much a 24-week-old fetus would weigh?"

I kept my eyes locked on him. He could not possibly have been finished asking me about the hysterotomy. "The average is around 750 grams," I said.

Flanagan then returned to what happened inside the patient's uterus. "Do you have an opinion that if a doctor put his hand inside of a pregnant uterus in performing an abortion, why that hand would remain motionless in the uterus for a period of three minutes?"

"I don't know why anybody would do that," I answered, looking straight into his tiny eyes.

"Assuming that the 'subject' was alive and the hand did remain in there, would that be good medical practice to just allow the hand to remain there?"

"First of all, as I said before, I can't imagine why anybody would do that. And secondly, the answer to your question would be no, it would not be good medical practice."

"From your definition of abortion, you, as the doctah, have the right to terminate the life of the fetus, is that a fact?"

Bill stood and objected to the question. McGuire agreed. Flanagan then tried a different approach.

"Do you have the right to leave your hand inside the uterus of a woman for three minutes?"

"No. It would be detrimental to the woman."

"Would it also be detrimental to the 'subject'?"

Bill objected again, but McGuire ordered me to answer it.

"If the fetus were alive before the placenta was separated, it would be detrimental to it," I said.

Flanagan sneered. "Isn't a fetus also called a 'baby'?"

"I have never referred to the products of conception to a woman who was asking for an abortion as a 'baby,'" I said. "When I talk to a patient who is going to follow through with her pregnancy, who wants me to deliver it, then I talk about a 'baby.'"

"So it's just a difference in words, is that correct?"

Hardly, I thought.

"It is a difference in intent *and* words," I said.

"What is the difference in intent?"

"When a woman comes to me to have me deliver her baby, she intends for me to give her and her unborn child the best care that I can. A woman who comes to me for an abortion does not have that intent."

"In this pahticulah case, what did you do aftah you removed the 'subject' from the mothah to determine whethah the baby was alive or not?"

Baby. He had slipped the word in again.

"I observed it and I touched it."

"With rubber gloves?"

"Yes."

"For how long a period of time?"

"Not very long."

"How long did you examine this pahticulah 'subject'?" he repeated.

"After the fetus was extracted from the uterus, I held it for three to five seconds. There were no spontaneous movements, there was no breathing and I felt no heartbeat."

"Was a birth certificate, a stillbirth certificate or a death certificate filled out in this case?"

"No, because this was an abortion and a death certificate was not required."

"Aren't these certificates required by law?"

"I object to this line of questioning, your honor," Bill cut in. "Mr.

Flanagan is asking him to testify on matters of law. He is not an expert in the law."

"He testified about *Roe v. Wade*, your honah," Flanagan shot back. "He must be an expert in law. Maybe he is a legal expert and we can qualify him." He looked back at me. "Where did you learn about the details of the decision in *Roe v. Wade*?" he asked.

"From a partial reading of the decision, medical journals, news reports and talking to other physicians."

Flanagan stood silently in front of me for a moment. "Thank you, Doctah. I have no furthah questions."

I was done, relieved. I had been on the witness stand for more than two days. I didn't think I had said or done anything to hurt my case. I had not let Flanagan intimidate me or trick me. I *was* smarter than he was. Thank you, Terrell.

As I took my place back at the table, Bill gave me a reassuring pat on the shoulder. He then stood up and said, "I would like to call Dr. Frank Fallico to the stand."

CHAPTER 31

February 3, 1975

Frank Fallico, the one who'd examined the fetus when it had first arrived in the pathology department, had dark hair, a youthful face, an effervescent personality and had been a resident in pathology at BCH at the time. Since then, he had completed his training at the world-famous Mallory Institute of Pathology—where surgical specimens from all of the operating rooms were examined—and was now working at the University of Minnesota.

His name and his examination of the fetus had become important elements of my defense. Though Bill had talked to him several times over the phone in connection with the case, he and I had never met or spoken before. When he flew into Boston's Logan Airport, I volunteered to pick him up. I was anxious to meet him, curious about him. Bill agreed, but warned me not to discuss the case with him.

We didn't. Not once. I remember only two things about that uneventful ride. I remember that I liked him—he was genuine, gentle and totally honest—and I remember that we talked about, of all things, the weather. He compared Boston winters with those in Minneapolis and said that they were both pretty bad.

The next time I saw him was when he took the witness stand. After he was sworn in, Dr. Frank Fallico sat easily and confidently in the chair.

After the usual questions about his education, training and credentials, Bill got into the substance of his testimony.

278

"What were your duties in September and October of 1973 as a resident pathologist in the Mallory Institute at City Hospital?"

Frank spoke clearly. "I was on the surgical desk, which means I was processing surgical specimens. I would inspect each specimen with the naked eye, then prepare a piece of the specimen so that a microscopic examination could be made. The remainder of the specimen was preserved in formaldehyde."

"How many surgical specimens have you examined?"

"About 1,500."

Bill showed him Evonne's medical record. "Do you recall receiving a surgical specimen related to this patient?"

"Yes, I do. The specimen consisted of a fetus and placenta. I received it on the morning of October 3, 1973."

Fallico described the condition of the fetus exactly as I remembered it. "I concluded my examination by weighing the fetus."

"What kind of scale did you weigh it on, Dr. Fallico?" Bill asked.

"It was a large, white Toledo scale. Written on the manufacturer's label were the words 'honest weight—no springs.' The scales were in good working order. I weighed the fetus on two different occasions and each time, I got a weight of 600 grams. The placenta weighed 170 grams and was separate from the fetus."

"What did you do after you weighed the fetus?"
"I put it in a small plastic container of formaldehyde solution. It stayed in the surgical pathology cutting room for a period of time—for several days, in fact."

Bill then produced the photograph Flanagan had introduced as evidence.

"Are you able to tell us whether or not this is the fetus referred to in your report?"

"No, I am not."

"What differences to you see?"

"The skin is wrinkled. The formaldehyde has wrinkled the skin."

"Did you then dissect the specimen, Dr. Fallico?"

"No. Because of the uproar in the Boston City Council over a research project carried out on aborted fetuses the pathology department instituted safeguards to make sure that no fetus was dissected unless an autopsy was requested by one of its parents."

"How did you determine the gestational age of the fetus?"

"I copied it from Dr. Edelin's estimate, which was recorded on the Pathology Request Form."

"I have no further questions. Mr. Flanagan, your witness."

Flanagan stood up, smoothed that horrible tie against his shirt and grinned at the witness. Dr. Fallico did not smile back.

"How many times have you examined a 'subject' of 22 weeks gestational age?"

"I know of two."

"Were both of them on Octobah 3, 1973?"

"No, they were not."

"When was the othah one?"

"October 4, 1973."

"The photograph of the 'subject' you just saw here, you would classify as just a surgical specimen, is that correct?"

"Yes."

"It represents a specimen?"

"It is a specimen."

"How many examinations of specimens did you do on Octobah 3rd?"

"Thirty-two."

I watched Flanagan as he paced in front of the witness stand, trying to figure out where his line of questioning was going.

"Of those 32, how many were on 'subjects'—if you know what I mean by the word 'subjects'?"

"No, I don't."

"Call it a fetus. How many on fetuses?"

"I don't recall the number fetuses that I examined on that date."

"Was it more than one?"

"I don't recall."

"How about Octobah 2nd?"

"I don't recall."

"How about Octobah 4th?"

"I know I examined one on October 4th, but I don't know the number other than that."

"When you received the specimen, did you weigh it?"

"Yes."

"Did you measure it?"

"No."

"What if I was to tell you that on the next day, you had a specimen of 22 weeks and you measured it, would that be any different?"

"It would be. Everything I do with these particular kinds of specimens is entirely optional."

"So you exercised your option on this pahticulah one, is that correct?"

"That's correct."

"Doctah Fallico, have you gone over your testimony befoah yesterday? Did you talk to anyone about it?"

"No, I examined my own records."

"You didn't talk to anybody about your testimony yesterday?"

"No."

"You didn't talk to Mr. Homans about what you were going to testify to?"

"Yesterday?" Fallico asked with surprise.

"At any time yesterday or befoah?"

"Yes."

"Sure you have. You talked to Doctah Edelin about what you were going to testify to, didn't you?"

"No."

"You didn't? What did you do Saturday with Docktah Edelin?"

"Rode from the airport with him."

"And just talked about the weather?" he asked with a sneer.

"As a matter of fact, yes. We did discuss the weather."

"The heat is on here," Flanagan said, his grin vanishing. "It's a lot hotter here than it is out in Minnesota, isn't it?"

Bill jumped up. "Your honor, I object!"

McGuire looked down at them both. "Wait a moment. Just a moment! Strike the whole—the entire colloquy."

Unfazed, Flanagan continued. "Doctah Fallico, what is your duty when you receive a specimen over 20 weeks of age?"

"My duties are twofold: to notify the chief resident and to not dissect the specimen."

Throughout his questioning, Flanagan badgered Dr. Fallico about his duties and the policies of the Mallory. Dr. Fallico remained cool, direct and honest. He answered every question simply, calmly and without hesitation.

"You ordered this pahticulah specimen to be transferred to the mortuary, didn't you?"

"No."

"Didn't you dictate this particular surgical pathology report?"

"Most of it, but not all of it."

A beat. I fought back a smirk. Once again, Flanagan had not checked everything over. "Oh, I'm sorry," Flanagan said, the red spreading from his cheeks into his hairline. "I must've misunderstood you. Didn't you dictate the note, 'Fetus transferred to the mortuary'?"

"No, I didn't."

"Somebody put that on aftah you dictated your note?" he asked, dumbfounded again.

"Correct."

"Who did that?"

"It was one of the attending pathologists."

"How'd you know that he ordered the fetus to be taken to the mortuary?"

"Because he told me."

Flanagan hesitated. He flipped through his own legal pad for a minute. "Doctah Fallico, as a pathologist, you are used to looking at specimens of tissues that are diseased, are you not?" he said, the heat rising in his voice.

Calm, cool and confident, Dr. Fallico answered, "Yes, I am."

"This was not a diseased specimen that you examined in this pahticulah case, was it?" Flanagan nearly shouted the question. He enjoyed taunting witnesses who were not helping his case. He was a master at that, but Fallico gave as good as he got.

Bill objected. McGuire agreed.

Annoyed, but not finished, Flanagan cleared his throat and forced his tone under control. "Were there any troubles with the scales in the Mallory Institute of Pathology that required repaihs in November 1973?"

"No."

"When you say this specimen weighed 600 grams, was that right on the nose, 600 grams?"

"Yes."

"There were no strings attached, right?" he said, chuckling at his own joke. Flanagan, the vengeful comedian, had made a pun on the label on the scales; it read "honest weight—no *springs* attached." He couldn't resist making a joke, again hinting that there was some conspiracy afoot to help me.

I was on trial for manslaughter and he was trying to be funny. He wasn't succeeding.

Thankfully, Dr. Fallico did not answer him. He did not even crack a smile.

"I have no furthah questions for this witness."

As Flanagan took his seat, Bill rose. "Your honor, I have one more question. Dr. Fallico, is there any question in your mind as to the weight of the fetus?"

Flanagan leapt to his feet, but Fallico got his answer out before Flanagan could open his mouth.

"No. There is no question in my mind."

"I move the answer be stricken!" Flanagan shouted.

"I will let it stand," McGuire said quietly.

"I have no further questions for this witness, your honor," Bill said. He sat back down.

The next witness called was Ellyn Curtis. Ellyn was an attractive, young nurse, with long, dark brown hair, who worked in the GYN OR. She was our first eyewitness, other than me, to testify as to what happened in the operating room on October 3rd.

She described the duties of the circulating nurse, which included assisting the anesthesiologists and surgeons, making sponge counts and getting instruments and other items needed for the operation. Operating room technicians could also do most of those things, but OR nurses handled medications and narcotics, whereas scrub techs could not.

Ellyn's account of the events matched mine, including Jim Penza's attempt at a saline infusion. She described who was in the operating room and what I had done to get ready for the operation. She described the incision I made into the skin. She also recounted when Gimenez came into the operating room and pointed out that he was standing behind me, looking over my right shoulder—not across from me, as he had testified. In describing the operation, she used the word "fingers," not "hand."

"Dr. Edelin then asked me to get Dr. Charles, which I did," she said. "Dr. Charles came into the operating room, conferred with Dr. Edelin, then left. Dr. Edelin continued with the case. The next thing I saw was the fetus."

"Where did you see it?" Bill asked.

"It was in his hand and he was placing it into a basin."

"What happened after that?"

"I took the basin from the scrub nurse and brought it into the back room. I placed the fetus into a paper container. When I returned to the operating room, the placenta was already in another basin. I took that as well and put the placenta in a paper container. Then I did a sponge count."

"What is a sponge count?"

"A sponge count is made in every case where the body is entered to be sure that there is no sponge left inside before closing the incision."

"How many sponge counts did you make?"

"There is a count made as the uterus is being closed, one after the peritoneum is closed and the final sponge count is made as the skin is being closed."

Ellyn told the jury which sponge counts she had made and ran them through the steps taken after the operation was complete. Her story matched mine, right up to me giving her the postoperative orders.

"Who signed the postoperative orders?" Bill asked.

"Dr. Edelin did."

"Who filled out the surgical pathology request?"

"I did."

"Who signed it?"

"Dr. Edelin."

"Did Dr. Edelin tell you what to put on the surgical Pathology Request Form?"

"Yes, he did."

"Miss Curtis, in reference to OR number two, do you remember the presence or absence of either or both of the two clocks at any time in 1973?"

"There was no clock on the wall in OR number two at that time."

"When you refer to a clock, do you mean a timer or clock?"

"As I recall, the timer wasn't working and the clock was missing from the wall."

"When?"

"It had been missing from the time I started working in the operating rooms in 1972 until this past June."

"What did you see Dr. Edelin do insofar as looking at the clock?"

"He never looked at a clock."

"Miss Curtis, while you were in the operating room on this case, did you ever observe everybody in the operating room staring at a clock?"

"No, I didn't."

"I have no further questions for this witness."

The missing clocks had become the joke of Boston. Morning radio hosts made up skits about it. The newspaper headlines shouted, "Where Are the Clocks?" or "The Case of the Missing Clocks."

We took a short recess, during which I approached my family and friends, looking very sullen and serious. They gathered about me, silent, waiting for me to say something.

"We have reached a plea bargain agreement."

No one said anything, but Ramona's eyes flashed. She was livid that I would even consider such a thing when I was innocent.

"I am going to plead guilty to stealing the clocks and they are going to drop the manslaughter charge."

A beat. Then uproarious laughter, led by me. I appreciated the humor in the situation. It was what I needed to keep my sanity.

Flanagan, on the other hand, was pissed.

His original case was falling apart. Gimenez swore that everybody in the OR was staring at a clock. I denied that, and so did Ellyn. Now Flanagan wanted to get her. He approached the witness stand, his sly grin spreading to show more of his pointed little teeth. He attacked.

"How many hysterotomies have you been a nurse on, Miss Curtis?"

"I think about four."

In rapid-fire succession, Flanagan asked Ellyn about specific dates, hardly giving her time to respond. Did she witness any hysterotomies in June of 1972? How about in October of 1972? How about all of 1973?

"How about June of 1972?" he asked.

"I might have," Ellyn said.

Bill was on his feet. "Your honor, I believe he has already asked that question."

Flanagan handed her the transcribed portions of her testimony before the grand jury. "Let me show you this papah and ask you to read it to yourself."

"Would you refer me to the page of the grand jury minutes, please?" Bill asked.

"Pages 45 and 46," Flanagan said, smirking.

Bill looked in his copy of the grand jury testimony. He looked again. He couldn't find those pages.

"I object, your honor. This is grand jury testimony which was withheld from us. Apparently," he said, his voice rising in a rare display of anger in the court. "The district attorney had never considered this line of questioning material to this issue because he never gave us this part of her grand jury testimony."

The devious Flanagan withheld grand jury testimony from us. He would do anything to win.

But McGuire overruled Bill and let Flanagan continue to question Ellyn from the grand jury testimony that we had never seen.

"You have seen a numbah of hysterotomies perfoahmed, isn't that correct?"

"A few," she corrected.

"A few? How many is a few?"

"I only recall about four or so."

"Is it fair to say that you are a friend of Doctah Edelin?"

The conspiracy again.

"I worked with him."

"I didn't ask you that. I asked if it's fair to say you are a friend of Doctah Edelin," Flanagan repeated.

"Yes, I am."

"How often is Doctah Charles called into the operating room in the middle of an operation?"

"I would say pretty frequently."

"So when Doctah Edelin called him, that was not unusual?"

"No."

Flanagan began to pace in front of the witness stand, rocking from toe to heel whenever he paused to turn.

"When the fetus is removed, who determines whethah it is alive or not?"

"The surgeon usually does."

"Does anybody else do it?"

"The circulating nurse in the room would notice if anything was unusual."

"Did you ever testify in connection with this pahticulah operation that the surgeon's hand was inside the patient's womb?"

"I don't remember. I don't think his hand could fit inside her uterus."

"I move the answer be stricken as not responsive to the question," Flanagan said.

"Let her answer stand, your honor," Bill countered.

"Try a different approach, Mr. Flanagan," McGuire suggested.

"In connection with this pahticulah operation, when was the first time you used the phrase 'the doctor used his fingers?'"

"I don't think I was ever asked to describe fingers or hands."

"I move that answer be stricken as not responsive to the question!" Flanagan hissed, glaring at Ellyn.

"I will let it stand," McGuire said.

Flanagan then began to repeat many of the questions he asked Ellyn before: questions about Dr. Charles, who else was in the operating room, sponge counts, the size of the incision, hands, fingers and what I was doing. He rambled and repeated himself over and over and over again. He asked about the postoperative orders I dictated, the Pathology Request Form and many of the same questions he had asked earlier. He repeated them again and again and again, hoping that Ellyn would change her story.

Finally, Bill interrupted. "I object. Mr. Flanagan is harassing the witness."

"Your honah, if I've been harassing the witness, I apologize." Without missing a beat, he continued, "Have you evah pahticipated in removing a fetus from the operating room that weighed 600 grams?"

"I have no idea what the weight is of any given fetus. I don't weigh it."

Flanagan just stared at her. I silently cheered her. She had not fallen into any of his traps. With frustration in his voice, he finally turned and began to walk back to his table. "That's all. I have no furthah questions for this witness."

The head nurse of the GYN OR was called to the stand, followed by the administrator of the GYN service. Both of them testified, under oath, that the clocks were broken and out for repairs. Flanagan found no way to use them against me.

It was now time to put the issue of clocks and people staring at them behind us so we could move on to discredit Flanagan's case. It was time to call forth our experts.

CHAPTER 32

EXPERTS

Each of our experts were giants in their respective fields and had contacted us, offering to testify. None of them asked for any payment, other than covering their travel costs. They knew I was innocent and that Newman Flanagan's indictment was an assault on doctors everywhere. Their willingness to do this for free saved the KEDF thousands and thousands of dollars.

February 5, 1975

The first was Dr. Jeffrey Gould. Jeff was the director of newborn services at BCH. He was not only a pediatrician; he was a neonatologist who, like Vernig the Vermin, took care of sick babies during the first 28 days of their lives. Vernig the Vermin couldn't compare to Jeff. Jeff had trained in all of the best hospitals and belonged to all of the most prestigious professional societies in neonatology and pediatrics. He had written many medical articles and chapters in textbooks. His credentials were sound.

We did not believe that viability was an issue in my case. The legislature had not passed any restrictions on abortion since *Roe,* therefore abortions could be performed at any time during pregnancy. More importantly, consistent with my own beliefs, I had never performed an abortion on a woman who was carrying a viable fetus. While I agreed that there were instances that it might be warranted, such as a severe illness in the mother or severe abnormalities in the fetus, it was not a procedure that I would perform. I would find someone who would, but I could not do it myself.

This issue had been forced upon us by Flanagan and his witnesses. Evonne's fetus was not viable. It could not have lived even if it had been born alive—which it wasn't. Therefore, Bill wanted Jeff to help the jury understand the concept of viability.

"What is the purpose of the Newborn Unit at City Hospital?"

"The function of the Newborn Unit is to ensure that every child born at City Hospital has the best opportunity to leave the hospital in the best possible shape and function as well as he or she can."

Jeff went on to describe the high-tech equipment in the newborn nursery. He told the jury about the monitors, respirators, incubators and all of the other special equipment there because of the high-risk pregnancies we dealt with. He described the training of people who worked in the high-risk nursery.

Bill asked if Jeff had any statistics about birth weight and survivability in the newborn nursery of City Hospital. Jeff had kept careful records. He had information for the years 1971, 1972 and 1973.

Flanagan objected. He argued these statistics about viability in the newborn nursery at BCH were not material to this case, especially the statistics from years other than 1973.

"Your honor," said Bill, "we would like the jury to understand what the potential for life is for a fetus at various weights and gestational age. We want to demonstrate that a 600-gram fetus would have no chance to survive."

McGuire allowed Jeff to give the information about the year 1973 only.

"Dr. Gould, what was the total number of live births at City Hospital in 1973?" Bill asked.

"One thousand seven hundred and seventy-four."

"For a birthweight range of 454 to 900 grams, how many live births and how many deaths of those live births occurred in 1973?"

"Of the 13 live births in that weight range, there were 12 deaths."

"Do you have information of a baby with a birth weight less than 900 grams that had the longest survival in 1973?"

"Yes, there was one that weighed 850 grams and lived 19 days."

"Could you tell us the survival times of babies born weighing under 1,000 grams in the year 1973, in the newborn nursery at BCH?"

Flanagan objected again, but McGuire let Jeff testify.

Jeff then rattled off a series of statistics. Of those born weighing less than 1,000 grams, not one lived longer than nineteen days. Most lived only minutes or hours.

Flanagan rose and objected to all the information that had been given to the jury.

Rather than striking all of the information, McGuire added a caveat to everything the jury had just heard.

"It is up to you to give this testimony such weight as you see fit. It is your job, your obligation, to find facts and to determine what weight, if any, shall be given to this testimony on the question of viability."

Bill turned back to Jeff. "Do you have any information as to whether or not there is a difference in the weight of black fetuses as opposed to white?"

Jeff Gould's research had discovered some interesting differences between white and black babies born at BCH. Jeff said that below 35 weeks of gestation, a black fetus tended to weigh more than a white one.

"Do you have an opinion as to the gestational age of a white fetus weighing 600 grams?"

"For a white fetus at 600 grams, that would be between 22 and 24 weeks."

"Do you have an opinion as to the gestational age of a black fetus at 600 grams?"

"At 600 grams, a black fetus would be between 18 and 23 weeks."

"I have no further questions for this witness, your honor."

Flanagan began asking Jeff questions before he was even fully out of his chair.

"Can a fetus be liveborn aftah an abortion?"

"Yes."

"How many have you treated at City Hospital following an abortion?"

"I have not treated any personally. I have heard that there was, over the last several years, perhaps one or two."

"I move that the lattah part be stricken from the answer, your honah," Flanagan said.

"His answer is, 'I have not treated any personally,'" McGuire said.

Flanagan turned back to Jeff. "Do you know the best mannah of determining age aftah delivery?"

"For a pediatrician, it would be weight. For a pathologist it might be something else."

"Does length have any value in determining gestational age?"

"Sometimes, but weight is better."

"Can you tell just looking at the child whethah it is viable or not?"

"At what age range?"

"At a range of 24 weeks gestation and 700 grams?"

"At 24 weeks and 700 grams, you could probably tell if the child was going to be viable."

"Is it fair to say that ovah the years, there have been instances where babies who weighed less than 700 grams lived to ripe old age?"

"Not in my experience, but I have heard of it."

"When you get a 700-gram infant, you do what you can for that infant, is that correct?"

"I do all that is *appropriate* to do for the infant. If you have an infant that weighs 700 grams and it comes to the nursery breathing, with a good heart rate and good muscle tone, we are aggressive in trying to help that infant to live. If, on the other hand, a 700-gram infant arrives in the nursery and the best it can do is gasp, is limp with no muscle tone and has a heartbeat of two beats per minute, we know the that infant has no chance of survival. In this case, we are less vigorous in attaching it to machines to prolong its death. In general, results with an infant that looks that bad have been very, very disappointing. Between 600 and 700 grams, an infant has very little chance of survival. Perhaps only one out of 250 will survive. To me, one out of 250 to survive is miraculous, really."

Flanagan interrupted. "I would ask that the lattah part be stricken, your honah."

"Strike *that* miracle," McGuire declared. There was a murmur of laughter and a few smiles in the courtroom as McGuire struck down another miracle.

This time, Newman Flanagan didn't think it was funny. He pressed ahead. "Is there any doubt in your mind that a baby of 700 grams and 24 weeks' gestation can survive?"

"Yes, there is."

"At what point in time?"

"At any time. At the time of birth, I think we have a good idea which one that is."

"You were not there when Doctah Edelin perfoahmed the operation on this pahticulah patient on October 3rd, 1973, were you?" Flanagan said. It was obvious he did not like Jeff's answers.

"Pediatricians don't attend abortions."

Flanagan then took Jeff over to the clerk's table to look at the photograph of the fetus.

"Assume this pahticulah 'subject' was alive outside of the mothah. What would you call it?"

"I object, your honor," Bill said.

McGuire sighed. "He is really being asked his definition under a set of circumstances. I will allow it if he has such a definition."

"I would call that a liveborn, low birth weight infant of extreme prematurity."

"You can't tell us whethah or not this pahticulah 'subject' had that special something that would permit it to continue to survive?"

Bill objected. McGuire sustained it.

Flanagan was finished.

"I have no furthah questions."

Bill stood up. McGuire looked down at him and asked, "Mr. Homans, do you have any redirect examination of Dr. Gould?"

"Yes, I do. Dr. Gould, what is your definition of 'viable'?"

"A viable infant is one that leaves the hospital alive."

"Do you have an opinion, if a woman was 22 weeks pregnant, whether the fetus she was carrying was viable?"

Flanagan objected, but McGuire let Jeff answer the question.

"The fetus is not viable."

"Do you have an opinion as to whether the fetus in the photograph Mr. Flanagan showed you was viable or not?"

"I object, your honah!" Flanagan exploded. He was on his feet, face purple with rage.

"He may answer it," McGuire ruled.

"It was not viable."

"If I told you that the fetus in the picture weighed 600 grams, do you have an opinion as to its gestational age?"

"Somewhere between 19 and 22 weeks. Probably closer to 19."

"I have no further questions for this witness, your honor."

With that, Jeff Gould was excused.

"I would like to call Dr. Arthur Hertig to the stand," Bill said.

———

Arthur Hertig was a revered Professor Emeritus of obstetrics, gynecology and pathology at Harvard Medical School. He was one of the legends of my specialty. He graduated from Harvard and trained in pathology and obstetrics at its hospitals. He also studied embryology at the Carnegie Institute. Eventually, he became chairman and professor of pathology at Harvard. He was board certified in pathology, obstetrics and gynecology, and had published more than 180 scientific articles.

He was soft-spoken, small, with thin, gray hair, a warm smile and a somewhat frail structure. He sat comfortably, but not arrogantly, in the witness stand. Under questioning by Bill, Hertig defined viability as occurring at 28 weeks, which is when the lungs are developed. At that gestational age, he said, the fetus weighs about 1,000 grams. He also said that, in his opinion, the fetus in this case was not viable.

Under cross-examination, Arthur Hertig became confused and couldn't understand or remember some of Flanagan's questions. After a humiliating round of questions, Flanagan ended with a low blow.

"When you say you are Emeritus, that means you are retiahed, doesn't it, Doctah?"

As a proud Harvard teacher, Hertig responded, "Emeritus is Latin, meaning 'to have served one's term.'"

"So your term is up, isn't it?" Flanagan said with disdain. Turning his back on Hertig and walking back to his chair, Flanagan said, "I have no furthah questions for this witness."

———

Dr. Charles Hendricks was our next expert witness. He was professor and chairman of the Department of Obstetrics and Gynecology at the University of North Carolina. He had done an extensive study of 29,000 deliveries and the relationship between gestational age and the size of the fetus, determining the average weight of a fetus at various stages of gestation and the range of weights at any given week of gestation. He also had information regarding the survivability of fetuses at various weights and gestational ages.

Hendricks testified that the fetus in this case was less than 24 weeks' gestational age. When Bill asked him about survival and viability, Hendricks said that in order to be considered viable, a fetus or baby would have to survive at least 28 days. In his experience, none who were less than 26 weeks' gestational age survived that long.

Under cross-examination, Hendricks admitted that a fetus that weighed 600 or 700 grams could be 24 weeks' gestational age.

"Are you aware of any 24-week-old fetus surviving outside of the womb?" Flanagan asked.

When Hendricks said he wasn't, Flanagan, implying that there were studies that indicated some 24-week-old fetuses had survived, began firing off his questions in rapid succession.

"Are you familiar with the study from the University of Washington regarding survivability?"

"No."

"Are you familiar with the Jackson Memorial Hospital in Florida?"

"No."

"Are you familiar with the study at the University of Colorado?"

"Yes."

"How about the New York City study in 1957?"

"No."

"I have no further questions for this witness."

I wondered what the jury thought of this exchange. Flanagan did not even point out what the studies were about, nor did he ask any questions about the study Dr. Hendricks was familiar with. Did it make a difference in their minds? Did they understand any of the testimony? Did they care?

———

Dr. Alan Barnes, our next expert witness, was the vice president of the Rockefeller Foundation, in charge of medical affairs, and had been chairman and professor of obstetrics and gynecology at Ohio State, Case Western Reserve and Johns Hopkins Universities. He had delivered over 6,000 babies during his career and had written over 200 books and articles, many of which had to do with abortion and the development of the fetus *in utero*. He wanted to testify on fetal development and the soundness of my medical judgment when taking care of Evonne.

Bill started by asking him to define the word "baby," which he did by saying that a "baby" only existed at birth. He went on to define "birth" as the emergence of the baby from the mother's body. He defined "abortion" and "viability" the same ways our other witnesses had. He, too, said the fetus in this case was not viable and pointed out that according to eyewitnesses, it was stillborn. He then went on to defend my decision to perform the hysterotomy.

"It was perfectly acceptable. The decision to abort had been made, the first technique used had failed. He was going to have to switch to a different one. That decision was made with the understanding and agreement of the pregnant woman," he said. "There were many factors pushing him toward the performance of a hysterotomy. There was the likelihood that with every passing day, infection would get into the uterus because there had been multiple attempts at amniocentesis and some bacteria could have gotten inside. Dr. Edelin could also have been influenced by the woman's mental state. She had been through a very traumatic series of events. All of these factors would be pushing overwhelmingly for an immediate hysterotomy."

"From your examination of the patient's record, do you have any idea as to why Dr. Edelin kept getting bloody taps?" Bill asked.

"Yes. I believe the needle was piercing the placenta and puncturing placental blood vessels, which would be very serious for the fetus."

Bill stopped his usual pacing to ask his final question. "Dr. Barnes, what happens to the fetus as the result of an abortion?"

"The pregnancy is terminated and the fetus does not survive."

Flanagan had an intense contempt for doctors who performed abortions. As he approached Dr. Barnes, he stared at him with the look of hatred he usually reserved for me. He spoke of the "subject" as if the word left a foul taste in his mouth and his sarcasm came in full force. Barnes, however, remained cool under Flanagan's barrage of questions. Not being able to discredit his testimony, Flanagan ended his cross-examination quickly.

Still seated at our table, Bill asked one more question on direct examination. "Dr. Barnes, was Dr. Edelin carrying out good medical practice in the management of this case?"

"His management was perfectly all right."

————

Next on the stand was Dr. Kurt Benirschke, the pathologist from California who had reviewed the slides of the fetal lungs for us. Born in Germany but educated at Harvard, he eventually became the chairman of pathology at Dartmouth Medical School, where he remained for many years, until he moved to San Diego. He had published over 200 articles in medical journals and several books on neonatal pathology, fetal pathology and the pathology of the placenta. He was the most renowned expert in fetal pathology in the world.

Dr. Benirschke had brought photographs and Kodachrome slides that we wanted to show the jury to help them understand what he found when he examined the slides. First, Bill had him explain his findings to the jury, then, over Flanagan's objection, McGuire gave Dr. Benirschke permission to project the Kodachrome pictures of the fetus' lungs.

A projector and screen were set up and with the flick of a switch, a large picture of a microscopic view of the fetal lungs appeared. Dr. Benirschke described the anatomy of the trachea and the various tubes leading to the immature air sacs—what would become the alveoli as the fetus matured. Did the jury understand? Were they bored? Did they care?

"Ultimately," Dr. Benirschke concluded, "at 7 months, or 28 weeks, the lungs reach a stage of development where they can serve their real life function, which is to be the place where the interchange between air and the blood circulating in the lungs can occur."

"Are there any fully developed alveoli present in this photograph?" Bill asked.

"No."

"Can you tell us if the fetus from which this lung came ever took a breath outside of the uterus?"

"This fetus did not take an extrauterine breath. Before birth, the alveoli contain fluid because the fetus inhales amniotic fluid containing a certain amount of debris. If it had inhaled air, the debris would be pushed against the walls of the immature alveoli and there would be air bubbles within them. I did not see any air bubbles and the debris is evenly dispersed throughout them."

"Was there any blood in the air sacs?"

"Yes. There are remnants of red blood cells in many of the premature alveoli in this lung. There are fragments of red blood cells in the process of being broken down. That blood came from multiple attempts at amniocentesis—which were described as 'bloody taps.' It is aspirated blood, blood that was in the amniotic fluid and inhaled into the lungs of the fetus. The red blood cells in the alveoli must have been suspended there for many hours."

Flanagan objected to Dr. Benirschke's testimony again. He said that the slides Dr. Benirschke examined were not the same ones that were seen by his expert, Dr. Ward, who said that the alveoli were distended with air, indicating that the fetus breathed.

McGuire looked as if he didn't know what to do. Which expert testimony should he allow entered into the record?

It was nearly lunchtime, so he declared a recess while he considered Flanagan's objection. Before we left the courtroom, Bill asked McGuire's permission to have Dr. Benirschke examine the same slides Dr. Ward had examined. Permission granted, Bill made a phone call and he and Benirschke crowded into a cab and went over to the pathology laboratory at the Mallory Institute of Pathology, where Dr. Stanley Robbins was waiting. There, using the Mallory's modern microscopes, Dr. Benirschke was able to examine the same slides Ward the Weasel had testified about. Bill and Dr. Benirschke made it back to the courthouse just in time. Bill resumed his questioning.

"Have you been able to examine the microscopic slides that both Dr. Curtis and Dr. Ward have seen?"

"Yes, I have."

"When did you examine the slides?"

"This afternoon, during the lunch break."

"Now that you have examined the same slides as Dr. Curtis and Dr. Ward, do you have an opinion as to whether this fetus breathed outside of the uterus of its mother?"

"It is my opinion that the fetus did not breathe after removal from the uterus."

"Could the lungs of this fetus have sustained its life outside of the uterus?"

"No. These lungs were too immature to sustain life."

"The medical examiner stated that he tried to float the lungs in water and they sank. What does that indicate to you?"

"The lack of floatation means that there was no air in the lungs."

"From all of the slides you have seen in this case, was the fetus live-born or stillborn?"

"It was stillborn."

"Mr. Flanagan, your witness."

Flanagan had been waiting to question Dr. Benirschke since October, when we'd made our first motion to dismiss the charges. He'd boasted then that he wanted to cross-examine him, to see if the findings he made by examining slides in California would stand up under his questioning here in Boston. Now he had his chance.

At our request, Benirschke had carried out an experiment which showed that fetuses gain weight when fixed in formaldehyde. Flanagan began by challenging the results of that experiment.

"Your study was based upon the weight of fetuses that had been preserved in formaldehyde for only three weeks. Do you know what would happen aftah three months in formaldehyde?"

"I think that after a small increase, the weight would remain the same."

"In this case," Flanagan said, "the fetus allegedly weighed 600 grams at the time it was first received and 700 grams several months later. That's a 15 percent increase. How do you explain that?"

"I can't explain it."

One for Flanagan.

He moved on to the final part of Benirschke's testimony. "If there was blood in the lungs, where did the blood come from?"

"The red blood cells within the air sacs must have been aspirated with the amniotic fluid."

"Are you assuming, Doctah, or do you know for a fact that this took place?"

"I know for a fact that it took place."

"Were you there?" Flanagan asked with a sneer.

"I can see it from the slides," Benirschke replied with confidence.

"Suppose that during the operation, the defendant had separated the placenta and left the fetus inside of the uterus for three minutes, then when he tried to remove the fetus, the amniotic sac broke. Isn't it possible that the red blood cells you saw in the air sacs were inhaled as the fetus was removed from the uterus?"

"If the fetus had inhaled blood into its lungs when the placenta was separated, as it was being extracted from the uterus, I would expect to find whole red blood cells in the air sacs. That was not the case here. The lungs showed degenerating debris from red blood cells, not whole cells. These were not fresh red blood cells in the air sacs."

One for us.

Flanagan tried a different approach.

"You spoke about the regular exchange of fluid in and out of the lungs of the fetus. That's just a theory, isn't it?"

"It's no longer a theory."

"No longah a theory?" Flanagan repeated with surprise.

"It's been established in the last two or three years that there is inhalation of amniotic fluid into the fetal lung. It has also been shown that any debris contained within the amniotic fluid is also inhaled into the lungs."

Another one for us.

Frustrated, Flanagan shifted gears again.

"How do you define 'viability'?"

"Viability is the ability to survive extrauterine life."

"What is your definition of an abortion?"

"The definition of 'abortion' is the termination of a pregnancy prior to viability."

"Do you agree that abortion is the termination of pregnancy before 20 weeks?"

"No, I do not."

"I have no further questions for this witness."

Flanagan gave up. He had boasted that he could get the best of Benirschke, and he could not.

Us, three; Flanagan, one. The round was over.

———

Dr. R. Gordon Douglas, our next witness, was professor of obstetrics and gynecology at Cornell University Medical College. He was the author of *Operative Obstetrics*, the best and most frequently used textbook on how to perform surgery on pregnant women. A copy of his book sat on Flanagan's table. Flanagan's experts tried to say, citing this book, that I was wrong in performing a hysterotomy on Evonne and that the surgical technique that I used was not in keeping with good medical practice. Douglas felt the opposite. He was the foremost expert in performing hysterotomies. He wrote the book on it—literally.

Bill went over to Flanagan's table and picked up a copy of Dr. Douglas' book. He made brief eye contact with Flanagan, who shot daggers his way, then turned back to the witness stand. He showed Dr. Douglas the book.

"Do you recognize this text?"

"That is a copy of the second edition of my book."

"Can you give us the indications for the performance of a hysterotomy for the purposes of abortion?"

"The most common reason would be the failure of a saline infusion."

Bill then produced blown-up photographs of the images in Dr.

Douglas's book that illustrated his technique for performing a hysterotomy.

"I show you these photographs and ask if you recognize them."

"Yes. These are pictures I used in the book you referred to."

"When in a pregnancy is it good medical practice to perform an abortion by hysterotomy?"

"From the 13th week to the 28th week."

"What does the 28th week signify to you?"

"It is the beginning of the period of viability of the fetus."

"Does the surgical technique for performing an abortion by hysterotomy change from the 13th to 28th weeks?"

"Yes, it does. The incision would have to be larger as the pregnancy progresses. In an early pregnancy, the incision would have to be made in the body of the uterus, but as the pregnancy advances, it may be possible to make a low transverse incision in the lower portion."

"Dr. Douglas, would you please describe the procedure for performing an abortion by hysterotomy?" Bill asked.

Using the photographs from his book, Dr. Douglas described the details of the operation exactly the way I had done it.

"I have no further questions for this witness, your honor."

Flanagan stood up, straightened his horrible little flowery tie, and approached the witness.

"What age and weight do you use to determine viability?"

"After 28 weeks and after the fetus has attained weight of 1,000 grams."

"Have you evah done a hysterotomy for the purpose of abortion aftah 20 weeks?"

"Yes."

"Have you evah done one at 24 weeks?"

"I can't recall for certain."

"What are the most hazardous types of operations for the termination of pregnancy?"

"Hysterectomy and hysterotomy."

"Would it be good medical practice to determine whethah there was a fetal heartbeat present prior to perfoahming a hysterotomy?"

"There is no advantage in doing that."

"If there was no fetal heartbeat, could you try to stimulate labor with the use of certain drugs?"

"You could try it. If contractions started up and the fetus was expelled, it would be less hazardous than a hysterotomy, but that doesn't work very often."

"I have no furthah questions for this witness, your honah."

"Your honor, I have a few questions on redirect," Bill said. He walked back over to the witness stand. "After examining the record of this patient and noting what Dr. Edelin did, especially after the failure of three attempts at saline infusion, do you have an opinion as to whether he was practicing good medicine?"

"Yes, he was. It was really the only practical way of terminating the pregnancy in these circumstances. That is certain."

"Considering the techniques described in your textbook for performing a hysterotomy, would this technique be good medical practice to terminate a pregnancy of 18 weeks?"

"Yes. That would be good medical practice."

"How about at 20, 22 or 24 weeks?"

"Good medical practice."

"I have no further questions for this witness."

We called Dr. Paul Weinberg, professor of obstetrics and gynecology at the University of Texas Medical School in San Antonio, to the stand. He was well trained, had practiced obstetrics and gynecology in Maryland, New York and Texas, was board certified and had published many papers on abortion. He said that he had performed or supervised more than 500 hysterotomies. His testimony repeated much of what had already been given by our previous experts. He agreed that the best choice for abortion after a failed saline infusion was a hysterotomy and that a hysterotomy could be performed up through the 24th week of pregnancy. He contradicted Gimenez's definition of birth by saying that it was the expulsion or extraction of the fetus from the mother.

"In your opinion, what was the quality of care delivered by Dr. Edelin in this case?" Bill asked.

"His care of this patient was consistent with good medical practice," said Dr. Weinburg.

"After examining the patient's medical record, have you found any reason why Dr. Edelin should have concluded that this patient was pregnant with a viable fetus?"

"This fetus was not viable," he said with certainty.

"Do you have an opinion as to why the fetus weighed 600 grams when it was first weighed by the pathologist and 700 grams four months later?"

"The difference in weight could have been explained by formaldehyde fixation. We did experiments in my laboratory using rabbit fetuses. We weighed them immediately after they were born and again after fixing them in formaldehyde for 42 days. The fetuses gained weight daily over that period of time. If we had continued the experiment, the weight gain would have continued."

"I have no further questions for this witness, your honor."

All of our expert witnesses were saying essentially the same thing. This was not a viable fetus, hysterotomy was the best choice for terminating the pregnancy after three failed saline attempts and my care of Evonne was good medical practice. I hoped the jury understood this.

Flanagan had very few questions for Dr. Weinberg, and the questions he did have had little impact. We moved on to the next witness, Dr. Jack Pritchard.

Dr. Pritchard was one of the best-known professors of obstetrics in America. He taught at the University of Texas Medical School and was director of obstetrics at Parkland Memorial Hospital in Dallas, where they delivered more babies than any other hospital in the country—the same hospital that President Kennedy was taken to after being shot. Pritchard had published hundreds of articles concerning the care of pregnant women and, most famously, was the co-author of *Williams Obstetrics,* the main text used by both Flanagan and us in defining terms. Jack Pritchard was a big man, wore a white cowboy shirt with pearl snap buttons and a string cowboy tie.

Pritchard repeated the definition of abortion that all of our other expert witnesses had given—the termination of pregnancy before viability, which he, like them, put at 28 weeks' gestation or 1,000 grams.

"Was it good medical practice for Dr. Edelin to go ahead with the performance of the hysterotomy?"

Flanagan objected to the question. "I don't mind if he testifies as to what he considers to be good medical practice, but I don't want him to testify if he thinks Dr. Edelin's actions were good medical practice."

Isn't that what this case is all about? I thought.

The exchanges between Bill and Flanagan were becoming sharper by the minute. It had been a long trial—nearly six weeks so far—and they continued to joust over the proper use of words, objecting at nearly every other question and answer. The heat in the courtroom rose. Flanagan was determined not to have Dr. Pritchard characterize my medical practice as being good. Bill was just as determined to have him do so. Eventually, Dr. Pritchard was able to say that what I had done was good medical practice. Flanagan seethed. He cast a hatred-filled glance my way.

"Why do you say that this was good medical practice?"

"For two reasons. First, an abortion was to be performed and this was the only practical alternative that was left. Second, there had been multiple attempts to enter into the uterine cavity for the purposes of instilling a hypertonic salt solution. These attempts were carried out over a period of 24 hours on three different occasions. In spite of the careful technique, the probability exists that bacteria were introduced into the uterus during one or more of these insertions. This increases the risk of infection. Had he not performed the hysterotomy, this young girl might have gotten really sick. The techniques available to him to perform an abortion were limited to hysterotomy."

"Dr. Prichard, do you have an opinion as to the condition of the fetus immediately prior to the start of the operation?"

"I think it is very likely that the fetus was dead."

"What is the basis of your opinion?"

"Because the pathologist said the lungs did not float in water, therefore there was no air in the lungs, meaning that it did not breathe outside of the womb. Furthermore, the two eyewitnesses said that there was no evidence of life when the fetus was removed from the uterus."

After a few more questions, Bill handed Dr. Pritchard over to Flanagan.

"Did you evah make the statement that abortion was the termination of pregnancy prior to 20 weeks?"

"I'm co-author of the textbook where that statement occurs."

Flanagan then turned the tables on us and produced an affidavit that Dr. Prichard had signed.

"Did you sign a statement that said that abortion is medically defined as the termination of pregnancy befoah the end of the 20th week?"

"I have already stated my definition of abortion," Jack Pritchard said defiantly.

"There's more than one definition for abortion, isn't that correct, Doctah Prichard?"

"Yes."

"How many are there?"

"I really don't know, Mr. Flanagan," Jack Pritchard answered, tossing some of Flanagan's condescending mock politeness back at him with his smooth, Texas accent. "*My* definition of abortion is the interruption of a pregnancy before viability."

"Can you tell us how long a fetus at 24 weeks' gestation and weighing 700 grams would live?"

"In my experience, I have never seen one that weighed 700 grams or less live."

"Do you agree that the survival of infants between 700 or 800 grams is unusual?"

"Yes."

"But they do occur, don't they?"

"Rarely."

"Do they occur?" Flanagan repeated angrily.

"Yes."

Flanagan opened *Williams Obstetrics* to the page containing the description of one very rare case. "Doctah Prichard, do you agree with the statement that infants weighing 400 grams or more may be regahded as capable of living?"

"Not necessarily."

Showing him the textbook, Flanagan asked, "Did you evah say that?"

"No, not me personally."

"Do you know who did?"

"Yes. It was Dr. Hellman, my co-author."

Obviously frustrated with Pritchard's testimony, Flanagan went back to the definition of abortion.

"Prior to January of 1973, your definition of abortion was termination of pregnancy before the 20th week?"

"Yes it was."

"Your definition of abortion was also the expulsion or extraction of a nonviable fetus?"

"Yes."

"Both of these were your definitions before January of 1973. Is that a fact?"

"The former was the definition of the state of Texas, a legal definition."

"I'm talking about your definition, Doctah," Flanagan snapped. "With all due respect, I don't care what the definition was in Texas!"

"My definition," Pritchard said slowly, his eyes flashing, "is before viability."

"Prior to January 1973, the medical definition of viability was up to 20 weeks, is that correct?" Flanagan asked.

"No, not my medical definition."

Flanagan raised his voice, "Do you agree with the statement that an abortion is a term referring to the termination of a pregnancy before the 20th completed week of gestation?"

"That's part of my definition."

"What is the othah paht?"

"Before viability."

"I have no furthah questions for this witness," Flanagan said with contempt.

———

Our next witness was Dr. Schuyler Kohl, a professor of obstetrics and gynecology at the Downstate Medical Center in New York. In addition to being a board certified obstetrician and gynecologist, he was also a biostatistician and an epidemiologist. He had carried out a study of the survivability of over 120,000 babies born at various birth weights. In that study, there were the 283 babies born who weighed between 700 and 800 grams and only six survived. Dr. Kohl further testified that of the 359 babies born weighing between 600 and 700 grams, only one survived—about a quarter of a percent. He defined viability as when the fetus has a very good chance of survival following delivery, beginning at around 800 grams. He said that a fetus born weighing less than that did not have a reasonably good chance of survival outside of the mother's womb.

Under brief cross-examination, Kohl repeated the definition of abortion that our other expert witnesses had given. Flanagan was not pleased.

February 11, 1975

Our final expert was Dr. Shirley Driscoll. She was a professor of pathology at Harvard Medical School and a pathologist at the Harvard teaching hospitals in Boston. She had performed more than 2,000 autopsies on fetuses and newborns. She, too, had reviewed the slides that Dr. Curtis, the medical examiner, had made as a result of his autopsy. She testified that the fetus never breathed air, described in detail the condition of the lungs by referring to photographs of the slides and said that the degenerating red blood cells found in the lungs were present because blood was in the amniotic fluid as a result of the multiple attempts at saline infusion. Finally, she concluded that the lungs of the fetus indicated that it was between 20 and 24 weeks' gestational age. Her testimony sounded very much like that of Kurt Benirschke. In his cross-examination, Flanagan picked up on that.

"If I told you that Doctah Benirschke said that in almost all spaces he found granulah debris, would that be consistent with what you saw?"

"Yes."

Then, in an offhanded manner, Flanagan asked, "Incidentally, have you examined the testimony of Doctah Benirschke?"

"Yes, I have."

"As a mattah of fact, you have co-authored a book with Doctah Benirschke, haven't you?"

"That is correct."

"Are you friends with Doctah Benirschke?"

"Yes."

"I have no furthah questions for this witness."

That was it for our expert witnesses. Their testimony had been much the same. Everything I had done was in keeping with good medical practice, the fetus was not viable, my decisions were the right ones…but what about the jury? I could only hope that the people sitting in judgment of me understood and believed them.

CHAPTER 33

TRIAL DAY 27

February 12, 1975

We had one more witness to place on the stand: Stephen Teich. Steve was the medical student who had assisted me during the hysterotomy. He was now in his final year of medical school. When he took the stand, he described how he became my first assistant in the operation.

"It was the morning of October 3, 1973, and I was in the first operating room on the GYN service watching surgery. From there, I went to OR number two because I heard that there was to be an attempted abortion on a black female who was about 22 weeks pregnant. I wanted to observe it."

"What did you see in the second operating room?" Bill asked.

"The first person I saw was Dr. Edelin and one of the attending physicians doing what appeared to be a saline abortion. I saw them attempting to pierce the abdominal wall with a long needle."

"How long did that take?"

"I don't recall exactly, but it lasted several minutes. They made at least one attempt, maybe more. Eventually, the attending physician left the room and Dr. Edelin asked for volunteers to assist him. I volunteered and left the room to scrub for surgery."

"When you returned to the operating room, what did you do?"

"I positioned myself on the side of the operating table, opposite to Dr. Edelin, which put me on the patient's right side."

"What did you observe Dr. Edelin do?"

"Dr. Edelin began the surgery on the patient with a small incision..."

Steve's detailed description of the surgery matched mine exactly. He used the word "fingers," not "hand," and never mentioned any clocks.

"During the surgery, did you ever observe Dr. Edelin stand motionless with his hand in the uterus?"

"No, I did not."

"Did you ever observe Dr. Edelin stand still looking at a clock for three minutes or for any other significant period of time?"

"No."

"During your time on the GYN service, did you ever make an observation with respect to a clock or timer in either of the operating rooms?"

"I recall that in one of the operating rooms, the clock was not functioning."

"Do you recall which operating room that was?"

"I don't recall."

"How did you know that the clock was not functioning?"

"At first, the clock was just wrong. The time always stayed the same. After that, there was a point when there was no clock at all in one of the operating rooms. There was just a hole in the wall with some wires sticking out."

Bill then had Steve examine the photograph Flanagan had introduced.

"Do you recognize this fetus?"

"No."

"I have no further questions for this witness," Bill said.

Flanagan stood up and my pulse quickened. Would Steve Teich, in his last year of medical school, be able to withstand Flanagan's attacks? See through his tricks? "Once Doctah Edelin put his hand in the uterus and aftah the circulah motion, what took place?"

Bill was ready. "Objection, your honor! The witness did not testify that Dr. Edelin had his hand inside of the uterus."

Flanagan tried a different approach. "How many fingahs did he have on the hand that was in there?"

Steve Teich apparently already had a distaste for Flanagan. "I don't know how many fingers he had inside the uterus, but he had five fingers on his hand as far as I know." There was a chuckle in the courtroom. Flanagan narrowed his small beady eyes.

"How long did it take him to delivah the fetus?"

"From the time that the sac broke and the time I saw the fetus, no more than several seconds."

"Did you talk to Doctah Edelin aftah the operation took place?"

Again Flanagan's conspiracy theory.

"Immediately after the operation, he thanked me for helping him," Steve said.

"When was the next time you talked to Doctah Edelin concehning the operation?"

"The next time we spoke was about a month ago."

"Where were you when you talked to him?"

"I was in New York."

"Did you call Doctah Edelin?"

"I'm not sure if I called him or he called me."

"I have no furthah questions for this witness."

Bill then slowly stood up from behind the table.

"The defense rests, your honor. May it please the court, on behalf of the defendant, the evidence is closed."

"May it please the court," said Flanagan, "on behalf of the Commonwealth, the evidence is closed."

After 27 days of being on trial, the only things left were the closing arguments, McGuire's charge to the jury, the jury's deliberations and the verdict.

Judge McGuire rapped his gavel on the desk of his bench.

"We will adjourn until 9:00 tomorrow morning, at which time we will hear the closing arguments."

McGuire left the courtroom. I stood up, stretched my back and beelined to the spectators' section, where my family and friends were gathered. They each hugged me, knowing that we had presented our best case. All of the facts were out in the open. Everyone was hopeful and optimistic—except me. It was difficult to say where I stood. I felt that the evidence presented and the testimony of the witnesses made it clear that I was innocent, but the fact remained that I was facing a potential conviction for manslaughter. My freedom, my career and my life were all at stake.

Bill, Frank and I walked in silence back to the office. The weather had turned unseasonably warm, so our pace was more leisurely than usual. We didn't go to the pub; we went straight to Bill's office.

We sat in the conference room, but no one broke the silence. We had presented a very strong defense. Medicine, science and the experts were on our side. The law was on our side. The truth was on our side. All that was remained was for Bill to summarize it all for the jury in his closing arguments.

Several of Bill's partners joined us, but no one said a word. After a long while, Bill finally spoke.

"I need to write out my closing argument. What do you think I should emphasize?" We all began to make suggestions as to what themes should be included. We wanted to contrast our case with that of Flanagan, our witnesses with his, our facts with his. As we sat there, all talking at once, Bill began to write.

CHAPTER 34

BILL'S CLOSING ARGUMENTS

"Mr. Homans, you may proceed."

"Thank you, your honor."

Bill rose from behind our desk, yellow legal pad in hand, and approached the jury box, where he rested his hand on the well-worn rail in front of the first row of jurors. He added his sweat to the seasoning of the wood.

His voice was clear, even and powerful. "Mr. Foreman, ladies and gentlemen of the jury, you have sat here since January 6th. We could hear cheers from your jury room when we completed the jury selection process. I'm sure there will be cheers when you finally come to a decision and can go home. This hasn't been an easy case. The issues have been complex and tough.

"You have heard the indictment read. You heard the charge that Dr. Edelin 'did assault and beat a baby boy and by such assault and beating did kill him.' Words have great significance in this case. This case, no matter what you have heard, is about an abortion. Mr. Flanagan will tell you that this is not an abortion case. He will tell you that this is a manslaughter case. But just because he said it, doesn't make it so.

"Whatever your personal views about abortion are, I am confident you will be able to put them aside in determining the issues in this case. But whatever your view, this case has to do with an abortion and the circumstances surrounding it. You heard in my opening statement that we will ask you to consider not words but facts. What is important in this case is what happened.

"This is not a case about a baby. You have heard that word throughout this case, but it is not about babies. This is not a case about speculation. Dr. Edelin has confronted the issues in this case with hard

311

facts. The Commonwealth didn't offer any evidence as to viability, but we did. We offered evidence about the ages at which a particular infant will survive. The Commonwealth will ask you to speculate and say that the 600-gram fetus in this case would have survived. What the Commonwealth means by survival, we don't know, but the Commonwealth is asking you to speculate. Don't speculate. This is a case involving facts and the judgments that physicians make on the basis of the facts that are available to them.

"This is a case not only about this physician, Dr. Edelin, but about thousands of physicians who have to make these decisions with the facts they have at the time. The questions is, can thousands of physicians—can your physician—embark on a medical procedure using his or her best judgment on the basis of the information at hand and after appropriate consultation? That, I suggest to you, is the simple issue in this case.

"The Commonwealth has brought their experts here to testify as to what Dr. Edelin should have done. Who were these experts? Consider Drs. Vernig, Mecklenburg, Cavanagh and the district attorney's neighbor, Dr. O'Connell. Each one of them had an ax to grind. And we certainly can't forget about Dr. Mildred Jefferson, who testified at the beginning of the case.

"They said she was here just to give definitions, which were supposed to guide you in understanding this case. But she isn't an obstetrician or gynecologist. She is a founding member of Massachusetts Citizens for Life. She, too, has an ax to grind. Dr. Mecklenburg was present at a meeting in Minnesota of a group campaigning against the present abortion law, where Dr. Jefferson was the featured speaker. Dr. Cavanagh acknowledged responsibility for an anti-abortion newspaper advertisement in St. Louis on the second anniversary of *Roe v. Wade*.

"You also heard about a speech given by Dr. Vernig. At first he denied it, but his memory was restored when he was shown a copy of the speech. Then he said, 'I didn't know it was being recorded.' In that speech, he said that 99 percent of infants under 28 ounces will die.

"All of these witnesses came here with the same ax to grind. They want to stop abortions.

"But there were other physicians with no axes to grind—like Dr. Curtis, who testified on behalf of the Commonwealth. He told you what he saw and what he concluded. Dr. Curtis was applying his best judgment to the task he had to do. You heard Dr. Kennedy talk about viability. He told you that in his opinion, the chance of survival of a fetus of 600 or 700 grams at the City Hospital nursery was nil. Those, in essence, were his words. You have heard from physicians like Drs. Barnes, Driscoll and Benirschke, who we brought here to testify, who have no axes to grind.

"Did Dr. Edelin perform the medical procedure within the bounds permitted him as a physician using his best judgment? A physician must determine when, how, where and in what fashion he can perform a particular medical procedure. It is not only Dr. Edelin who is on trial here. It is your physician, my physician, thousands of physicians throughout the country who act on the basis of the information available to them and according to good and accepted medical standards. It is of the utmost importance that physicians have knowledge of the legal requirements and prohibitions to which they are subject. It is not only the strict medical facts that a physician must base a decision on—he has to be aware of what the law says he is permitted to do and what he is prohibited from doing. The testimony of Dr. Edelin showed you what was in his mind concerning these laws. He told you that on January 22, 1973, he became aware of the decision in *Roe v. Wade.*"

Bill glanced down at his legal pad, and then looked back up at the jury.

"The district attorney has been pushing hard in this case. Sometimes, in his eagerness to push, he missed some facts. Dr. Gimenez's testimony in this case is the best example of that. You recall that I asked Dr. Gimenez, 'When you testified in front of the grand jury, you said you *thought* he looked at the clocks. You were uncertain that he looked at the clocks?' to which Dr. Gimenez responded, 'I was certain. It's…just…probably, at the time, I didn't say 'yes,' but he *pushed* me and then I said the truth.' Think back to that. 'He pushed me…'"

Bill paused to allow his words to sink in, then began to pick apart Enrique's testimony, starting with his uncertainty about which operating room the procedure took place in, then continuing on to the issue of the clocks and me standing there with my whole hand inside the uterus.

"Was Dr. Gimenez telling the truth? I leave that to your judgment.

"I suggest to you that you could find beyond a reasonable doubt that the clock was not there. But, if your whole decision is made upon the basis of clocks, that would not be fair to the Commonwealth and that would not be fair to Dr. Edelin because there are other issues here, much more important issues."

Bill returned to Flanagan's tactics, citing his mistake in calling Helen Horner to the stand.

"The district attorney misread the sponge count book. He was pushing so hard that he was confused. She answered their questions because she also was confused; they were pushing so hard. After her testimony in front of the grand jury, she went back and checked the hospital records and discovered that she was not the scrub tech on this case. When she testified to that in this courtroom, the district attorney was dumbfounded and tried to make it look as though she's engaged in some kind of conspiracy to protect Dr. Edelin.

"Dr. Gimenez was pushed and Helen Horner was shown the wrong record. This is the nature of the Commonwealth's case."

As Bill pressed through his summation, his emotions rose and his voice cracked. He knew Flanagan's case against me was as weak as his experts. But the jurors—the jury of Flanagan's peers—were the ones who had to be convinced.

Bill criticized Dr. Ward's testimony and pointed out our experts' counter-explanation as to why there were red blood cells in the lungs. He cited fact after fact and reminded the jury to listen to those facts, to draw their own conclusions, not to speculate.

Bill then moved to the essence of my defense.

"What was Dr. Edelin aware of at the time of the hysterotomy procedure? He was aware that Dr. Holtrop had said, on the basis of his examination, that the patient was between 20 and 21 weeks pregnant. You have heard Dr. Edelin state that he, too, examined the patient and estimated that she was 22 weeks. The patient said that her last menstrual period was on the 28th of May, which would make her 18 to 19 weeks pregnant. Dr. Edelin was also aware of what Dr. Gimenez and a third-year medical student had estimated—24 weeks. But in *his* judgment, it was 22 weeks.

"Dr. Edelin has told you that he would never abort a viable fetus. It is not what anyone else tells you about weight or measurements, it is what Dr. Edelin *knew and believed* at the time he performed this procedure that is important in determining viability.

"The district attorney may argue that the record in this case shows that the operative note was not made until December 12th, two months after the operation, and that Dr. Edelin is trying to pull the wool over someone's eyes. In that operative note, Dr. Edelin said the fetus was 20 weeks, when in reality it was 22 weeks. But if you look at the note that he dictated to Ellyn Curtis, the nurse, immediately following the operation, he said that it was 22 weeks. The pathology sheet also, in Ellyn Curtis' own handwriting, says '22-week pregnancy.'

"If bad record keeping is a crime, then I know where I would be."

Bill went over other important points in the various testimonies, to make sure the jury understood the implications of everything. He paced in front of the jury box, letting his fingers run along the worn railing.

"These are the facts we have presented to you over and over again. Not the Commonwealth. We presented you with the results of experiments, showing an increase in weight after formaldehyde fixation. The Commonwealth did not.

"As you go into the jury room, think about the facts and hard evidence here. Don't speculate. When you have done that, you will find that Dr. Edelin, without question, engaged in a procedure which, in his best judgment as a physician, was sanctioned not only by good medical practice, but also by the law. Unless you feel that Dr. Edelin is some kind of ogre who went about killing babies with malicious intent, I suggest that you will find that Dr. Edelin acted in accordance with his best judgment and good medical practice. That is the issue in this case. Under those circumstances—under all of the circumstances you have heard—you will find him 'not guilty.' Thank you."

He stood there in the emotional silence of the courtroom, looking at each juror in turn. He then returned to his chair and dropped his yellow legal pad on the table. I gave him a nod. He had put his mind, heart and soul into this closing argument—into this entire case. I had every confidence that he had done his absolute best.

I jumped at the sound of McGuire's gavel.

"We will take a recess and after lunch, Mr. Flanagan will present his closing argument. Court will resume at 2:00 p.m."

CHAPTER 35

FLANAGAN'S FINAL ASSAULT

———

I dreaded having to sit through Flanagan's closing argument. I had no doubt it would be a continuation of his distortions and his own motives. He knew this jury. They were his people. They were not like me. They were not like Bill Homans or Frank Susman. This was Flanagan's jury, and all I could do was hope they could see and recognize the truth.

After lunch, Flanagan began.

"Mr. Foreman, ladies and gentlemen of the jury, what Mr. Homans told you this morning and what I am about to say to you now is not evidence in this case. This is the time in the case when the lawyers try and bring your attention to certain facts that they feel are important. You will then sit and deliberate to decide what is important and what is not.

"The duty and task of the jury is to find the facts, apply the law and reach a verdict. How do you do that? What tools do you have? The most obvious is the testimony that is elicited from the witnesses as to what took place. You have heard from a great numbah of expert witnesses, and they gave their opinion on certain facts. As the supreme judges in this case, you can completely disregahd what any one of them said, completely believe them, or believe part of what they said and disbelieve the other part. You have the right to look at *any* witness and ask yourself, 'Is he telling the truth?' Size the witnesses up. Recall how they said things. How did they impress you? Were they speaking right? Do they have an interest in this case? Would they be prejudiced one way or another?

"Finally, in helping you reach a verdict, you have evidence, real evidence—photographs, records, *et cetera*. These are the tools that will assist you in finding the truth.

"Let's look at the facts in this case. Remember the witnesses who testified on the facts—Doctah Gimenez, the defendant, the Curtis woman, Doctah Holtrop, Doctah Penza. Ask yourselves, do they have an interest in this case. Would they be prejudiced in testifying one way or anothah?

"What interest does Doctah Gimenez have? What interest does the defendant have? Do they stand to gain by their testimony? That's for you to determine.

"This is the case of the Commonwealth of Massachusetts versus Kenneth Edelin. This is not the case of Doctah Gimenez versus Kenneth Edelin. This is not the case of Doctah Mecklenburg versus Kenneth Edelin."

He paused, then spouted out the most blatant lie I had heard throughout the entire trial: "This is not the case of pro-life versus Kenneth Edelin. This is not the case of anti-abortion and pro. This is a case of manslaughtah, not abortion. It involves the killing—unjustifiably—of an independent human being *following* an abortion, not during the termination of the pregnancy. Don't forget that we're not here trying Doctah Gimenez against the defendant or anybody else against this defendant. This is a crime that the Commonwealth has alleged and a grand jury has seen fit to indict. A crime has been committed, and the Commonwealth must prove that that crime has been committed beyond a reasonable doubt.

"When I say 'the Commonwealth,' I am including you, the defendant and everybody in our society. I include the victim in this case. He has the right to be protected, if he is a person.

"From the beginning, there has been a lot of talk about clocks. Why do they keep harping on a clock, a clock, a clock? Because that is not the basic issue in this case. It is a side issue. It is to take your mind off what actually took place here. It is the same reason I wear a bright tie—to hide a dirty shirt."

He paused. No one laughed. The jurors did not even crack a smile.

"Doctah Gimenez said that he was not sure whethah there were one or two clocks in the operating room. Then the nurse—the Curtis woman—said there was a clock out; Doctah Teich said that he remembahs that there was a clock out with wires sticking out from a hole in the wall. But ask yourself this: there was only one person who testified that two clocks were broken and out for repairs. Only one witness mentioned two clocks, the defendant, Doctah Edelin. Has he got anything to gain by testifying that there were two clocks out?"

The knot in my stomach tightened as Flanagan continued to play his jury like a violinist plays a Stradivarius.

"Mr. Homans mentioned something about a conspiracy here. Let's look at that issue. Let's take the witnesses as they first started out in this case. Doctah Holtrop, Doctah Penza, Alan Silberman, Helen Horner—those were the first four of the witnesses. What did they say? Do you recall their testimonies? This is one of those 'not me—him' kind of situations. 'Not me—him.' Because every time I asked certain witnesses, 'Who was in the operating room?' That was their answer. 'I wasn't there—he was.' 'Who was the operating nurse?' 'It wasn't me, it was Miss Bloom.' 'Who was there?' 'Not me—her.' 'Who made the statement in the book Hellman and Pritchard wrote?' 'Not me—Doctah Hellman made that statement.' Doctah Holtrop said, 'She was not my patient.' But the record shows that she was his patient. It was always the other one. Mr. Homans says that the Commonwealth would say that this was a conspiracy. I didn't say that. But I do say this: if something looks like a duck and waddles like a duck and quacks, then it's a duck. Keep that in mind in your consideration of the testimony and the statement that there may be a conspiracy. I didn't say that, Mr. Homans did.

"Now, let's get to Doctah Gimenez's testimony. Mr. Homans wants you to think that I was pushing Doctah Gimenez to mention a clock in the grand jury room. Let me say this to you: it is awfully easy to criticize an individual for taking a stand and testifying in a case. It's awfully easy to criticize an individual who happens to be a docktah for taking the stand and testifying against another doctah. It is not easy to actually do that—to get on the stand and testify against a fellow doctah. What does Doctah Gimenez have to gain by taking the stand and testifying that a certain doctah who worked with him did something? Ask yourself, what does he have to gain by that?"

I knew exactly what Enrique Gimenez had to gain by it, but I was forced to keep my mouth shut, lest I hurt my case. I ground my teeth as Flanagan went on.

"Maybe he's telling the truth as to what took place in this case. Did I push him to say that she was 24 weeks pregnant, four fingerbreadths above the umbilicus? Doctah Gimenez found a fetal heart rate of 140, the heartbeat of a fetus within its mothah's womb, attached to the mothah and a part of the mothah. If a woman, at that time in her pregnancy, wants to have an abortion, under the law, she's got a right to it. Whethah we like it or not, the law says she's got that right. So what happens? Multiple attempts to terminate the pregnancy by a saline infusion, unsuccessful, resulting in bloody taps. Prior to that, the defendant testifies that he made a personal examination of the patient. He had in mind what Doctah Holtrop had done when he measured the uterus to be 22 centimeters—he had written it in the chart. The defendant knew what Mr. Silberman had put down, he had in mind what Doctah Gimenez had put down, and he tells you that he made a clinical diagnosis of one fingerbreadth above the umbilicus—22 weeks. Where is it in the record? Why *isn't* it in the record? Where and when does he say that for the first time? Here. January 1975. When did the abortion take place? Octobah 3rd, 1973.

"So she wanted an abortion. What is an abortion? You heard the testimony of a great number of experts as to the definition of an abortion—the termination of pregnancy prior to the end of the 20th week, resulting in either a stillborn or a liveborn infant. That was the testimony of almost all of the expert witnesses. There was only one who made a little variation in that and that was Dr. Pritchard. But who was the first one to say that an abortion culminates in the termination of whatevah is in the mothah? The defendant, Doctah Edelin, was the first one to testify that not only is an abortion the termination of pregnancy, but it involves the termination of whatevah neonatal life is in there.

"Doctah Edelin tried a saline abortion two different times and he got back bloody taps. You've heard a lot about 'bloody taps.' When the second one didn't work, he asked Doctah Penza what to do and he said, 'Put her on the schedule tomorrow and I will try again.' What did Doctah Edelin tell the patient? He said, 'We are going to perfoahm a hysterotomy if the saline doesn't work.' Did he tell the patient anything else?

"A hysterotomy is major surgery. You heard several opinions about what a hysterotomy is and how they are done. Hysterotomy is a way of terminating a pregnancy for the purposes of abortion. Doctah Mecklenburg testified that he has perfoahmed hysterotomies for the purpose of abortions—'You open her up, you take out the fetus and then you go back and get the placenta. And you put the fetus in the nursery,' or words to that effect.

"In December of 1973, we received information from City Hospital about abortion practices there. It was discovered that there was a body at the morgue. Two weeks after we subpoenaed hospital records, the defendant dictated the operative note—two months after the operation. Is it important? Ask yourself.

"Remembah what Mr. Homans said in his opening statement? He said that no baby boy ever existed, no baby boy was killed and that the existence of this fetus was terminated by anoxia. We agree with him.

"How do you die from anoxia? You heard the testimony. Ask yourselves this question: when the placenta was detached from the uterine wall was the baby—oh, *excuse me*," he said sarcastically. "Was the 'subject' alive or dead? When the placenta is detached, what happens? You lose oxygen. You lose that lifeline to the mothah. What does that cause? Anoxia. Well, isn't it common sense that in order to die from anoxia, you must be alive at the time that the placenta is detached? Is there any evidence in that record that from the time the fetal heartbeat was taken on September 30th until the time the placenta was detached from the uterine wall that the fetus was anything other than alive?

Flanagan went on and on, twisting the words of our other expert witnesses to confuse and conquer the jury. He repeated their testimonies out of context, distorting meanings and placing undercurrents where they didn't belong.

He brought up Ward the Weasel's testimony and how Dr. Driscoll and Dr. Benirschke disagreed with the notion that the fetus lived outside the mother. He hinted again at a conspiracy, since they knew each other, had co-authored a book together and considered one another a friend. He criticized the 30 minutes Dr. Benirschke spent studying the same slides that Dr. Ward had looked over—when they were denied to us in the first place.

This was his final attack, and he came on full force.

"Let's get back to the case," Flanagan said. "The defendant tells us that after he separated the placenta, he removed the fetus—the 'subject.' Take a look at the picture of the 'subject.' Is this just a subject? Just a specimen? You tell us what it is. Look at the picture. Show it to anybody. What would they tell you it was? Use your common sense when you go to your jury deliberation room. Are we speaking about a blob or a big bunch of mucus? What are we talking about here? 'Subjects'? I respectfully submit that we're talking about an independent human being—a baby—that the Commonwealth of Massachusetts and anyone else in this courtroom—including the defendant—must protect.

"What took place? Ask yourself if this defendant was trying to determine whethah or not the subject was alive. Two seconds? Hand over. Rubber glove. Put it in the pan. Then there was an autopsy four months latah. What did it show? No abnormalities. Like you and me.

The autopsy described everything—the heart, the brain, the spleen. Everything. The curly hair. Just a 'subject'?

"We are in a society where if you are alive, you have a right to continue to live. There is no greatah right in our society than the right to life, and there is no more heinous thing than to deprive an individual of that right. *That's what this case is all about.*"

I couldn't agree with him more. This case *was* about the right to life versus the right of a woman to control her own body. But Flanagan didn't care about that. He was lost in his self-righteous right to life world.

"Although a woman has her rights and we have our rights," Flanagan continued, "so does any independent human being, in this case the baby boy, the male child, as indicated in this pahticulah indictment. He has those rights once he is on his own, and no one has the right to take it away from him. Not even a docktah.

"The fact that the defendant in this case happens to be a docktah shouldn't be to his advantage or to his detriment. You should not use the fact that he is a docktah to be prejudiced for or against him. You can't use sympathy, because obviously, what's the most sympathetic thing in the entire case? Look at the picture and then answer that question.

"Mistah foreman, and ladies and gentlemen of the jury, it has been a long and tedious trial. I respectfully say to you that your job is about to begin aftah the judge instructs you tomorrow on the law. You will have 12 minds of citizens in our society that know essentially what life is all about. You will sift through the evidence and find the truth.

"Listen to the judge's instructions on the law and apply them to the facts that you find. On all the evidence presented, you would be more than warranted in finding this defendant guilty of the crime with which he is charged. We are a land of laws, and all must abide by that. Whethah it is a back street, white collah or white coat killing, you must make that determination. Thank you."

As Flanagan sat down, the words "white coat killing" hung in the air, reverberating like the last note of a symphony. No one moved. After an eternal minute of silence, McGuire rapped his gavel and told the jury that he was going to recess the proceedings for the day. In the morning, he would give them their instructions before they began their deliberations. For the final time, he warned them not to discuss the case until after his instructions.

CHAPTER 36

McGuire's Instructions

February 14, 1975

On the 29th day of my trial, at 10:25 a.m., Judge James McGuire looked over at the jury and began his instructions. We focused all of our attention on every word—listening for hope.

"On January 10, 1975, after the selection of this jury had been completed and the foreman had been appointed, the clerk rose and read to you an indictment against the defendant, Dr. Kenneth Edelin, who is charged with the crime of manslaughter. This trial has occupied your time and your attention from that day to this. You are the jurors in this case. You sit here in open court listening to the proceedings, sitting in judgment upon a fellow citizen. The doors have been open to the public to come and go at all times while you have been sitting in the courtroom.

"The grand jury sits in a room in the courthouse from which the public is excluded. It meets in secret. The only persons permitted in that room are the members of the grand jury, a witness who may be giving evidence, a stenographer who records that evidence and one or more representatives of the office of the district attorney, who present the evidence. The grand jury sits and hears only the evidence the prosecutor wants to present to it. If the grand jury believes that the evidence is sufficient to require a person under investigation to be brought to trial, it indicts that person. The grand jury has never passed upon the innocence or guilt of this defendant. The indictment is not evidence in any way against the defendant. You are the first body of jurors to have the question Dr. Edelin's innocence or guilt posed before it.

"You are to judge the facts of this case. You must act fairly. You must not allow yourselves to be influenced by bias or prejudice or sympathy or emotion for or against anyone connected with this trial. When you go to your jury room, all that you take with you is your memory of what was said, the exhibits and a copy of the indictment.

"The opening statements of the lawyers and their closing arguments are not evidence. You are the sole judges of the credibility, the truthfulness and the veracity of every witness who testified during this trial. You likewise are the sole judges of the weight to be given to various portions of the evidence that have been presented. You had a chance to observe and size up each witness when he or she was on the stand. You should consider whether any witness who appeared at the trial would be affected in any way by the outcome. You should also consider whether any feeling exists between witnesses and the defendant, or witnesses and other witnesses.

"Ordinarily, a witness is not allowed to give an opinion. However, there are certain exceptions to that rule. One of those exceptions is concerned with the testimony of people such as physicians, who are allowed to express opinions based upon their education, training and experience. One witness's opinion should not be given greater consideration than another's. You will regard such opinions as evidence and weigh it as carefully as you would weigh any other testimony in the case. You may accept it, reject it or accept only part of it.

"By virtue of our state constitution and the Constitution of the United States, every defendant in a criminal case is presumed to be innocent. The burden of proving the case is on the Commonwealth, to prove guilt beyond a reasonable doubt. Unless the Commonwealth does just that, the defendant is entitled, as a matter of right, to a verdict of 'not guilty.' The presumption of innocence is with the defendant before and all throughout the trial. Therefore, the defendant has no burden whatsoever in establishing his innocence. He cannot be convicted on conjecture, surmise, speculation, suspicion or rumor.

"If, in the search for the truth, you end up with a reasonable doubt as to the existence of any essential fact of the crime charged, then the verdict of 'not guilty' must be returned.

"The defendant in this case has been indicted for the crime of manslaughter. Manslaughter is the unlawful killing of another without malice.

"Negligence is the failure of a responsible person to exercise the care, vigilance and forethought that he should under particular circumstances. But negligence or carelessness is not sufficient to prove the crime of manslaughter. Negligence is different from wanton or reckless conduct. The essence of wanton or reckless conduct is acting or failing to act, knowing that doing so involves a high degree of likelihood that substantial harm will result to another; it has been described as indifference to or disregard of the probable consequences to the right of others. Wanton or reckless conduct is the legal equivalent of intentional conduct. If the result of by wanton or reckless conduct is death, the person guilty of such conduct may be guilty of manslaughter."

I watched the jurors' faces as McGuire gave his speech. None of them gave any hint of what they were thinking. Were they listening? Daydreaming? Had they already made their decision or would there be a long deliberation?

McGuire went on to explain *Roe v. Wade* and *Doe v. Bolton*, reminding the jury that those decisions made all existing Massachusetts laws regarding abortion null and void and that between the date of those decisions and the date of Evonne's hysterotomty, the state had not passed any laws restricting abortion in any way.

"Thus," he continued, "we have in the consideration of this case, the law of manslaughter which is inextricably intertwined with the January 22, 1973 decision in *Roe v. Wade*.

"During this trial you have had expert witnesses give you definitions of words. They may have been helpful in listening to their testimony, but they were not legal definitions. The definitions I am about to give you now must be accepted by you as the legal definitions under the decision of *Roe v. Wade*.

"Let me first discuss the word 'person.' One of the essential elements of the crime of manslaughter is the death of a person. The Constitution of the United States does not define 'person' in so many words. There are several references, however. In nearly all these instances, the use of the word is such that it has meaning only after birth. None of the definitions indicates that it has any possible prenatal application.

"It is implicit that the word 'abortion,' as used by the United States Supreme Court in *Roe v. Wade*, is the termination of a pregnancy at any time during the pregnant woman's nine months of that pregnancy. In *Roe v. Wade*, the Supreme Court said—and it is the law of this land and of this Commonwealth—that the abortion process and its effectuation must be left to the medical judgment of the pregnant woman's attending physician. Because the Commonwealth of Massachusetts had no statute or laws in effect to regulate abortion, abortion at the time of this case was protected by the decision in *Roe v. Wade.*

"If, in your consideration of the facts of this case, you determine that the terms 'viability' and 'potential for life' have any applicability, their meanings are to be taken as such: first, as to viability, the ability to live after birth. Second, a child's potential for life means the power to live outside of its mother, dependant only on its own systems.

"A fetus is not a person, and not the subject of an indictment for manslaughter. In order for a person to exist, he or she must be born. Unborn persons are not the subject of the crime of manslaughter. Birth is the process which causes the emergence of a new individual from the body of its mother. Once outside the body of its mother, the child has been born within the commonly accepted meaning of that word.

"Killing or causing the death of a person who is born alive and is outside the body of his or her mother may be considered manslaughter. In order for the defendant to be found guilty in this case, you must be satisfied beyond a reasonable doubt that the defendant caused the death of a person who had been alive outside the body of his mother. If you believe beyond a reasonable doubt that the defendant, by his conduct, caused the death of a person, as I have defined the word for you, you may find the defendant guilty of the crime of manslaughter, if that death was caused by wanton or reckless conduct on the part of the defendant. Otherwise, you must acquit him of the crime charged.

"If you find that even though death occurred, it was not due to any wanton or reckless conduct on the part of the defendant, then you likewise must acquit."

McGuire paused and looked at each juror in turn. He spoke louder, slower.

"You have the final judgment of the facts in this case and this is an onerous responsibility. I charge that you must decide those facts and reach your conclusions without sympathy and without any prejudice, animosity or ill feeling against any party in the case or any of the witnesses that have appeared before you. Divorce from your mind any outside emotion that may affect your judgment. You are here in an intense search for the truth—12 independent minds of various backgrounds, all seeking to determine where the truth lies by your impersonal judgment, dictated by your consciences, your intellect, guided by your oath and nothing else.

"Your verdict *must* be unanimous. The foreman has one vote just like everyone else. In the course of your deliberations, do not hesitate to re-examine your own views and change your opinion if you are convinced that your opinion is erroneous. However, do not surrender your honest conviction as to the weight or effect of evidence solely because of the opinion of fellow jurors or for the mere purpose of returning a verdict.

"You have been asked to make a finding in a most sensitive area of human relations. But whether a case has national significance or merely is of neighborhood interest, it is essential that each and every case receive the same honest, careful logical considerations from you, the jurors."

McGuire's instructions seemed to be in our favor. I dared to hope. If we managed to convince James McGuire, a member of the Knights of Columbus, surely we would be able to convince the jury.

"Mr. Foreman, ladies and gentlemen of the jury," McGuire said, "one final matter remains before I finally submit the case to you. In the beginning of this trial, I directed that 16 jurors be impaneled. The clerk will now draw four names and those jurors will retire from the jury panel and the case will be submitted to the remaining 12 jurors. Mr. O'Leary? Will you place the names of all the jurors except that of the foreman, Mr. Shea, in the usual receptacle and then draw out four names?"

When the names were in, Paul O'Leary said, "When I call your name, please step down and take your place in the front row here with the officer in attendance."

The clerk put his hand in the small barrel, pulled out a slip of paper and read the name.

"Frederick Spencer."

He then pulled another.

"Ralph Mischley."

And another.

"Michael Ciano."

And finally, "Michael Seifart."

As I watched the four men stand up and leave the jury box, I couldn't help but wonder if they would have made a difference—for good or for ill—in my case. Hope was beginning to evaporate again. It didn't matter if we convinced McGuire. What mattered was the jury.

"You four are now hereby designated alternate jurors, and are to be kept separate and apart from the other jurors unless you are called to replace one," said Paul O'Leary.

McGuire nodded. "Mr. O'Leary, you may escort the ladies and gentlemen of the jury to their deliberating room, and the court will be in recess."

The jury was taken to room 9M in the Suffolk County Courthouse for their deliberations at 12:35 p.m. on Friday, February 14, 1975. They gathered around a wooden table in a "lousy, plain" room to begin the process of finding the truth and reaching a verdict—my fate was in their hands.

CHAPTER 37

The Verdict

I had been under indictment for nine months and on trial for six weeks. We put on a strong defense that parried nearly every move Flanagan made. Now all that was left was waiting—waiting for this jury to find the truth and pronounce it. I sat in silence in a little windowless room in the Suffolk County Courthouse and replayed the trial in my mind. My heart was pounding so hard, I wondered if they could hear it in room 9M.

These strangers had lived together for six weeks, but they were told that they could not discuss the case amongst themselves—the very thing that brought them together in the first place. They were cut off from the outside, forbidden to know what the world was thinking and saying about the trial. They were ordered not to read any news about it, listen to radio broadcasts that discussed it or watch television reports on it. Their only contacts were the court officers who were assigned to take care of them for the six weeks that they were sequestered at the Lenox Hotel in Boston. What was that like? What kind of relationships had formed between the jurors and the court officers?

Did they toss their instructions aside and talk about me and the case amongst themselves anyway? Probably. If they did not have open, full discussions about me or the case, there were certainly some secret and private conversations. That is human nature. I wondered if they talked about race.

From the beginning, Bill and I made the decision not to play "the race card." We felt that the facts in my case were more than sufficient. Although we had heard that when Garrette Byrne and Newman Flanagan were told that I'm black, one of them said, "Oh. Shit." I think Flanagan thought I was Jewish.

There were only two or three black people in the jury pool from which the 16 were selected. Flanagan used one of his preemptory challenges to keep the only black person McGuire declared impartial off my jury. Flanagan and the system stacked the deck.

The foreman of the jury was Vincent Shea, a physically big man, with the large hands of a mechanic—which he was for the MBTA. His neighborhood was caught up in the busing crisis. Did that play a part in how he saw me and what he thought of me?

The rest of the jury was made up eight men and three women—10 were Catholic, some were married, most were blue-collar workers without a college degree. Some were old, some were young…and all were white.

What was happening in that room as the jury deliberated? Manslaughter. It was absurd. It was a ridiculous accusation—but it was happening.

At 4:30 p.m., Bill came into my little room and told me that the jury had not yet reached a verdict. McGuire asked them if they needed more clarification about the law. They said they did not, but they were going to resume their deliberations the next morning. I had scheduled a few prenatal patients the next morning, so I called my secretary to have them come in early. Bill, Frank, my sister, brother and I retreated to our corner in the basement of our pub in the Old City Hall to try and guess what it meant for the jury to suspend their deliberations for the night. Bill thought it was a good sign and that the extra time meant that they were carefully considering the facts in this complicated case. Frank felt that it was an ominous sign and became increasingly pessimistic. I ordered another martini. There was nothing else to do.

The next morning at 10:00, after seeing my patients, I returned to the courthouse and went back to my small windowless room to wait for the jury's verdict. Visitors came in and out to check on me. I was in no mood to talk. What was taking so long? Didn't they see the truth? Wasn't my innocence obvious? I sat alone and asked that question over and over again. No answer came. My silence was interrupted at 1:00 p.m., when the door opened and Bill and Frank walked in.

"The jury's got a verdict. McGuire is calling them in," said Bill.

It was done. I stared at Bill and Frank for a moment as the twin feelings of relief and fear infused my body, mind and soul. I steeled my being for the very worse. We walked through the side door of the courtroom and took our places behind our table where we had spent six long weeks. The ordeal was about to come to an end. Or was it? On either side of me were my lawyers, my defenders. Behind me was a room full of supporters—family, friends, doctors, lawyers—and activists on both sides of the abortion divide. Everyone was waiting for the decision in this case.

The jury filed into their box, walking right behind me. There was no connection, no contact, no feeling. Flanagan and his gang were milling around their table, confidently fidgeting.

McGuire came into the courtroom with his long, black robe flapping behind him, his white hair standing out against it, lips curved into a frown.

It was Saturday, February 15, 1975, 1:25 p.m. Forty weeks after my indictment and 40 days after my trial began. After seven hours of deliberation, the jury was going to deliver its verdict.

"Mr. foreman, please rise," Paul O'Leary said. Vincent Shea stood up. "Has the jury reached a verdict?"

"Yes, we have," Shea said in his rotund, baritone voice.

"Will the defendant rise?" directed the officer.

As I rose from my chair, I rested the tips of my fingers on the table in front of me. I needed to feel something real. Everything all around me was surreal and dreamlike.

Bill Homans and Frank Susman rose and stood on either side of me. They had been my bookends every day for six weeks. My defense. The evidence they presented, McGuire's charge to the jury, the law, the people—all of it was on my side. Yet I had a sense of dread, fear and foreboding that rose as a wave from my stomach to the back of my throat as I stood there. I tasted bile. I had prepared myself for the worse, the illogical, the unthinkable, the unexpected and the extraordinary.

"Mr. foreman, how say you in indictment 81823, *Commonwealth v. Dr. Kenneth Edelin*, on the charge of manslaughter in the death of Baby Boy Roe? Guilty or not guilty?"

None of the jurors looked at me. No sign. No signal. Not a glance. No courage. In that instant, I knew.

"Guilty!"

Like a jolt of electricity to my ears, the words burst through my brain, down my spine, through my arms, hands and fingers and into the table. *There's a mistake*, I thought. *He meant to say, "Not guilty."* I waited. He did not correct himself. *What are you saying?* I wanted to scream.

Guilty!

The word ricocheted off the high ceiling of the old New England courtroom and cut through the thick air of anticipation, fear and hope which had filled it. It flew from the mouth of Vincent Shea, standing no more than 10 feet from me, and engulfed this place of justice, poisoning the air and corrupting everything the courthouse was supposed to stand for.

There was a shriek behind me. Gasps.

"No!" someone cried. Groans. Wailing. Sobs.

I was afraid to turn around to look. As I stood, I was numb. I did not want the reality to hit just yet. I heard the cries and shouts, the words vaguely registering in my brain.

"Guilty!"

"Injustice!"

"That nigger's guilty as sin!"

"He is guilty of sin!"

There was a loud scream and I turned, just in time to see Michael Ciano, one of the alternate jurors, bolt from the courtroom, shouts of outrage trailing behind him like the wind.

Bill Homans grabbed my arm, though to this day I am not sure if it was to steady himself or me. Perhaps it was both.

I stood there frozen, immobile, straight, unbelieving. I felt as if my fingers were seared to the tabletop.

"Your honor, I would like to have the jury polled," Homans managed to say.

"Guilty."

"Guilty."

"Guilty."

"Guilty."

"Guilty."

"Guilty."

"Guilty."

"Guilty."

"Guilty."

"Guilty."

"Guilty."

"Guilty."

Not one looked in my direction. Their words came at me blindly.

Though I had hoped against hope that the jury would see the truth, I was prepared for the worst—for the reality. I stood there, hearing the words flung at me like thunderbolts. I refused to show the pain they caused, but there was nothing I could do to prevent the scar that would be caused by the word—by all the words—as they settled into my heart and into my soul. Guilty. Of manslaughter.

Over at the next table, Newman Flanagan was gloating, smiling with that chipmunk smile, his upper teeth over his bottom lip. The little man with the flowery tie. The one, the only, ambitious assistant district attorney, Irish Newman Flanagan, assisted by his gang of three—Joe Mulligan, Charlie Dunn and Donald Brennan. They had saved their city, their way of life—at least for now.

There was chaos in the courtroom. People were openly crying and loud wails reached all the way up to the high ceiling. Some sat alone in stunned silence. Others gathered in small groups. Still others hugged to console each other. It was like being at a funeral. Judge McGuire, who had sat stone-faced, high on his bench for six weeks, stared at the jury in disbelief. He rapped the gavel and excused the jurors, but did not thank them.

Bill said that McGuire's thankless dismissal of the jury indicated his displeasure with their verdict. I did not think so kindly of him. So what if he was displeased? We gave him more than enough chances to end this case in my favor.

McGuire scheduled my sentencing for early the following week. I faced 20 years in prison.

"God bless the Commonwealth of Massachusetts," O'Leary bellowed.

"It sure needs it!" someone from behind me yelled.

After a brief moment of recovery, I went into the spectators' area to console my sister. She was sobbing. My brother's face was ashen, his eyes large and red. Ramona was there, too. Silent tears were streaming down her face. I wanted to put my arms around all of them. They had come every day to sit on the hard chairs, listen to the testimony, watch as the story of my case unfolded. I hugged them and thanked them for their support. I couldn't cry. The reporters who had been there from day one gave us our time and space alone. They waited for me outside of Room 906.

Once we were finished talking to and consoling "our" people, Bill and I walked towards the open doorway. On the other side, the rest of the world waited.

We could see that the marble hallway outside was jammed with people—people crying, people shouting, people with cameras, people with microphones and tape recorders. There were bright lights—bright, white, hot lights.

Flanagan was at the bank of microphones that had been set up in the corner of the hallway.

"This was not a case about abortion. I have maintained from the beginning that the defendant was guilty of manslaughtah. I maintained from the beginning that the defendant had the right to perfoahm an abortion, that the patient had a right to have an abortion. This case involved the termination of a life following the termination of a pregnancy.

"There is no question that a woman has a right to terminate a pregnancy, and in most cases, the fetus is dead befoah it is removed from the mothah, but, if you get a person who is an individual, who is separated from the mother, then it is a person undah the Constitution and that person has rights, too."

He then left the crowded area and sought out the sanctuary of his office.

I stepped out of Room 906 with Bill Homans at my side, into the hallway of another world—my new world as a convicted felon.

Someone led us to the bank of microphones. Flash bulbs were popping, cameras were clicking and tape recorders were turning.

I did not stutter. My voice did not shake, crack or break. "We started with a steep uphill battle and we're not through. The war is not over. For those people who are trying to find a hero or a martyr in this case, let me tell you that the heroes and martyrs are the women who, before January 22, 1973, put their lives on the line. I just hope that this decision today will not throw us back to where women will once again have to risk their lives and their hopes. I have done nothing that was illegal, immoral or bad medical practice. Everything I did was in accordance with the law and with good medical practice."

Someone yelled a question about the impact of my guilty verdict on other physicians who perform abortions.

"I'm sure it will discourage many from performing abortions," I said.

Someone asked Bill for his reaction.

"This verdict is a great disappointment to me and we will appeal. Dr. Edelin's actions fell completely within medical standards, but the facts have somehow been perverted in this court, twisted into some kind of illegal conduct. He was protected by *Roe v. Wade*. I think this verdict will have a terrible impact on women seeking abortions in Massachusetts. I've hesitated to say this before, but Mr. Flanagan has used this case as an end run for himself and certain other parts of the community to demonstrate their dissatisfaction with the Supreme

Court decision. Frankly, I'm surprised with the vehemence with which the foreman shouted out the word 'guilty.' I think it shows something of the temper on the part of the populace from which at least some members of the jury came. I was disappointed that the jury did not respond to the judge's invitation to ask for more specific information during their deliberations if they needed clarification on the law. There must have been disputes on the jury with respect to the principles that ought to be applied. In his charge to the jury, Judge McGuire did his best to settle those disputes. I'm not sure that he was successful, but I don't think any judge could have been successful."

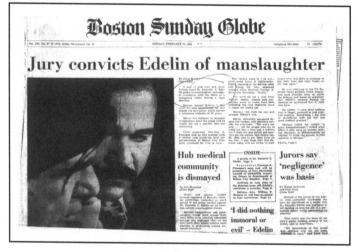

Boston Globe Headlines
February 16, 1975
Bill Homas and me.

CHAPTER 38

DELIBERATIONS

After the verdict, reporters chased after the jurors to get their stories. Several were found trying to relax and unwind in the bar at their home for the last six weeks, the Lenox Hotel in Copley Square. The reporters described the atmosphere as part carnival, part funeral, as the 12 jurors and four alternates—13 men and three women—were reunited with their families. They expressed relief at the trial's conclusion as they said goodbye to each other and the sheriff's deputies, who they referred to as their "keepers."

"We determined at the outset that abortion was not the issue" said one of jurors. "Manslaughter was the issue."

Nearly all of them said the picture of the dead fetus had an effect on them and disturbed them when Flanagan dramatically introduced it at the trial. But some of them said that they had no animosity toward me and called me a "capable doctor."

The initial vote was eight to four for conviction. Vincent Shea, the jury foreman, voted guilty on the first ballot. One of the four original "not guilty" votes was the mother of four, Liberty Ann Conlin.

"Yes, I was one of the four voting 'not guilty' at the beginning," she told reporters. "I was very sympathetic to the doctor and I wasn't sure he was guilty. It took me quite a while. Although the picture looked like a baby, it didn't play a major role in my decision. I came to the conclusion that the fetus was alive when Dr. Edelin went in and he neglected to do his duty to save life. We all thought that was negligence."

Others who voted "guilty" from the beginning said they believed that the fetus was a person. "It couldn't be manslaughter unless the fetus was a person," one of them said. "The picture made an impression. It helped people draw their own conclusions."

Francis McLaughlin, the bartender from Dorchester, said that he was surprised that the three women voted "guilty," although he said Liberty Ann Conlin expressed a lot of sympathy for me. He said that she finally decided to vote guilty, but wanted to recommend to the judge that he show mercy in sentencing me, because she did not want me sent to jail.

"It was negligence. I don't think he did a thorough job of examining the fetus for signs of life once it was removed," McLaughlin said. He then went on to say that he thought the trial was "boring."

He added, "During the deliberations, there was plenty of screaming and hollering. There were heated arguments with everyone trying to talk at once during that first day."

An hour later, a second vote produced a nine-to-three tally for conviction. The arguments continued.

Francis McLaughlin said that the "picture of the dead baby" swayed the jury.

"They called it a fetus and we always called it a baby. I think the picture really hurt him the most. None of us wanted him to go to jail. One reason I voted the way I did is because I felt he would not go to jail. Maybe he made a mistake and in the future he'll be more careful to determine if the baby is alive or dead, instead of taking it for granted. I have a lot of sympathy for the guy. He's a good doctor."

At 4:30 Friday afternoon, John Kelly, the unmarried bank teller, was the only juror left who voted 'not guilty.' He said he had not changed his mind and couldn't see any sense in holding further deliberations that day. After some more argument, the jury remained deadlocked at eleven to one. The others agreed that it might be a good idea to let Kelly sleep on his decision.

When the jury reconvened at 10:00 on Saturday morning, Kelly said his mind was still unchanged. They began discussing his hang-ups in the case. The big issue with him was the viability of the fetus. Kelly was also concerned if the fetus had taken a breath inside or outside the womb.

Kelly eventually agreed that he had some doubts as to whether I lived up to my duties to the baby. He asked each of the other jurors why they felt so strongly for conviction. One by one, they told him. It was repetitious. Kelly recalled that most of the jury felt the fetus was alive during the operation and when it was removed, and that I was negligent for not thoroughly checking for a heartbeat. They thought my examination of the baby was too short. Kelly listened to all the arguments of the other jurors and was no longer confident of his own judgment. He said it was very difficult for him to feel confident when he was standing alone against 11 other people. They had listened to the same evidence, but he had drawn a different conclusion. They repeated over and over again that I was negligent. They then broke for lunch. When they had finished eating, Kelly made a speech.

He said he disagreed with the other 11 as soon as they started deliberating the manslaughter charge. But eventually, with 11 other jurors arguing hour after hour for a verdict of guilty, Kelly wondered if he could be wrong...that maybe I was unconcerned about the fetus and that this is where his own feelings were out of order. He said he thought the fetus was not capable of sustaining independent life. He also said that he found our witnesses objective and the Flanagan's witnesses less so. Kelly said he believed that the stated purpose of abortion is to terminate a fetus' life. Then he said, "I have never made a decision in my life. This decision is the first I had ever been called upon to make."

He paced the room. The foreman then called for a vote. Kelly changed his mind. He joined the other jurors on the fourth ballot and voted to convict me.

He came to believe that I was negligent, and that despite the fact that I was performing an abortion, I should have made every effort to preserve the fetus' life.

Kelly told the reporters, "I went in there with strong feelings that he was innocent of doing anything wrong. I felt in the end that he should have been more concerned about the baby, about the potential for life. I said it often in there that he was doing an operation and that it was a hard fact, but this death was a part of the operation. This was completely unpersuasive to the rest of the jurors. I came around to feeling that the doctor was negligent partly because of his own testimony. I believe the majority thought Dr. Edelin was a very fine doctor, a very competent doctor, but thought he was really unconcerned about whether the fetus was alive. There was shouting, and of course that was unproductive, but I wasn't intimidated at all. I did stand up and review my feelings and everybody's. I concluded I must be wrong when most of them felt the opposite—there wasn't anybody on the jury who felt as

I did. I explained to them when I was changing my decision that I had followed the medical testimony completely and perhaps this kind of case is beyond the scope of a jury without experts to make decisions. I believe a lot of them felt they couldn't judge it."

As the beer and liquor flowed in the bar of the Lenox Hotel, the tongues of the jurors became looser.

"Three broads on the jury," said Paul Holland, the Boston Edison clerk, "and look who I get for a roommate." He pointed toward William Sokolowski with his beer bottle. The crowd in the booth laughed. Michael Seifart, one of the alternate jurors, had little to say except that he would have liked to have made his views known.

"The charge was manslaughter," said Sokolowski, swirling the ice in his drink. "When the judge gave his edict as to what manslaughter entailed, we had to decide if this fell within that realm."

When asked by a reporter what manslaughter entailed, Holland took a sip of his beer and said, "Right now I'm so tired, I don't know. In a couple of hours from now, I could tell you, but right now I couldn't say."

When Sokolowski was asked the same question, he nodded toward Holland and said, "I feel just like him."

McLaughlin, the bartender, came rushing over to the booth. "I'm on national TV now, kids!" He laughed.

Holland grinned. "Ya never thought you'd make good, huh Frank?"

Another one of the reporters asked Holland how he would define a "person." Holland paused for a moment as he lit a cigarette. "I don't know if I'm qualified to define a 'person' in words."

After another round of drinks and after questions about the photograph of the fetus, which most agreed helped them determine whether it was a person or not, one of the reporters asked if viability became an issue.

"Yes, it did," one of them said.

"Did the jurors come up with an age or weight when a fetus becomes viable?" the reporter asked.

"If all those doctors couldn't come up with a figure, far be it from me to know," said Sokolowski.

McLaughlin, the bartender and new TV star, best summed it up. "I got nothing against Dr. Edelin. What he did's been going on for thousands of years and will be going on for thousands of years more. He was just unlucky; he was in the wrong place at the wrong time. Maybe he did the thing wrong. He's a good guy. So he aborted a broad, maybe he didn't do it right."

After his conversations with the jurors, Gary Griffith, a reporter for the *Real Paper*, a Boston weekly, came to the conclusion that my trial had not been decided on the legal issues at all; the charge from the judge had either not been understood or deliberately ignored, and it seemed the jury hadn't paid much attention to the testimony.

Griffith said that after the judge had given his charge to the jury, he watched as Paul O'Leary drew the names from the barrel to see which of the 16 jurors would become the four alternates—a procedure which turned out to have been crucial. As O'Leary called out the names, Griffith could not believe what he was hearing.

Two days earlier, in a casual conversation in the corridor, Griffith asked Assistant District Attorney Charles Dunn, one of Flanagan's gang, who they would like to see eliminated if the choice were up to them.

"The little guy with the whiskers, first of all," Dunn said.

"Ciano?" Griffith asked.

"Yeah. Him," Dunn said.

"Who else?" Griffith asked.

"The other guy with the whiskers. The first one."

He was talking about Michael Seifart, the telephone installer for New England Bell. When Griffith pressed for the third and fourth name, Dunn said that he couldn't think of anyone else. When O'Leary drew the names out, both of those jurors were eliminated.

Three of the four alternate jurors told the reporters that they would have voted to acquit me.

Later on, Kelly, the holdout, was asked by the press if he thought right to lifers among the prosecuting staff or the jury were using the manslaughter charge as a means of striking out against abortion.

"I really don't want to answer that," he said. He also added that he was alone among the jurors in considering Flanagan's medical experts less objective than ours. "I did not hear any racial epithets. You would expect to find some small amount, and there were, but not in any way connected with Dr. Edelin or any of the issues in the trial.

"At the beginning of the deliberations, I felt that the baby was never alive and that the defense had proven this. I will never be sure I made the right decision. I'm not sure Dr. Edelin's conviction will hold up when it is appealed to a higher court."

Vincent Shea, the foreman, had very little to say. "We went

through a good six weeks of testimony and the verdict speaks for itself."

When asked how he felt now that the trial is over, he said, "Tired. That's it."

Francis McLaughlin said he was glad the trial was over because it was very boring.

Michael Ciano, who became an alternate juror and ran screaming out of the courtroom when the verdict was announced, insisted that racial prejudice was a factor in the verdict and quoted one of the jurors saying, "That black nigger is guilty as sin."

Ciano said this happened on the Thursday night before they heard the judge's instructions and before they started their "official" deliberations. Ciano's allegation meant two things: that race *was* a factor and that the jurors *did* discuss the case contrary to McGuire's admonishment and order.

The jurors finally left the bar and the Lenox Hotel, and headed home. That evening, it was reported that four of them received death threats. Holland moved his family in with relatives "for their own safety." The windows of his car were smashed.

The next morning, February 16, 1975, the headlines of the Sunday papers shouted the outcome of the trial. Across the top of the front page of the *Boston Globe*, in big, black letters, were the words:

JURY CONVICTS EDELIN OF MANSLAUGHTER

The headlines were repeated in Sunday newspapers across the country and around the world. *The London Sunday Times* said, "The American law on abortion was thrown into confusion yesterday when a doctor was found guilty of manslaughter for killing a foetus in a legal abortion."

The papers were full of opinions and quotes on both sides of the abortion divide. Ray Flynn, who took credit for getting the case against me started, praised the courage of the jury, who, he said "spoke for those whose voices are never heard in a court of law."

Dr. Kenneth Ryan, chairman of the department of obstetrics and gynecology at Harvard and a strong abortion rights supporter, said, "We have too long degraded women on the issue of compulsory childbirth, even in cases of rape, incest and ignorance."

Roy Scarpato, president of Massachusetts Citizens for Life, said the conviction "puts the pressure on the US Supreme Court, where it belongs." He said he didn't take pleasure in my conviction because I was not the real culprit. He blamed the US Supreme Court.

John Cardinal Krol, the Archbishop of Philadelphia, said that he hoped the guilty verdict would stop abortions.

Dr. Mary Ellyn Avery, the president of Children's Hospital in Boston, said, "I don't know when I've been so upset. This decision could lead to extraordinary efforts to sustain life against all odds of the successful outcome of an intact human being."

Dr. Salvado Luria, a Nobel Laureate in medicine and a cancer researcher at MIT, said, "I am very upset. I think the verdict is a reflection of a complete misunderstanding of the practice of medicine. It attempts to force a specific narrow ideology on medical practice."

Other physicians gave their opinions as well. "I think it's a travesty of justice," one of them said. "Edelin was working within the context of what we know the Supreme Court has laid down as guidelines. What makes it even more amazing was that I thought the defense had proven their case pretty well and the prosecution had not. It's a devastating result, and in most of the medical community, quite unexpected. The verdict could change medical practice in ways that could become permanent."

The executive director of the Boston Hospital for Women said that his institution "would not limit the number of abortions performed up to 20 weeks of pregnancy, but they would limit the involvement of residents in the performance of abortions."

Physicians in private practice said that the verdict was "shocking," "a shame" and "a great pity."

"I think the man was crucified," one of them said.

Dr. Leon White, Boston's commissioner of health and hospitals said, "I just think Edelin has been made a fall guy in an issue that should be or could be decided without damaging what I consider a very fine doctor's career."

The president of the interns and residents section of the American Medical Association pledged the organization's support during my appeal.

Even committed anti-abortion advocates said they had not expected the verdict. One of them, Rabbi Samuel Fox of Lynn, predicted that I would be cleared on appeal.

"I'm sure the case will go to a higher court," he said. "I have a feeling he might even win the appeal, but the fact that he was convicted indicates a moral consciousness of humanity that the Supreme Court cannot legislate away."

He went on to support Flanagan's contention that I was on trial for manslaughter, not for having performed an abortion.

Lawyers weighed in on the commentary, too. One said that he felt that the prosecution had made a valid charge, but that Bill Homans had discredited the manslaughter accusation. "I'm amazed," he said. "I thought Bill Homans put on an absolutely solid case. The defense not only disputed every point, but put forward a far better case. This verdict will have a chilling effect on individual hospitals and physicians. How can it not? I don't see how the jury could convict on that evidence, but it did."

Women spoke out as well. "I see it as a temporary triumph for the right to lifers," one woman said. "They clearly sought this trial. I hoped that Dr. Edelin would not be found guilty, because he isn't guilty. This decision will not last, just like their Human Life Amendment to the Constitution will not prevail. If it does, then women will become the slaves of their own reproductive organs. This will rally women who are upset by the decision, but who haven't felt a personal involvement in the matter before."

She was right. Rally they did!

On Monday evening, February 17, 1975, 48 hours after my guilty verdict, more than 2,000 people, mostly women, staged a candlelight march and rally on Boston Common to condemn the guilty verdict and support legal abortion. The rally was co-sponsored by 25 different organizations. They carried signs in support of women's right to choose and blasted the trial. They chanted slogans.

"Not the church! Not the state! Women must decide their fate!"

Bumper stickers were distributed that said "Edelin Framed, Women Chained" in red, bold letters. The crowd collected signatures on a petition that accused Flanagan of being actively engaged in a campaign to deny women their basic rights since he began his investigation.

One of the speakers at the rally proclaimed, "We see this as an attack on the rights of all women to decide when and if to have children. It is particularly harmful to those women unable to afford private medical care and who so depend on the minimal services that City Hospital provides."

The next morning, Tuesday, I sat on the couch in my Cambridge apartment, watching the news accounts of the rally and reading more accounts of it and the aftermath of the trial in the newspapers. The phone rang. It was Bill Homans' office telling me that Judge McGuire wanted to see us in court that day.

Bill and I arrived in Room 906 just after noon. He and Flanagan were ushered immediately into McGuire's chambers.

As I sat alone in the courtroom, I looked around at this place where I had spent the last six weeks. The high-ceilinged courtroom bore little resemblance to the way it looked when my trial began. It had been packed every day with spectators. There had been three rows of tables to accommodate newsmen covering the trial, which had caught the attention of the nation. Now, it was nearly empty, silent. My every breath seemed to echo throughout the room. I sat there with a solitary and horrifying thought: was I going to jail?

Flanagan and Bill emerged from McGuire's chambers. Following behind them, McGuire came in and mounted his bench.

Before I could make eye contact with him and get some hint as to what this was about, Bill spoke. But not to me.

"Your honor, we didn't realize why we were called here today. That explains the informality." He gestured toward me. I looked down at my gray turtleneck sweater and silently admonished myself for not putting on a suit. "Your honor has heard the evidence. You heard Dr. Edelin testify on his own behalf. You have heard him describe his life, his education and his practice of medicine. I think I have nothing to say other than my personal experience with Dr. Edelin, as well as everything I have heard from others associated with him—not only in the practice of medicine, but also in his personal life—demonstrates that he is not the kind of individual who has any malice in his heart. Everything I have heard indicates that Dr. Edelin is a person with a long, fruitful and charitable career ahead of him in the practice of medicine. I hope you will bear that in mind when you make your sentence."

McGuire looked unimpressed. He handed clerk Paul O'Leary the order. I stood and watched him unfold the paper. My heart dropped to my stomach. I held my breath.

"Kenneth Edelin, the court, in consideration of your offense in indictment 81823, orders you placed on probation for a period of one year. The execution of this order is stayed until further order of the court, pending the final determination of your appeal, and the case stands continued on the same bail."

Relief spread from my heart out to my fingers and down to my toes. I was free on $1,000 bail. No jail.

But I still did not know if I would be allowed to continue to practice medicine. Later that day, I had my answer. The Board of Registration in Medicine said they would wait until after the appeal process before deciding if my license should be revoked.

As we left Room 906, reporters were waiting to ask our reaction to the sentence.

"I'm still numb from Saturday's verdict," I said. "Although I don't think I should have been indicted or brought to trial in the first place, I appreciate the judge's decision on what sentence to impose." I started to walk away, then stopped and turned back to the reporters. "One more thing: I am outraged and angered at the verdict, but I don't believe that the lives or safety of the jurors should be threatened. I ask those who share my outrage and anger not to retaliate against the jurors. That has no place in a civilized society. We will get our vindication through the courts. Now I must go back to work at City Hospital."

Reporters sought out the jury to get their reactions to the sentence. Vincent Shea, who had been described by some of the other jurors as the most outspoken in arguing for a guilty verdict, said, "I was tickled pink that Dr. Edelin got a light sentence. I wish him no harm."

Mrs. Liberty Ann Conlin of West Roxbury said she regretted her guilty vote.

"I wish Edelin could be exonerated completely," she said. "I wish I'd had the strength to stick to my not guilty vote. I regret my guilty vote, but I was sick and tired and couldn't fight."

She had taken to her bed immediately after the trial and her daughter said she was quite sick. "The trial was an emotional and physical ordeal for my mother," she said.

For me, too.

"I'm glad he got off without going to jail," said Frank McLaughlin. "I hope he wins his appeal. He hasn't done anything that a thousand other doctors haven't done. It's too bad to make an example out of him."

Also applauding McGuire's leniency were William Sokolowski, Paul Holland and Anthony Alessi of Roxbury. Sokolowski, the 26-year-old meat market employee, said, "I clicked my heels, I was so happy. He had no intention of killing the baby. I feel a hundred percent better now that the judge was lenient. If I'd had to sentence him I would have given him five minutes probation."

Frank Guiney, the executive director of BCH who had originally suspended me after I was indicted, only to have his suspension reversed by the board of trustees, said that I was free to return to work at the hospital. "There is nothing to prevent him from returning, but he probably needs some rest after this."

The executive committee of the City Hospital medical staff said that my "actions and clinical practices have been consistent with the highest standards of medical care."

On Tuesday afternoon, after the sentencing, I returned to BCH for the first time in more than six weeks. Although I usually entered the hospital directly into the maternity building, this day, I decided I was going in through the front door, between the columns, into the building containing the mural of James Michael Curley, the powerful Irish Mayor of Boston. As I approached the entrance on Harrison Avenue, a crowd of nurses, interns, residents, nurses' aids and janitors had gathered outside in the cold. They began to applaud.

"Welcome home, Dr. Edelin!" someone yelled.

"We love you, Dr. Edelin!" said someone else.

I dove into the crowd of smiling faces. I shook their hands, hugged and thanked them for their continued support. It was good to be *home*.

That afternoon, Bill Homans filed our notice of appeal.

And that night, I delivered a seven-pound, eight-ounce baby girl to Helene, a patient and friend I had seen each Saturday morning for prenatal care throughout the trial. It was the perfect ending of this phase of my life, and for beautiful little Ayanna, it was the perfect beginning of hers.

CHAPTER 39

THE APPEAL

During the hours of Helene's labor, I received telephone calls every 30 minutes from one of the producers of the *CBS Evening News with Walter Cronkite*, wanting to know if the baby had been born and whether it was a boy or girl. They wanted to end that evening's newscast with a report on my sentencing and conclude the story with news of my delivery of Ayanna. But Ayanna was having none of that. She was born in the late evening, on her own time, and not according to any TV schedule.

For six weeks, my picture or stories about the trial had been on the front page of all the Boston newspapers. It was often the lead story on the local TV news. There was no place I could go in Boston without being recognized. During the trial, my life was limited to the courtroom, Bill Homans' office and my apartment. The end of the trial freed me to speak out against the right to life agenda and the tactics Flanagan used to convict me.

There were lots of requests for interviews. I gave my first on a live, local, black TV news show hosted by Maurice Lewis that aired on Sunday afternoon, 24 hours after the verdict. This audience would know that racism was rampant in Boston. They would understand that for black people, the justice system was broken. Michael Ciano's revelation that one of the jurors had said, "That black nigger is guilty as sin," proved that, and I wanted the world to know it.

On Monday, I appeared live on a women's TV show hosted by Pat Mitchell. Women were the other audience I wanted to reach because the verdict affected their lives the most.

I was determined not to let Newman Flanagan get away with using me and my trial as an end run around the Supreme Court's ruling. He got the jury he wanted, sequestered them so that they would be insulated from the public's opinion—which was clearly in my favor—and skillfully distorted the scientific facts to reinforce the biased opinions the jury brought with them to my trial.

In hindsight, it was easy to see that there was little chance that Flanagan could lose this trial. It was his jury, his judge and his skill as a manipulative prosecutor that assured his victory. We never connected with the jury on an emotional level. We presented our defense as if the trial were a scientific debate bolstered by the law. That strategy did not work with this jury. For them, this was an emotional issue that they saw through the lifetime lenses of their religious biases.

My relationship with Bill Homans was complicated, because he was a complicated man with a complicated life. He was a brilliant, intellectual lawyer who relied heavily on alcohol to numb the pain in his life. His law practice skated on the edge of financial ruin, and his personal life also perched on that precipitous cliff. By the time the trial began, our relationship had evolved from one where I needed his support to one where he needed mine to keep going. I had a deep affection for him and his two daughters, and got caught up in the tangled mess of his life and couldn't get out of it. I had to keep him functioning because my life depended on him.

I needed to get away from the publicity of the trial and verdict, the loss of my privacy, the complications of Bill's life and the frigid gloom of the Boston winter, so I booked a flight to Jamaica to clear my head, to think about my future and the appeal. Almost immediately, I decided that Bill Homans and Frank Susman would not handle my appeal. I wanted a new start and needed a new lawyer.

Most people I spoke to about this, even lawyers close to Bill, understood and agreed with my decision. The appeal to the Supreme Judicial Court of Massachusetts was not guaranteed to overturn the verdict in spite of the law, science and the public sentiment in my favor.

I spent my first several days in Jamaica talking by phone to Bert Lee and lawyers from the Harvard Law School about my appeal. One of them suggested that I talk to a professor on the faculty at Harvard named Charles Nesson. I called him and we instantly connected. After several conversations, I set up a time to meet with him on my return to Boston. With those decisions made, I could relax and enjoy the warm sunshine of Jamaica and the anonymity that the island provided me.

My escape was interrupted by a phone call from Bert. Bill Homans had suffered a heart attack.

He and Bill were on the phone, having a heated conversation about the KEDF and the expense of the trial when Bill interrupted the argument.

"Bert, I'm having pain in my chest and can hardly breathe. I have to hang up now." He made his way to Mass General Hospital, where they determined that he was having a heart attack and admitted him.

I called the hospital over and over again until I was put in touch with him. "How are you doing, Bill?" I asked.

He sounded very fragile and described the conversation with Bert and the onset of his pain. I promised to come see him on my return to Boston. My brief Jamaican respite from worry ended abruptly.

Now what do I do?

I couldn't tell him I was going to replace him and Frank Susman as my lawyers—not over the phone, from Jamaica, while he was lying in a hospital bed. The disappointment might've killed him.

On my return to Boston, I met with the BCH officials and resumed my job as the director of ambulatory services for the OB/GYN department. I also met with the KEDF to talk about the expenses of the trial and the management of the fund. By this time, Bill was out of the hospital and staying with a friend in her Cambridge apartment to recuperate from his heart attack. I visited them and talked to Bill about the appeal and the approach he was going to take.

I also met with Charlie Nesson and liked him immediately. He was my age—36—boyishly attractive, soft-spoken and very, very smart. He had attended Harvard College as an undergraduate, and Harvard Law School. He graduated at the top of his law school class with one of the best academic records in the history of the school. He spent a year as a law clerk for a Supreme Court justice, and after working in the Department of Justice, joined the Harvard Law School faculty in 1966 and became a tenured professor in 1969.

I explained to him the dilemma I was facing with Bill and asked him if he thought the two of them could work together. He, of course, knew of Bill Homans, his defense of the defenseless and passion for civil rights and liberties. Charlie believed they could work together and agreed to be an equal co-counsel for the appeal. I told him that I wanted to wait a while before telling Bill of my decision. I wanted to be sure he was fully recovered and could handle the news.

A month later, Bill and I met. It was not a happy meeting. He did not want Charlie on the appeal. I told him that it would be foolish for me to proceed with him alone as my lawyer.

"Suppose you get sick again or, God forbid, your next attack is fatal. I think the only smart move for me is to bring someone else in as co-counsel, just in case. You need help with the appeal so that the full burden and stress of it doesn't fall on you."

Bill resisted, but I stood firm in my decision. In hopes of easing his resistance, I suggested that he meet with Charlie soon. Reluctantly, he agreed, and I set up the meeting.

The meeting went as well as could be expected and, in a subsequent meeting with the two of them, we agreed that if ever there were ever a dispute over the handling of the appeal, I would be the final arbiter. Bill was not happy and, because he was not going to be involved with the appeal, Frank Susman remained angry with me for years.

The other parts of my life—taking care of patients at BCH and seeing my children as much as possible—filled my days and weeks. The KEDF had raised enough money to pay all of the costs of the trial, from Bill Homans' fees, to the cost of bringing the expert witnesses to Boston, to the preparation of the exhibits, to paying for the daily transcripts and all of the motions and briefs that flowed from Bill's office. In all, it amounted to $65,000. The appeal to the SJC would cost another $100,000. If we lost and had to go to the US Supreme Court, the costs would be even higher. I set off on a whirlwind speaking tour to explain the trial, the issues and the importance of a woman's right to choose to any group of people who would listen. I had speaking engagements in Connecticut, Georgia, New York, Ohio, Illinois, Washington, D.C., Tennessee, Wisconsin, California and, of course, Massachusetts. In all of my travels, there were interviews with newspapers, radio call-in shows and television. Gloria Steinem interviewed me for an article published in the August, 1975 issue of *Ms. Magazine*. I appeared on *The Today Show*, interviewed by Barbara Walters. I also appeared on *Good Morning America*. In every city and every venue, the responses to my talk and my interviews were overwhelmingly positive. I explained the history of abortion and the consequences of it for women when the procedure was illegal. I shared my experiences with abortion, starting with medical school and ending with the case of Evonne Gilbert.

"Women have been trying to control the number of children they have for as long as women have been on this earth. And some women, when they find themselves pregnant and don't want to be, will go to any length, putting their lives and their health on the line, to terminate that unwanted pregnancy. Women have always assumed that right and that responsibility. The decision to have an abortion is not one that should be made by religious leaders, judges, legislators or district attorneys. The decision has always been and should always be one that is made by women. What the Supreme Court did in its ruling in *Roe* was to assure that once a woman had made that decision, it could be carried out safely, legally and with dignity."

Everywhere I went, I received standing ovations, and at the end of every meeting, donations were collected to pay for the appeal. The travels, speeches and media interviews always resulted in more money being sent into the KEDF. But speaking out also gave me the chance to denounce the enemies of a woman's right to choose—the so-called right to life movement. They were not only women's enemies; they were my enemies, too. I was determined to speak out against them and the tactics they used to convict me. I had my voice and a stage, and I used them. I wanted them to be sorry that they decided to pick on me to advance their cause to restrict the rights of women and doctors.

Back in Boston, Bill and Charlie were working together to present one final motion for Judge McGuire to set aside the jury's decision and enter a "not guilty" verdict. This would be an important test of the arguments we would make before the Supreme Judicial Court. It would also be an important test of how Bill and Charlie would work together. They both failed.

From Charlie, I got phone calls complaining about Bill. From Bill, I got long, detailed letters complaining about Charlie's tactics. It took everything I had to keep them together and moving forward to get the verdict overturned.

On April 30, 1975, two and a half months after the guilty verdict, I again entered Room 906 in the Suffolk County Courthouse, presented myself before Judge James McGuire and listened as Charlie argued our final motion that the verdict be overturned. Charlie argued eloquently, thoroughly and beautifully, using new approaches and understandings of the law. He was brilliant. Two weeks later, McGuire denied our motion, for the last time sidestepping his chance to repair the broken justice which had occurred in his courtroom. The next step was to prepare and file our brief with the SJC and make our arguments to them.

Charlie Nesson's approach to the appeal was fresh and insightful. He wanted to fully understand the nuances of every facet of the case. At his request, I arranged for him to come into the operating room at BCH to observe while I performed surgery. He wanted to understand, see and hear the dynamics of that special place.

WGBH, the public broadcasting station in Boston, had decided to produce and broadcast a dramatic reenactment of the trial. Throughout the spring and summer, I worked with the writers and producers on the script, helping them bring to life the dryness of the trial transcript.

The relationship between Bill and Charlie continued to be tense and full of friction. Finally, it exploded in a meeting when Charlie told Bill that he thought it was a mistake to have attacked Gimenez and his testimony so forcefully. Rather than trying to discredit him in cross-examination, Charlie said that Gimenez's testimony that the fetus showed "no signs of life once it was removed" was in our favor.

Bill was livid that his handling of the case was being criticized. It was the first time anyone had done that, but Charlie made a good point. If it were not alive when I removed it, it could not be a person, and, therefore, not the victim of manslaughter. Still, I did not need my lawyers arguing like this. I struggled to keep Bill and Charlie focused on the appeal and not on each other. I reminded them that we had a September deadline to meet for submitting our brief to the SJC in preparation for oral arguments in December.

WGBH announced that it would air *The Edelin Conviction* in November. They were able to reduce the six-week trial to a two-hour dramatization, which they wanted to premiere on Monday November 17, 1975, and repeat two more times after that.

Flanagan was furious. He went to court to get a restraining order to prevent them from showing the film. He had the audacity to argue that the showing of the film "will have a direct, immediate and inevitable prejudicial effect on a subsequent fair and impartial trial" if I were granted one. WGBH argued that Flanagan was attempting to "censor events which took place in a public forum." The judge ruled against Flanagan and let the film be aired as scheduled. It received critical acclaim and won several awards for the station.

Around the same time, we received word that the SJC had postponed our oral arguments until the spring of 1976 because one of the justices was retiring. It was their hope that a replacement would be appointed and seated by spring. Because of the importance of the case, the SJC wanted their full complement of judges to hear the appeal.

This gave Bill and Charlie more time to prepare the brief. Many other lawyers contributed to it and many organizations wanted to submit amicus briefs on my behalf. There were so many facets to the case that these organizations wanted to be sure that the SJC considered them. In all, 19 amicus briefs were submitted from such diverse organizations as the American Ethical Union, the American Jewish Congress, the United Methodist Church, the Union of American Hebrew Congregations, the United Church of Christ, the Center for Constitutional Rights, the National Jury Project, the National Medical Association, medical school deans, professors and individual physicians, the NAACP Legal Defense and Educational Fund and Planned Parenthood Federation of America.

The completed brief was submitted to the SJC in December of 1975 and oral arguments were held on Monday, April 5, 1976. The written brief was brilliant, and Bill and Charlie were each allotted 30 minutes to present our case to the six judges. There was so much interest in the oral arguments that the SJC designated special elevators for those going to the courtroom and set up an additional room where those who could not fit into the courtroom could hear the arguments over loudspeakers.

Our appeal began with a simple truth.

"The manslaughter prosecution of Dr. Edelin was a trial of his professional judgment during the course of an abortion. From the day of the indictment, this case became a central focus of the abortion controversy, and that controversy became very much a part of this case," Charlie said. "Although the district attorney protested that this was not an abortion case, he injected the issue throughout the trial. He even asked his star witness if he was 'an abortionist.' Moreover, almost all of Flanagan's experts were affiliated with the right to life movement and were opposed to legal abortion."

We blasted Flanagan for using my indictment and trial to threaten all physicians who provided abortions. We said that the threat of criminal charges was being used as an instrument of ideological and religious warfare by Flanagan and all of those who were vehemently opposed to abortion. We argued that physicians who provide abortions must have their judgments protected from a second-guessing prosecutor and jury.

"Flanagan's prosecution was an abuse of the criminal law," the brief pointed out, "because it wanted to prevent women and doctors from exercising the fundamental rights the Constitution guaranteed them."

Although we criticized Flanagan's tactics and motives, our most scathing criticism was saved for Judge James McGuire and his handling of the case. We started gently.

"The trial judge rejected the Commonwealth's theory of the prosecution by instructing the jurors that, to find Dr. Edelin guilty, they must find that Dr. Edelin killed or caused the death of the fetus once it had been born alive outside its mother. Yet under these instructions, Dr. Edelin was clearly entitled to a directed verdict of acquittal."

We pointed out that the only two doctors who were eyewitnesses to the operation, Enrique Gimenez and me, testified that the fetus showed no signs of life when it was removed. Furthermore, there was no proof of any conduct which could be considered wanton or reckless. Finally, turning up the heat on McGuire, we showed that his instructions to the jury were totally at odds with the accusation brought against me. I was never accused of the offense of which I was convicted—wanton or reckless conduct after the fetus had been removed from Evonne. Flanagan had stated that the manslaughter occurred before the fetus was removed. That was his charge against me and he was unable to prove it. As a result, McGuire should have directed the jury to bring back a verdict of "not guilty," especially in light of the instructions he gave to them.

"Dr. Edelin's conviction must be reversed because the trial was full of evidentiary error. There was fundamental confusion from the beginning to the end of the trial over what were the material issues. Not until his instructions to the jury did Judge McGuire decide that the prosecution's theory of the case was untenable. But at that late date, a mass of testimony had been admitted in support of the prosecution's erroneous theory that the fetus became a person when the placenta was separated. The case was presented to the jurors by the prosecution on one theory, and then submitted to them by the trial judge on another. The result was inevitable confusion and an invitation to the jurors to decide the case according to their own standards."

We brought up the photograph and pointed out that it had no probative value whatsoever and that Judge McGuire vaguely indicated that the jury might consider the photo on the issue of personhood, but subsequently instructed that "personhood" required birth alive outside the mother.

"There is absolutely no way in which a juror could be assisted by looking at the photo in determining whether the fetus had been born alive outside its mother. Mr. Flanagan's extraordinarily inflammatory use of the photo, capped by his closing plea to the jury to 'humanize' the fetus, shows that the true thrust of the photo was directed to the passions and emotions surrounding the powerful, yet extraneous ideological issue of the right to life of the unborn fetus."

Throughout our argument, we emphasized again and again that I was entitled to a directed verdict of acquittal because I was not charged with the crime of which I was convicted. The Constitutions of both Massachusetts and the United States stated that I could not be accused of one crime and convicted of another. Since there were no laws in Massachusetts that prohibited the kind of surgical procedure I used, prosecution for that procedure was "lawless." Flanagan used his indictment to circumvent due process. In the entire history of Massachusetts, there had never been a manslaughter prosecution for the death of a fetus in the process of being born. Regulation of abortion should have been the business of the legislature, not the district attorney.

We argued that McGuire failed to define "viability" for the jury in terms of the Supreme Court's ruling in *Roe v. Wade*. Viability, we contended, was a judgment made by others and me prior to the procedure. McGuire, in effect, left the determination of viability up to the jury. If they chose to, they could ignore it altogether.

McGuire should have confined the trial to the material issues from the beginning. He should not have waited to define the issues at the very end, especially when his definitions were different from those he had allowed Flanagan to enter for the 28 days of testimony. As a result, the case went to the jury on a confusing record which effectively set the jury free to decide the case on the basis of misapprehension, emotion and prejudice.

Our appeal concluded with a request that the SJC set aside the guilty verdict and enter one of "not guilty." In the alternative, we suggested the SJC should at least set aside the verdict and order a new trial.

That was it. My fate was now in the hands of the six justices of the SJC. All that was left now was to wait.

December 17, 1976

As I left the operating room at BCH, my pager went off and flashed Bill Homans' telephone number. When I called back, Judi Bernstein answered the phone.

"The SJC has reached a decision. We don't know what it is. Bill has gone over to pick it up."

I quickly changed out of my scrub suit and ran down to the street to hail a cab. I was too nervous to drive.

As I got into the back seat of the cab, the driver looked at me in his rear view mirror. "How you doin', Doc?"

"Fine," I said. I was still a little uncomfortable with the recognition.

"What's happenin' with your case?"

"I'm about to find out. Old City Hall, please."

The cab driver sped off down the narrow streets of Boston, to Bill Homans' office. He was as excited as I was. Panicking as I did at the way he weaved in and out of traffic, turning sharply around every corner, I was left with little time to think about the answer I was about to receive from the SJC. I was more worried about whether or not I was going to make it to Bill's office in one piece—though we did make it there in record time.

My heart thudded as I made my way to Bill's office. I paused before I entered and took a deep breath. It was hard for me to feel confident after being indicted and convicted in the first place. I needed to brace myself for the worst.

I walked through the office door.

Judi glanced up, saw me and screamed. Beaming, she jumped from her seat and gave me a long, victorious hug, tears of joy screaming down her face. As she cried, she repeated it over and over again:

"It's over. It's over. It's over."

She handed me a single sheet of paper from the court.

In the case of the COMMONWEALTH versus
Kenneth Edelin
Rescript received from the Supreme Judicial Court:
The judgment is reversed and the verdict set aside.
Judgment of acquittal is to be entered, filed.

I could not contain anything. I joined Judi in crying out and sobbing with relief. After our tears stopped and the screaming quieted down, I sat down to read the full opinion of the SJC:

> All six Justices who heard the appeal, holding that there was error in the proceedings at trial, vote to reverse the conviction. Five justices also vote to direct the entry of a judgment of acquittal; the chief justice (Hennessey) dissenting in part in a separate opinion, would order a new trial. The five justices are agreed that there was insufficient evidence to go to a jury on the overarching issue whether Dr. Edelin was guilty beyond a reasonable doubt of the "wanton" or "reckless" conduct resulting in a death required for a conviction, and that motions for a directed verdict of acquittal should have been granted.

The rest of the 30-page opinion reviewed the details of my trial and the multiple errors made in bringing the charges against me in the first place, the weakness of Flanagan's expert witnesses and the way Judge McGuire handled the trial. The opinion ended with these final two paragraphs:

> In the comparative calm of appellate review, the essential proposition emerges that the defendant on this record had no evil frame of mind, was actuated by no criminal purpose and committed no wanton or reckless acts in carrying out the medical procedures on October 3, 1973. A larger teaching of this case may be that, whereas a physician is accountable to the criminal law even when performing professional tasks, any assessment of his responsibility should pay due regard to the unavoidable difficulties and dubieties of many professional judgments.

> The judgment is reversed and the verdict set aside. Judgment of acquittal is to be entered. So ordered.

It was over. I could now go back to being what I wanted to be—a doctor who took care of the women who needed me the most. I was free. As Charlie Nesson inscribed on a copy of the SJC decision, "A battle never sought, a victory justly won."

I never asked for this fight. All I was doing was my job. It was all I'd ever wanted to do. It was the legacy of my mother's all too brief life and early death.

I returned to BCH relieved. A huge burden had been lifted from my shoulders, but the anger remained. The wound from the original verdict was still fresh. And although broken justice has been repaired, the scar on my soul has never gone away.

Welcome home! (Boston City Hospital).

EPILOGUE

In 1978, Bill Homans called to tell me that he was going to endorse Newman Flanagan, who was running to be the district attorney of Suffolk County. I was outraged, angry and pleaded with him not to do it. I didn't understand how he could support a man who used underhanded tactics to get convictions. Despite my pleadings, Bill endorsed him. Flanagan won the election with the slogan, "A Man of Convictions." It disgusted me. He served as the DA from 1978 to 1992.

I severed all ties with Bill after that and only saw him once before he died in 1997.

My divorce from Ramona became final in 1977. She moved to Washington, DC, and became an important leader in the Civil Rights movement. Together and apart, we raised two wonderful children, Ken and Kim, who have grown up to be extraordinary adults and parents. I am very proud of them.

In 1978, I married Barbara Evans. We have two children, Joseph and Corinne who have also grown up to be extraordinary adults and of whom I am also very proud. Barbara is not only my lover, but my love, my best friend and my life partner. Without her, this book would never have been finished.

In 1979, three years after the SJC made its decision, I was chosen to be the chairman of the Department of Obstetrics and Gynecology at Boston University School of Medicine. At the same time, I became the director of OB/GYN at Boston City Hospital and gynecologist-in-chief at University Hospital. These positions gave me the opportunity to further improve the lives and health care of women, especially black women. I increased the size of the full-time staff of doctors at BCH, thereby improving the care of patients and the education of resident doctors and medical students. The residency training program received full accreditation twice during my tenure. I hired doctors specifically to work in the neighborhood health centers around Boston, to improve

358

the quality and continuity of care to the most vulnerable of women. I invited midwives to perform hospital deliveries for their patients as soon as the law was changed to permit them to do that. I was able to improve the educations of medical students and provide them with proper supervision as they learned the specialty and art of obstetrics and gynecology.

I was especially interested in health care for teenage girls and women. Many of them were sexually active and needed birth control and education. Preaching only abstinence would have been folly. I had to deal with them and their lives as I found them, and give them information to help them take control their lives. Along with the Department of Pediatrics, we established an adolescent OB/GYN clinic to provide the specialized care that these young women needed.

I was able to finally establish an ambulatory abortion clinic at Boston City Hospital, to meet the needs of the hundreds of women who came to us for help. The clinic is still operating today.

I also had to deal with the reality of drug abuse in pregnancy. I did so by establishing a methadone maintenance program for women who were pregnant and addicted to heroin. We provided them with prenatal care and helped them reduce or eliminate their use of heroin so that their babies would not be born addicted. I established a residential drug treatment program for the most difficult of these cases and gradually weaned the pregnant women off of all drugs. This was especially helpful when crack cocaine invaded Boston in the early 1980s.

I wanted our resident doctors to be able to see their patients in a more holistic light. With a grant from the Cox Foundation, I established a "house call" program so that they could visit their pregnant patients in their homes, to see the circumstances under which they lived and the challenges they dealt with every day. They discovered that many of their patients had little financial support, lived cramped in small rooms with their other children, often had no meaningful relationships with the fathers of their babies and many had little food to eat. That which they had was grossly inadequate to provide the necessary nutrition for a pregnant woman and the baby growing inside of her. As a result, we established a food pantry in the prenatal clinic at BCH, to give poor pregnant women free food during their pregnancies.

In 1989, I was chosen to become the chairman of the board of Planned Parenthood Federation of America. In this three-year, voluntary position, I oversaw the operation of the largest private family planning organization in the country, which operated over 900 clinics throughout the nation.

When I was chairman of the PPFA, the American government tried to dismantle publicly funded family planning programs and muzzle doctors and nurses, to prevent us from providing full, unbiased information to our patients. We fought back with marches, demonstrations and promised that we would not allowing ourselves to be censored. It was during this time that the organization became more actively involved in electoral politics as a means of protecting a woman's right to choose and doctors' rights to practice medicine without unwarranted government interference.

The rights of women to make choices about their pregnancies and doctors to be able to offer their patients the most appropriate care continues to be under attack. Recent Supreme Court rulings have further restricted a woman's right to choose. There is no question efforts will continue to be made to overturn *Roe*. I believe that the Supreme Court has invited such challenges.

In 1990, after 11 years of being chairman and chief at BU and BCH, I stepped down from these positions and became the associate dean for students and minority affairs at Boston University School of Medicine. Over the next 16 years, programs were expanded to increase the number of minority students—particularly black and Hispanic students—admitted to the medical school at BU. Issues of cultural competency and health care disparities were introduced into the curriculum. My career in that position culminated when BU admitted more minority students to its medical school than any other medical school in Massachusetts and most other medical schools in the country.

I never saw Evonne Gilbert after she was discharged from the hospital in 1973. She called me once as the trial was beginning and offered to testify on my behalf. I was grateful for the offer, but decided that her privacy was more important than having her take the witness stand. I only hope that the dreams that she, her parents and I had for her came true.

INDEX